A Traveller's Guide to
PLACES OF WORSHIP

A Traveller's Guide to
PLACES OF WORSHIP

Charles Kightly & Michael Cyprien

ROUTLEDGE & KEGAN PAUL
London, Boston, Melbourne and Henley

CONTENTS

Introduction 5

The Featured Sites 6

*National map showing the location
of sites described in the gazetteer*

Places of Worship 8–125

*A gazetteer to the sites
including the special articles listed below*

Glossary of Terms 126

Further Reading 128

First published in 1986 by Historical Times Incorporated,
2245 Kohn Road, Harrisburg, PA 17105, USA
and by Routledge & Kegan Paul plc
11 New Fetter Lane, London EC4P 4EE and
29 West 35th Street, New York, NY 10001, USA

Text by Charles Kightly
Photography and Art Direction by Michael Cyprien
Filmset in England by BAS Printers Limited,
Over Wallop, Stockbridge, Hampshire
Printed in England by Balding + Mansell Limited
Wisbech, Cambridgeshire

Library of Congress Cataloging in Publication Data

Kightly, Charles.
  A traveller's guide to places of worship.

  1. Shrines — Great Britain — Guide-books.   2. Great
Britain — Description and travel — 1971 —   — Guide-
books.   I. Cyprien, Michael.   II. Title.
BL980.G7K54   1986   914.1′04858   86–14853
ISBN 0-918678-18-8

British Library Cataloguing in Publication Data also available
ISBN 0 7102 0941 X

INTRODUCTION

Wherever the traveller through Britain journeys, places of worship are always at hand, be they prehistoric stone circles, medieval parish churches and great cathedrals, or buildings of the Georgian, Victorian and later eras. In compiling this Traveller's Guide, I have tried to include as wide as possible a geographical range of such places, though I have sometimes deliberately included several in the same small area for ease of comparison. I have likewise attempted to represent every major period of Britain's long religious history, and to provide a linking series of backdrops to the site entries by means of special subjects briefly recounting the story of the nation's religious development. No conveniently portable guide, however, can hope to describe more than a tiny fraction of Britain's hundreds of thousands of places of worship: and while the selection made is designed to help the traveller gain an insight into the many different ways in which Britons have honoured God, it has inevitably been a personal and subjective one.

Some of the sites included are justly famous internationally, while others are less well known and a few – often the most rewarding – are so far off the beaten tourist track that to find them requires a modicum of perseverance: though here I trust that the especially detailed directions, recorded during my own visits, will be of assistance. Medieval places of worship – churches great and small, cathedrals, abbeys and pilgrimage shrines – account for rather more than half the entries, a proportion which accords with their ubiquity and inherent interest: but prehistoric and Roman sacred sites are also well represented, as are the Christian churches of the Celts and Anglo-Saxons. I have made a point, moreover, of including a score of unrestored "Prayer Book Churches", which remain substantially as they were built or converted for Protestant worship during the sixteenth to eighteenth centuries. These I particularly recommend to the traveller, not only because their splendidly unspoilt interiors bring the past almost within touching distance, but because many of them possess in good measure that indefinable atmosphere of peace and sanctity which is the hallmark of a place of worship, whatever its date or origin.

This atmosphere is better experienced than described, and the extent to which the traveller will experience it will plainly vary from person to person: some may even feel, with the Quaker George Fox, that no one place is holier than another, while others hold that the prayers of many generations cannot but imbue a building with an aura of sanctity. What is certain is that visits to places of worship must, if at all possible, be unhurried, and at best should combine inspection with a period of quiet thought or if so inclined of prayer. Should travellers wish to attend a service, moreover, they will generally be most welcome to do so, whatever their religious views.

Charles Kightly, York 1986

PLACES OF WORSHIP IN BRITAIN

The numbered list on this page keys
the places featured in this book to
the accompanying map of Great Britain.

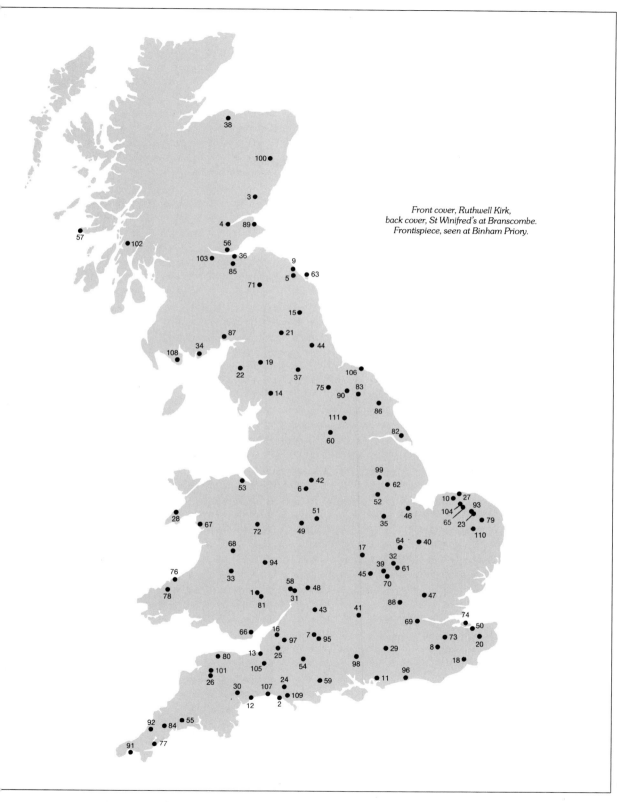

Front cover, Ruthwell Kirk,
back cover, St Winifred's at Branscombe.
Frontispiece, seen at Binham Priory.

ABBEY DORE Hereford and Worcester

OS 161 SO 386304

The small village of Abbey Dore is eleven miles south-west of Hereford, via the A465 to Pontrilas and the B4347 up the Golden Valley – so called from the river Dore, whose Welsh name "dwr" (water) the Normans misunderstood as "d'or" (golden)! The outstandingly beautiful surrounding countryside is full of historical interest: five miles to the east (off the A465) is the famous Norman church at Kilpeck; one and a half miles north is Bacton church; and to the west are Longtown Castle, Llanthony Priory and the Black Mountains.

At first glance, St. Mary's at Abbey Dore appears to be an unusually grand and exceedingly odd-shaped parish church, with a curiously positioned and rather irrelevant tower. Closer inspection, however, reveals it as the eastern two-thirds of a splendid Cistercian abbey church, built between *c*.1180 and *c*.1240 – and thus in a style transitional between late Norman and early Gothic – for a monastery which initially prospered by trading in the incomparable Herefordshire wool, the most costly in medieval Britain. Battered during the later middle ages by Anglo-Welsh border warfare and the murderous feuds of this notoriously lawless frontier region, Dore Abbey was already dilapidated when Henry VIII dissolved it in 1535, granting its buildings to a local squire named John Scudamore: and during the following century its church became little more than a cattle shelter, its altar slab used for cheese-making and its stone monuments for sharpening scythes.

By this time possession had descended to

John Lord Scudamore, a traditionalist churchman who suffered pangs of conscience over his ancestors' profiteering in confiscated ecclesiastical lands. So in 1632 he began to restore the originally cruciform church, blocking off its hopelessly decayed nave and re-roofing the remainder to form the present T-shaped building from its chancel and transepts, to which he also added a tower. The unique amalgam of medieval and late Jacobean this process produced is immediately apparent on entering the church, whose lofty medieval transepts – now serving as the nave – are decorated with seventeenth century wall paintings and texts,

and separated from the chancel by a massive and ornate Jacobean screen. With its 'table-leg' columns, elaborate curlicues and obelisk pinnacles, this is the work of the famous Herefordshire carpenter and woodcarver John Abel, who also furnished the church and re-roofed it in local oak: his ingenious method of capping medieval stone pillars with timber is best seen near the altar, above which is an unusual seventeenth century window, also dating from the Scudamorean restoration.

From here, too, the magnificence of the Cistercian church can best be appreciated. Its most strikingly beautiful feature is the proces-

sional walkway round three sides of the choir, made up of aisles to the north and south – the southern containing an effigy of the founder, Robert Fitz Harold – linked by an eastern "ambulatory" passing behind the altar, where it becomes a double corridor with a roof vault supported on slender columns. Between these columns, against the east wall, were five little chapels: and here are now placed sculptured fragments from the lost nave of the church which Scudamore so laudably saved and so delightfully restored. *See* **Dundrennan, Inchcolm, Monasteries and Religious Houses, The Prayer Book Church.**

Far left, the south front of St Mary's, and above, the font in the nave.

ABBOTSBURY Dorset
OS 194 SY 572848

Abbotsbury is situated in a dramatic section of the Dorset coast, eight miles north-west of Weymouth on the B3157. The village's many attractions, including the Sub-Tropical Gardens (open daily mid-March to mid-October) and the fascinating Swannery (open daily mid-May to September, when hundreds of birds may be seen) are all well signposted. The church, abbey ruins and barn (SY 578852) are all at the east end of Abbotsbury; and St Catherine's chapel is accessible (after a ten minute climb) from a footpath beginning near the Post Office in the main street. Winterbourne Abbas is four miles north, via a minor road: and the great Iron Age hillfort of Maiden Castle six miles north-east, just south of Dorchester.

A village of thatched and honey-coloured houses in the high chalk hills overlooking Lyme Bay, Abbotsbury has much to draw the traveller. Here, in 1026, one of King Canute's courtiers founded a great monastery: and though few of its buildings survive – with the magnificent exception of the great thatched tithe barn south of the church, once twice as long as it is now and thus among the largest in England – the monks have left their mark on Abbotsbury. It was they, for example, who established the unique and still operational Swannery, whose birds provided them with fresh meat: and who built the fine late medieval parish church of St Nicholas, which has a striking monument to an abbot in its porch. Their successors the Strangways family (who acquired the monastic estates at the Reformation, and whose descendants still own Abbotsbury), added the church's Jacobean pulpit, scarred by musket balls in a Civil War skirmish; the curious seventeenth century plaster vault over the chancel, with its rustic-looking angels; and the towering Georgian reredos behind the altar.

But the monks' most noticeable legacy (and indeed one of the oddest and most dramatically-sited places of worship in the West Country) is St Catherine's chapel, on the summit of the steep hill south-west of the village. Reached by a stiffish climb, it commands sweeping views to seaward and down the Chesil Beach to Portland, and one of its purposes was doubtless to serve as a watch-tower against the French pirates who so plagued the abbey during the late fourteenth and early fifteenth centuries. A need for defence, too, may partly explain its paucity of windows, massively thick greenstone walls, and mighty buttresses: though these last also have a structural function, namely to support the chapel's weighty and most unusual roof, which is not of wood but of tunnel-vaulted stone. Unknown elsewhere in southern England, such stone tunnel-vaults were frequent in medieval Scottish churches as a precaution against fire: a necessary precaution here, for the chapel's turret once carried a blazing beacon, a sea-mark for ships and a warning to the countryside of approaching raiders.

St Catherine's on Chapel Hill.

ABERLEMNO Tayside
OS 54 NO 522557

Aberlemno is some sixteen miles north of Dundee and five miles north of Forfar, on the B9134 from Forfar to Brechin. The kirk and cross-stone are just south of this road (at NO 522557), while the remaining stones stand by the roadside at NO 523559. There are also two castles in the parish, ruined Flemington tower (just north-east of the kirk) and the larger and better preserved Melgund Castle; this stands near the Mains of Melgund at NO 545563, and is reached via a minor road turning south off the B3194 about two miles north-east of the roadside stones.

The scattered hamlet of Aberlemno in the heartland of the Picts, the most obscure of the peoples of Dark Age Britain. Known by the Romans as "Picti", the painted ones, but by the Irish simply as "Cruithni" or Britons, these inhabitants of north-eastern Scotland seem to have been a fusion of Celtic incomers with an aboriginal Bronze Age race. For though they spoke a tongue related to British, they also used (probably for religious or ritual purposes) an ancient and so far indecipherable language of pre-Celtic type, and likewise retained the ancient custom of choosing their rulers not from the male but from the female line. Another important but little understood element of their culture was the use of a series of mysterious symbols, found expertly carved

on stone slabs all over eastern Scotland from the Forth to the Shetlands. Whether they served a territorial, memorial, or (more probably) a religious purpose is uncertain, but a fine collection of them remains to be seen at Aberlemno.

Probably the oldest of these stands by the roadside, about three hundred yards north-east of Aberlemno's little kirk. This is a roughly-shaped monolith, incised on one side with the Pictish symbols known as "the serpent", "the double disc", and the "Z-rod", as well as with a mirror and comb, sometimes held to represent a woman. The Z-rod and double disc appear again, now in conjunction with a crescent and V-rod, on the reverse of a much finer and more accomplished slab

nearby. Below them is a spirited hunting scene, complete with stags, hounds, and men blowing horns: but on the other side of the nine foot high stone is a beautiful Celtic cross, surrounded by interlacing patterns and flanked by mourning angels. This second roadside slab therefore belongs to the period after the Picts had been converted to Christianity by St Columba of Iona, and may well have been set up during the eighth century. Of approximately that period also is the finest of the Aberlemno stones, which stands alone immediately west of the kirk. Here, too, Pictish symbols (a Z-rod and "brooch") are carved on the reverse, above a splendid battle scene which may depict some local event, the martial deeds of a hero, or even an incident from the Bible. Clearly the principal subject of the red sandstone slab, however, is a superb seven foot Celtic cross, covered in intricate ornament and flanked by spirals of entwining monsters: and whatever the links with the past implied by the accompanying symbols, both the subject of the stone and its position in a churchyard seem plainly to demonstrate that (like the great Ruthwell standing cross) its main purpose was to mark a Christian place of worship.
See **Abernethy, Iona, Ruthwell.**

The village of Abernethy is now chiefly famous for its soaring Celtic round tower, one of only two on the British mainland, though there are over seventy in Ireland. Seventy-three feet high, it tapers from forty-eight feet in circumference at its base to thirty-two feet at its summit: its internal diameter is no more than eight feet, and within were originally six storeys of timber flooring. This remarkable structure was raised (probably in the eleventh century) as a steeple, watch-tower and place of refuge for a community of Celtic monks – known as Culdees or "servants of God" – which had perhaps been established at Abernethy by Irish missionaries as early as the fifth century, when the place was one of the capitals of Pictland. At one time, indeed, it was also the seat of a bishopric, and virtually the headquarters of the Scottish church: but as the power of Rome increased in Scotland the Irish-inspired Culdees fell out of favour, and in 1272 they were replaced here by Augustinian canons. By then Abernethy had long since ceded its ascendancy to St Andrews, and now only the impressive tower remains to commemorate its past glories.
See **Monasteries and Religious Houses, St Andrews.**

ABERNETHY Tayside
OS 38 NO 190164
Abernethy stands near the south coast of the Firth of Tay, some eight miles south-east of Perth and four miles east of junction 9 of the M90 motorway, via the A912 and A913.

Less than five miles south of the Anglo-Scottish border, St Anne's at Ancroft is one of the most impressive of the fortified churches of that fiercely disputed region. The main body of the church is much-restored Norman, built by the monks of nearby Lindisfarne: and its massive square fortress-tower, added during the Scottish Wars of Independence of the late thirteenth and early fourteenth centuries, was designed both as a permanent stronghold for the vicar and a safe refuge for his parishioners when raiders crossed the frontier. Its ground floor (which could not originally be entered from outside) is therefore vaulted in stone, to minimise the danger of fire: while its upper storeys were only accessible via a winding and easily-held stair from inside the church, which thus served as a second line of defence. The original windows, moreover, are all small and high up for safety, and it is surprising to learn that the rooms they dimly light were still being used as Ancroft's vicarage in the early nineteenth century, long after the danger of raiders had passed.

ANCROFT Northumberland
OS 75 NU 003452
The church stands by the B6525, five miles south of historic Berwick-on-Tweed and a mile and a half south-west of the main A1 trunk road. Ford, six miles to the south-west, has a fine thirteenth century church and a medieval castle, with the battlefield of Flodden (1513) another three miles to the west: while Norham (six miles west) has a Norman church and another impressive border fortress.

Lonely and rather sinister on its grassy hilltop, Arbor Low is one of the most important and certainly among the most atmospheric prehistoric places of worship in the English midlands. Probably raised in about 2000 B.C., towards the end of the New Stone Age, it is technically known as a "henge monument", and consists of an egg-shaped (or perhaps womb-shaped) earthen bank about 250 feet in diameter: within this is a wide ditch surrounding a circular plateau, and on the plateau great recumbent limestone slabs lie tumbled in an uneven ring round a central setting of four fallen stones called a "Cove". Whether the circle of stones ever stood upright is uncertain, and excavation has revealed no rock-cut sockets for them: but they may once have been supported by blocking-stones, and it has been calculated that the horseshoe-shaped central Cove originally opened directly towards the point where the moon set at Midsummer. Near it lay the skeleton of a man, probably a priest or chieftain, though possibly a sacrificial victim buried to give the circle power: and it seems likely that (as at Avebury and Stanton Drew) this Cove was the most important feature of the henge, a real or symbolic burial chamber used in rituals of death and rebirth.

Whatever Arbor Low's purpose, it clearly retained its importance for some time: for the later "round barrow" built into its southeastern rim was raised in the Bronze Age by a people anxious to bury their dead as close

ARBOR LOW Derbyshire
OS 119 SK 160636
Arbor Low is in the dramatic hill country of the Peak District National Park, some ten miles south-east of Buxton via the A515 and a minor road turning east towards Youlgreave (whose fine medieval church has some notable monuments). It is roughly signposted from this minor road, and reached through a farmyard where a fee must be paid: the traveller is also advised to wear stout shoes or boots, especially in wet weather, but the effort of a visit will be well rewarded. Eyam and Tideswell are both some ten miles to the north.

as possible to the sacred site. The much larger mound some 350 yards across the fields to the south-west – called Gib Hill from the gibbet or gallows erected there in the eighteenth century – was also used for a Bronze Age burial, but is probably contemporary with the henge, from which a low earthen bank wanders towards it. Originally it covered only burnt offerings of animal bones and flints, and it may well have borne the same enigmatic relationship to Arbor Low as Silbury Hill does to Avebury.

See **Avebury, Silbury, Stanton Drew, Prehistoric Religion.**

AVEBURY Wiltshire
OS 173 SU 103700

The great circle is eleven miles south of Swindon via the A4361, and one mile north-east of the Beckhampton roundabout off the A4, midway between Marlborough and Calne: it can also be reached from exit 15 of the M4 motorway, via the A345 south to Marlborough and then the A4 west. Much the most dramatic approach is via the minor road turning north off the A4 at West Kennet, which passes between the stones of the West Kennet Avenue. The site, in the care of the National Trust and English Heritage, is open all year round; and also includes the largely medieval church of St James, an excellent museum, and Elizabethan Avebury Manor (open April–October). Nearby are Silbury Hill (by the A4 and also accessible by a half mile long footpath from Avebury car park) and the great prehistoric communal tomb called West Kennet Long Barrow (accessible by the same path or from the A4).

"This old Monument doth as much exceed in bigness the so renowned Stonehenge, as a Cathedral doth a parish church: so that by its grandeur one might presume it to have been an Arch-Temple of the Druids." So wrote John Aubrey in the seventeenth century, and Avebury is indeed much the largest prehistoric monument not merely in Britain but in the whole of Europe: a great ring of earth and stone a quarter of a mile across and four-fifths of a mile in circumference, enclosing enough space for more than a dozen Egyptian pyramids. Outermost is a mighty earthen bank, which once rose some fifty-five feet above its wide internal ditch – now silted up to half its depth, but still vastly impressive: and within the ditch was a concentric ring of about a hundred colossal unshaped stones – thirty of which survive, principally in the north-western and south-western of the four quadrants into which the ring is divided by modern roads passing through prehistoric entrance-gaps. Inside the bank, ditch and outer circle were two more rings of stones, now fragmentary and obscured by the

modern village: the southern inner circle, once centred on a stone "obelisk"; and the northern, originally a double circle focused on the three huge stones of "the Cove".

Nor is this all: for the huge Avebury circle was only part of a still vaster complex of sacred sites. From its southern entrance the "West Kennet Avenue" of a hundred paired stones (many now re-erected) ran a mile and a half to a smaller circle, "the Sanctuary" on Overton Hill: and another stone avenue of similar length (now almost destroyed) marched westward to an unknown destination. Just over a mile to the north, moreover, is the prehistoric "causewayed camp" on Windmill Hill, which is older than Avebury – as are enigmatic Silbury Hill and the great communal tomb called West Kennet Long Barrow, both within a mile and a half to the south; while the hills all around are crowned with ancient tree-grown burial mounds.

Aubrey was wrong, however, in associating Avebury with the Druids: for it was apparently raised between about 2600 and 2300 B.C., towards the end of the New Stone Age; and had most probably been abandoned for at least a thousand years before the shadowy (and largely mythical) Druid priesthood began their late Iron Age ministrations. Wrong, too, are the theorists who over the centuries have asserted that the great stones were erected by Egyptians, Phoenicians, or even far-wandering Red Indians; or that it is the burial place of Arthur's knight's, a set of stone needles for "earth acupuncture", or a focus for telepathic rays, to mention only a few of the 'interpretations' that Avebury has attracted by its grandeur. The more plausible notion that it was some kind of astronomical observatory can likewise not be proven: but a place of worship it most certainly was, constructed with infinite care and almost unimaginable effort – for some of the largest stones are almost twenty feet high and weigh up to sixty tons, so that to raise them with levers, ramps and hide ropes required not only great muscle power but also considerable organisation.

This argues that a numerous and comparatively unified people dwelt amid these well-watered and easily farmed downlands, readily accessible from the ancient track called the Ridgeway a mile east of the circle, and that they had some compelling reason for building on so immense a scale. The area was already sacred when they did so, and a desire to add to its (and therefore to its inhabitants') prestige may have been a contributory factor: yet Avebury must primarily have been a focus for vitally important religious rites, doubtless designed both to ensure the fertility of the worshippers and to preserve them from the terrors of death and the unknown. Exactly how such rituals were performed we shall perhaps never know – though they probably centred on the two inner circles, and perhaps particularly on the Cove within the northern circle, with its similarity to a megalithic tomb: but whatever they were, they bequeathed an atmosphere of pagan mystery to Avebury which was slow to disappear, and has perhaps not entirely gone yet.

When the Anglo-Saxons founded Avebury village, indeed, they built their church of St James (well worth a visit in itself) just outside the earthwork, as though they doubted whether Christianity was yet strong enough to overcome the pagan past. But as the Church's confidence grew – a confidence perhaps symbolized by the carving on St James's Norman font, showing a bishop vanquishing two dragons of evil – came the counter-attack: and by the early fourteenth century "the Devil's stones" were being deliberately and laboriously pushed over and buried. Then, in about 1325, a travelling

barber-surgeon was crushed beneath a stone he was helping to fell, his corpse remaining there until the "Barber Stone" near the south entrance was excavated and re-erected in 1938. This shockingly ominous incident seems to have temporarily halted the destruction: but during the seventeenth and eighteenth centuries it continued apace, as less pious but more profit-conscious farmers and innkeepers demolished the stones to make plough-room, or smashed them with fire and hammers to sell as building material. Only in 1934 was the site finally secured from damage: yet despite the ravages of time and of man the bones of Avebury remain (as Stukely put it in 1743) "equal to any of the noted wonders of the world".

See **Arbor Low, Castlerigg Carles, Knowlton, Prehistoric Religion, Silbury Hill, and Stanton Drew.**

Far left, stones within the massive bank and ditch that ring the modern village. Below, many of the standing stones are colourfully decorated with lichen.

One of the comparatively few substantial monastic ruins in south-estern England, Bayham Abbey stands in a picturesque valley site exactly astride the Kent-Sussex border, and originally had gatehouses leading into both counties. It was founded in the first years of the thirteenth century for the "white canons" of the Premonstratensian order, so called from their mother-house at Prémontré in France, and had a fairly uneventful history.

Its church, however, was twice altered, and the remains now present a curious aspect. For in the later thirteenth century the cruciform chancel was doubled in length by simply adding to the old east end, so that it became a double cross with two sets of transepts: while in the fifteenth century alterations to the south nave wall necessitated the support of buttresses so wide that the cloister walk cuts through them via a series of arches. Consider-

BAYHAM ABBEY East Sussex
OS 188 TQ 651366
The abbey is four miles east of Tunbridge Wells, via the A267, the B2169 towards Lamberhurst, and a signposted track. Three miles further east (beyond Lamberhurst and off the A21) is Scotney Castle, a medieval fortress likewise incorporated into a romantic landscape.

able portions of the monastic buildings also remain, most notably the "Kentish gate-house" some distance north-west of the church. At that time, indeed, the already attractive situation of the ruins was enhanced by landscaping, in order to provide a "romantic vista" for the mansion on the hill above: while the Kentish gate became an eye-catching lodge for the battlemented Gothick Dower House which stands just to the south.

BERWICK-ON-TWEED
Northumberland
OS 75 NU 001533

Still entirely surrounded by its unique Elizabethan ramparts, Berwick is one of the most interesting and unspoilt of Britain's historic towns: it stands on the Anglo-Scottish border, the river Tweed and the A1 trunk road, sixty-seven miles north-west of Newcastle-upon-Tyne and fifty-eight miles east-south-east of Edinburgh. Holy Trinity church is to the east of the town centre, in Church Street and opposite the early eighteenth century Ravensdowne Barracks military museum (open to the public April–October).

Just inside the splendidly-preserved Elizabethan fortifications of Berwick-on-Tweed stands one of the most unusual parish churches in England. It is exceptional, first, because it was built between 1650 and 1652: which is to say during the Commonwealth period, when a Puritan Parliament ruled without a king and the Church of England as such did not officially exist. Raised by Colonel George Fenwick, Governor of Berwick, it replaced a medieval parish church which was too small and dilapidated to serve both the citizens and the large garrison stationed here to guard the border against the Scots: and was constructed largely of old stone brought from the ruins of Berwick Castle, so that the walls appear weathered within as well as without. Because it was designed for Presbyterian rather than Anglican worship, Holy Trinity's external appearance is also most unusual, for it is essentially a rectangular "preaching box" with aisles, which originally had no chancel and never had a tower: Cromwell himself, it is said, for-

bade one to be built when he passed through in 1650, on his way to defeat the Scots at Dunbar.

Yet Holy Trinity is by no means a dull church, and it was indeed built in the very latest style of the day: perhaps its most distinctive feature being its many "Venetian" windows, each consisting of a round-headed central light between two lower rectangular ones. Within, too, it is more Classical than Gothic, with round arches on 'Greek' columns: but its original internal furnishings have been sadly altered. For, as part of the process of de-Puritanising the building, the originally central pulpit has been moved to one side, while of the galleries which formerly extended round all four sides only one remains, at the west end. At the east end, moreover, an irrelevant chancel was tacked on by the Victorians, to house the altar which the Presbyterian citizens of Berwick once indignantly refused to allow into their distinctive church.

See **The Prayer Book Church.**

Prehistoric Religion

The study of prehistoric religion is fraught with mysteries. This is first of all due to the very fact that it *is* "pre-historic", which is to say that its practices, cults and beliefs passed away before the advent of writing, so that all our knowledge of them derives from the bare bones of archeology, clothed with what can at best be only enlightened speculation. Unenlightened speculation, moreover, has laid many misleading trails. For though we no longer possess the confidence to state (as did Bishop Ussher in the seventeenth century) that the world began on the evening of October the twenty-second in 4004 B.C., or that all stone circles were built either by giants or druids, several conveniently comprehensive "interpretations" of prehistoric belief still continue to be propounded. These tales of extra-terrestrials, of magical "ley-lines" linking holy places and of vast Zodiacs, however, rarely take into account that the sites they purport to explain may be separated in time by thousands of years, or that religious practices must have passed through countless changes during the twenty or so millenia of man's existence in Britain.

One of the very few near-certainties about prehistoric religion, indeed is that it was much concerned with death, rebirth and fertility. Thus the earliest known deliberate human burial in Britain, thought to date from around 1700 B.C., was carefully laid in a deposit of blood-red oxide, as though to revitalise the bones for some future existence: while other finds hint at rituals designed to guarantee the fertility of humans, hunted animals, or even flint mines – at Grimes Graves in Norfolk, for example, the figure of a heavily pregnant mother goddess was laid at the entrance to a new tunnel in about 4000 B.C., perhaps in the hope of increasing its productivity. Other rituals, probably intended to free the spirits of the dead from their bodies, seen to have been practiced in connection with the great communal burial places – the earthen long barrows and megalithic tombs lined with massive stones – which began to be raised at about the same period. One of the most impressive and accessible of these is at West Kennet near Avebury, in an area which contains a very large number of interconnected sacred sites built over a long period of time, including Silbury Hill and the vast stone circle at Avebury itself.

Such stone circles, occasionally built within the earthwork ring banks called "henges" but far more frequently freestanding, are the most striking and best known of all prehistoric monuments. Raised during the third and second millenia B.C., when the New Stone Age was giving way to the Bronze Age, they were all but certainly used for important religious ceremonies, which may well have included dancing and festivities. A distant memory of such rituals, indeed, is discernible in the many legends (like those told about Castlerigg Carles, the Hurlers and Stanton Drew) which explain them as groups of revellers turned to stone. The theory that they were laid out for the purpose of complex astronomical calculations, however, remains unconfirmed: though the careful arrangement of stones in circles like Sunhoney indicates that some at least of them were used for rites connected with the movements of the sun and moon, and thus with the passage of the seasons.

By the time prehistory passes into history with the Roman invasion of A.D. 43, these stone circles had long since been abandoned, and the Celtic peoples who inhabited Britain worshipped their multifarious gods in oak groves and by holy wells and springs.

To this late Iron Age period belongs the mysterious priesthood known as the Druids, whose name apparently means "men of the oaks" and around whom much romantic myth has gathered: very little, however, is reliably known about them, since all our information concerning their practices comes from generally hostile Roman sources. According to these, the Druids carried out human sacrifices as a means of placating the gods and divining the future, sometimes burning men and animals in wicker cages or slaughtering them in the oak groves where they venerated the sacred mistletoe. Some classical authors, nevertheless, depict them in an altogether less sensational light: as philosopher priests who preserved an ancient tradition of learning handed on by word of mouth, and who believed above all in the transmigration of souls – which is to say that the soul never dies, but simply passes from one body to another by the process of reincarnation. As the mediators between men and the gods, they seem also to have wielded very considerable political power, rallying the Britons against the invading Romans. The latter, therefore, extirpated them without mercy, mounting a campaign specifically designed to destroy their headquarters on their holy island of Mona or Anglesey.

Some of the less controversial elements of Celtic belief, however, were adopted with enthusiam by the Romans, while here and there the old gods – demoted to demons or transmogrified to local "saints" – maintained a shadowy existence even after the coming of Christianity. That prehistoric places of worship long continued to be held in awe as places of power, moreover, is clear from the strenuous efforts the medieval church (as at Knowlton and Rudston) made to exorcise them: and some of that power lingers even yet, to be experienced by the modern traveller.

BINHAM Norfolk
OS 132 TF 982399

Binham is some twenty-two miles north-west of Norwich, and eight miles north-east of Fakenham via the B1105 and the B1388. Walsingham and Little Snoring are respectively four and six miles to the south-west: while Cley-next-the-Sea (on the beautiful north Norfolk coast) is some six miles to the north-east.

The parish church of St Mary and the Holy Cross rises majestically amid the ruins of Binham Priory, and once formed the nave of the much larger priory church. Founded in the late eleventh century by a nephew of William the Conqueror, the Benedictine priory was subordinate to the great abbey of St Albans – a situation which produced many disputes, and even a full-scale siege – and afflicted with several eccentric priors, including an alchemist and a "wandering vagabond". Yet it nevertheless contains some remarkably fine architecture, most notably the famous and richly decorated west front of the present church: this was built during the second quarter of the thirteenth century (when the Priory was doubtless benefiting from pilgrims travelling to nearby Walsingham) in the very latest style of Early English Gothic.

Within, the east end of the church is disappointing by comparison – a blank wall raised in 1540, when the priory was dissolved and its chancel, transepts and aisles allowed to fall into ruin, leaving only the nave for parish use. But the soaring triple tiers of arches along the north and south walls do much to compensate for these losses, and also provide an unusually clear demonstration of the transi-

The richly decorated font at the west end of the nave.

tion between the Norman and the newer Gothic styles. For the lowest tiers of arches are all round in the Norman fashion, but at the west end the last two of the middle storey are pointed Gothic, as are the three above in the uppermost tier: thus proving that the change came when the lowest storey had already been built, and continued upward and westward. Within too are some fine carved medieval bench ends, and a font sculptured (like so many in Norfolk) with the Seven Sacraments of the Church, the marriage scene on its north-east face being particularly clear: but perhaps the most telling of Binham's possessions are the panels from the fifteenth century rood screen set into the rearmost pews. Once richly painted with saints (as, for instance, at Cawston), these panels were considered "idolatrous" at the Reformation, when they were whitewashed and covered with Biblical texts: but the saints (or superior medieval paint) triumphed in the end, for fourteen of them now wholly or partly appear through the overlay, including St Helena with her cross and the revered royal martyr Henry VI, with an antelope at his feet.

See **Monasteries and Religious Houses, The Reformation, St Albans.**

An outstandingly attractive village overlooking Chichester Harbour, Bosham possesses the only English parish church represented on the famous Bayeux Tapestry. There, Earl Harold Godwinson is shown entering the church to pray before sailing from Bosham on his fateful journey to Normandy in 1064, which culminated in his being forced to swear allegiance to William the Conqueror and thus helped to precipitate the subsequent Norman invasion. At that time much of the present building (which is said to stand on the site of a Roman basilica and a seventh century monastery) already existed: namely the tower (topped by its pretty shingled spire in the fifteenth century), the nave, and part of the chancel. Like many Anglo-Saxon churches, it is somewhat haphazardly planned, for none of its corners are right angles, no two walls are parallel, and there is a pronounced skew between nave and chancel. Yet the great chancel arch is one of the very finest of the Saxon period in England: dramatically wide and lofty, with twenty foot pillars resting on massive plinths, it probably dates from just before the Conquest. Scarcely less impressive is the long and largely thirteenth century chancel, which has at its east end five graceful lancet windows graduated in size towards the centre, and separated by dark Purbeck marble shafts in a manner characteristic of the Early English style of architecture. Most memorable of all, however, is the distant view of the church across the water, with the Downs as a backdrop.

See **The Anglo-Saxon Church.**

BOSHAM West Sussex
OS 197 SU 804039
Bosham stands on a tidal inlet of Chichester Harbour, just south of the A27 some ten miles east of Portsmouth and four miles west of historic Chichester, with its splendid cathedral: also nearby (two miles to the east via the A27) are the well displayed remains of Fishbourne Roman Palace.

BRANSCOMBE Devon
OS 192 SY 195885
The scattered combe-side village of Branscombe is sixteen miles east of Exeter and five miles east of Sidmouth, via the A3052 and signposted minor roads turning south. Whitchurch Canonicorum is some fourteen miles to the north-east, via the A3052, the A35, and minor roads north.

The transepts of St Winifred's are set back to the west of its Norman tower.

Its situation alone – in a steep wooded valley scattered with attractive houses, dropping down to a particularly beautiful part of the south Devon coast – would make St Winifred's at Branscombe well worth a visit: yet it is also an uncommonly interesting church, with architecture or fittings of every period from the Norman Conquest to the nineteenth century. Norman, for example, are the sturdy central tower with its distinctive round stair-turret, and part of the nave; while the transepts – not flanking the tower as usual, but set back to the west – are of the thirteenth century and the chancel is of the fourteenth, with triple-stepped priests' seats and a grand fifteenth century east window. This last is best seen from within, lighting the unusual eastward vista produced by successive transept and tower arches, with the screened-off sanctuary beyond – where the altar stands out from the wall, surrounded on all four sides by railings in the "Protestant" fashion of the seventeenth century.

Back at the west end – by the late medieval "Morality" wall-painting of a devil spearing a courting couple – the magnificently carved oak gallery is Jacobean: it was perhaps by the son of Joan Wadham ("a virtuous and ancient Gentlewoman descended from the ancient House of the Plantagenets") whose Elizabethan monument oddly depicts her twice, kneeling with some of her "much issue" behind both her successive husbands. This is in the north transept, and there too – completing the extraordinary range of fittings in this history-book of a church – are a fine three-decker pulpit and some "horse-box" pews, erected by the formidable Parson Puddicombe who made erring parishioners wear dunce's caps and do penance in white sheets.

See **The Prayer Book Church.**

*Lying at the foot of the distinctive hill
of the same name, Brent Knoll village
is seven miles south of Weston-super-
Mare via the A370 and the B3140,
and just over a mile north of the M5
motorway via junction 22 and the
A38 north. The church stands above
the south end of the long village, on
the slope of the hill. Nearby East Brent
also has an interesting church with a
fine spire and an unusual seventeenth
century nave roof: and from its
churchyard a footpath leads to the
prehistoric hill fort on the summit of
the Knoll.*

Set on the south-western slopes of Brent
Knoll itself – an isolated and hillfort-crowned
eminence which dominates the marshlands
all around – St Michael's is an essentially fifteenth century church with a fine angel roof
over its north aisle. On its south wall is a quite
delightful piece of local folk art: the highly-
coloured plaster monument to John Somerset (d.1663). He glares belligerently from a
central oval, surrounded by all the panoply
of war and flanked by his two wives, one in
a large and fashionable hat and the other in
a widow's hood: while in the panels below
his whole family kneels at prayer, and the Last
Trump summons his shrouded corpse from
its coffin. Still more graphic, but rather more

mysterious in origin, is the famous series of
"political cartoons" carved on three of the
late medieval bench ends opposite the monument. The easternmost of them shows a wily
fox disguised as a mitred abbot and preaching
to a congregation of birds, while pigs in
monks' cowls look on: above, a chained ape
offers a money bag, and below two more spit-
roast a pig. On the next bench-end westward
the fox-abbot has been unmasked and foot-
cuffed: he is then set in the stocks and
guarded by an ape, with his mitre hung mock-
ingly before him. Finally, on the third bench
end, he is hanged by the birds, while dogs
bark in triumph and a face above grins
derisively. Whoever commissioned these

*The John Somerset monument on
the south wall of the nave.*

carvings, then, obviously regarded abbots (and perhaps especially the Abbot of Glastonbury, a great landowner hereabouts) as hypocritical deceivers ruling over greedy pig-monks, intent on luring their bird-parishioners to destruction. The development of the fable is doubtless a piece of wishful thinking: and doubtless too its finer points – including the identity and role of the apes – would have been instantly understood by the late medieval inhabitants of Brent Knoll. Yet the modern traveller can still enjoy it for itself, while speculating on the circumstances which allowed this outspoken attack on churchmen to be introduced into a church.

One of the three political cartoons carved on bench-ends opposite the Somerset memorial.

Brigflatts, the oldest Quaker Meeting House in northern England, stands at the historic heart of Quakerism, only a few miles from the open hillside where the first ever meeting of the Society of Friends was held in 1652. At that exciting time, with both Monarchy and Established Church overthrown by the Civil Wars, all England was bubbling with new ideas about Man's relationship to God, and with new sects impatient of traditional "organised religion". Among these were the "Seekers" of the high Pennine Dales, groups of men and women who met together in houses or fields to hear one of their number preach, but who also seem to have been expecting some special message or revelation. When the wandering preacher George Fox was led by a vision to Brigflatts hamlet (where he lodged at the grey-rendered farm which still stands opposite the Meeting House) he was therefore received with interest; and soon afterwards, on June the thirteenth 1652, was invited to attend a Seeker gathering at the now ruined chapel on nearby Firbank Fell. He refused, however, to enter the chapel, which he declared to be no more holy than the surrounding mountainside: and instead preached for three hours from the roadside rock now known as "Fox's Pulpit" and marked by a plaque.

The message that he there proclaimed was, in brief, that "something of God's Spirit" dwells in every human being, if only they will allow it to operate. Without this "Light Within", this first-hand knowledge of God grounded on personal experience, all religion is in vain, and outward doctrines, rules and ceremonies are at best distractions. "What canst *thou* say of Christ?", he demanded of his thousand-strong congregation, many of whom were so convinced of "God's Everlasting Truth" that they resolved to spread it not only throughout England but also into Europe and across the Atlantic. Thus was

born the Religious Society of Friends, nicknamed "Quakers" because they were said to tremble at the name of God: and despite (or perhaps because of) the fierce persecution their revolutionary notions and their pacifism provoked from Anglican and Puritan alike, Fox's followers went on from strength to strength.

In 1674, though still forbidden on pain of imprisonment (or worse) to gather for worship, the local Friends decided to build a specialised Meeting House at Brigflatts, where the present – intensely moving – Quaker burial ground already existed. Wishing both to avoid unwelcome attention and to shun the conventional forms for places of worship, what they raised with their own hands was and is quite literally a house: a simple whitewashed building in a little garden, amid a once-thriving hamlet which has shrunk to a handful of dwellings. Nor does its plain and dignified interior resemble that of a church or chapel: there is, of course, no altar or communion table, since Quakers observe no set form of service whatever, sitting in silence unless and until the spirit moves one or more of them to speak or to pray. The oak-panelled meeting room, however, has elders' seats along its south wall, and a gallery round the other three sides, and many of its fittings date from the seventeenth or early eighteenth century. They include, at the foot of the gallery steps, a feature highly unusual if not unique in a British place of worship – a pair of doors which form a pen for the sheepdogs of hill-farming Friends.

Such sound practicality, typical of Quakers, has helped to prevent Brigflatts from becoming a mere museum, despite its fame and associations. It continues, rather, to be a place of peace and of power, where "meetings for worship" are still held every Sunday morning: the traveller of any religion, or of none, is most welcome to attend them.

BRIGFLATTS Cumbria
OS 97 SD 641913
The Meeting House is three miles east of junction 37 of the M6 motorway and just over a mile west of Sedbergh, down an unobtrusively signposted lane turning south off the A683 Sedbergh to Kirkby Lonsdale road. Visitors are welcome seven days a week in summer (the Meeting House being closed on winter Mondays only), and are invited to attend the "meetings for worship" held every Sunday at 10.30 a.m.. "Fox's Pulpit" (SD 619937) stands immediately to the east of a narrow minor road over Firbank Fell, at a place marked by a ladder-stile over the roadside wall and the remains of a chapel: this road turns north off the A684 two miles east of the M6 and about two and a half miles west of Sedbergh, opposite a house painted with a black horse (SD 621918).

The Gods of Rome

During the four centuries of Roman dominion over Britain, more different deities were worshipped here than at any other time in recorded history. For the Romans were nothing if not tolerant in matters of religion: they had many gods of their own, and had no objection whatever to adding almost infinitely to their number, so long as certain simple rules were kept. The new deities must not, first of all, threaten Roman power in any way, and their worship must be carried out without offending the somewhat elastic Roman notions of public decency. Neither must they claim exclusive power (as did the God of the Jews and Christians), for this would be to detract from the official state religion which all citizens were expected to observe, whatever other gods they chose to worship in addition.

The especial importance of this last rule sprang from another characteristic of Roman religion, its hard-headed practicality. Their gods were (so to speak) extremely human: if properly honoured, they could reasonably be expected to extend their help and protection to mortals; but if ignored or derided, disaster was almost sure to follow. This attitude produced the thousands of altars which even now survive in British museums, vowed to the various gods by men and women who hoped for such benefits as health, wealth, promotion or good hunting; or who, having received these favours, were fulfilling their side of the bargain by having the altar carved and inscribed. It also produced Roman official religion. Since the benefit which all Roman citizens ought to desire most was the well-being of Rome itself, it was clearly necessary that the City's particular guardian gods should be regularly and publicly placated lest they withdraw their support not only from the City but from the whole Empire. These guardian deities – Jupiter "Greatest and Best", Minerva, and Juno – therefore had temples in most large Roman towns, and at least an altar in every Roman fort. They were soon constrained, however, to share public worship with a being who personified even more precisely the Roman state, namely the Emperor himself. For most emperors were deified by decree after their death – the dying Vespasian is supposed to have joked, "Dear me, I must be turning into a god" – and though during their lifetime they were not exactly worshipped, divine honours were paid to their "genius" or guardian spirit, which amounted to much the same thing. The birthdays of current emperors and the anniversaries of their most famous predecessors (like the great Augustus) were thus occasions for public sacrifices of oxen, and for official rejoicings organised by magistrates or garrison commanders, which all good citizens were expected to attend.

Perhaps the most famous Roman temple in Britain, indeed, was that of the deified Emperor Claudius at Colchester, whose remains can still be seen beneath the great Norman castle later built on its site. Constructed within a decade of the invasion as the centrepiece of a showpiece Roman city, this huge and lavish place of worship attracted the particular hatred of the conquered Britons, who viewed it as "a citadel of perpetual slavery". When the warrior-queen Boudica of the Iceni rose against Roman rule in A.D. 61, therefore, the temple of Claudius became a prime target, especially since the garrison of Colchester attempted to make a last stand there. After two days of fierce fighting, however, the temple was stormed and taken, its defenders being either massacred out of hand or preserved only for sacrifice in the groves of the Celtic goddess Andrasta. The life sized statue of the god-emperor himself was symbolically decapitated, its head being carried off in triumph as a trophy. It came to light as recently as 1907 in the bed of a nearby river, where it had either been thrown as an offering to the water god or, more probably hastily deposited as incriminating evidence after the defeat of the revolt. When more peaceful times returned, emperor worship soon ceased to rouse stong passions, and increasingly came to be seen as a necessary but fairly meaningless aspect of Roman state religion.

This formalised state religion has been appositely compared to Victorian churchgoing, and like Victorian churchgoing it had very little to do with faith. To satisfy their deeper spiritual needs, the inhabitants of Roman Britain might turn to the classical deity of their particular trade or calling, such as Mars for soldiers, Vulcan for blacksmiths, or Nemesis for gladiators: or to the gorgeous ceremonial and secret rites of eastern "mystery" cults. London certainly had a temple of the Egyptian goddess Isis, and perhaps others dedicated to the orgiastic wine-god Bacchus and to the equally abandoned worship of Cybele, with its self-castrating priesthood. Doubtless these last deities had originally been imported by citizens who originated in other parts of the Empire, for the population of Roman Britain was remarkably cosmopolitan – Roman York had inhabitants born as far afield as Greece, Sardinia and North Africa – and the army was more cosmopolitan yet, each unit tending to cling to its own gods. Thus, on rainswept Hadrian's Wall, homesick Syrian archers dedicated altars to Hittite weather gods and to a Syrian version of Venus, while German auxiliaries invoked the Mother-goddesses, of their native tribe. Nearly always, the worshippers of these visiting deities equated them with the classical gods they most nearly resembled in appearance and powers, endowing them with a dual personality and a double-barrelled name like Jupiter Dolichenus or Venus Syriaca.

Others, perhaps feling that the gods of their homeland were too far distant to provide really effective aid, adopted the local deities of Celtic Britain as their own, a practice common to Roman soldiers wherever in the Empire they were stationed. To equate these British deities with the gods of Rome, however, was not so easy. For whereas the latter all had clearly defined fields of influence – war, love, family life and so on – the Celtic gods were much more shadowy and indefinite beings, sometimes shifting from single to triple form and rarely consenting to be tied down to a consistent line of work. The horned deity Belatucadros ("the bright beautiful one"), admittedly, was usually regarded by his Roman worshippers as a version of their war god Mars, but in other cases the same Celtic deity might sometimes be equated with Mars, sometimes with Mercury, and sometimes with the woodland spirit Silvanus. Very often, indeed, the rustic gods of northern Britain were linked with this Silvanus, the Roman Pan: and since they might be presumed to know the countryside better than any foreigner, were frequently invoked by off-duty soldiers who hoped for good hunting or who (like the cavalry officer who erected an altar on the Durham moors) wished to give thanks "for killing an enormous wild boar, which had eluded many of his predecessors".

British dieties, indeed, seem to have found particularly favour among the Roman garrison of Hadrian's Wall. One of the most popular of them was Brigantia ("the High One"), the guardian goddess of the northern British tribe called the Brigantes: usually depicted as a warrior queen, she was often worshipped by the Romans as a personification of Victory, or of their own war goddess Minerva. Other native warrior dieties recognised by the newcomers included Camulos and Lugh, who gave their names respectively to "Camulodunum" (later Colchester) and "Luguvalium" (now Carlisle): while Maponus, "the divine son", appears to have been venerated particularly around the western end of Hadrian's Wall, where he is still commemorated by the town name of Lochmaben in Dumfries and Galloway. All over Britian, too, Roman and Romanised Britons honoured the mysterious trio of Celtic gods called "the hooded ones", who are invariably shown swathed in hooded cloaks. Among the many other British gods whose worship persisted into Roman times were Taranis, probably a thunder god; Mataunus, "the sacred bear"; the stag headed Cernunnos; and Succellus "the good striker", who the Romans may have equated with their club-bearing Hercules, and who is perhaps represented by the famous Cerne Giant at Cerne Abbas.

Some of these part-Romanised British gods were worshipped over a fairly wide area, but others – including the guardians of holy wells and sacred springs – were very much more localised. Among these were Coventina, who enjoyed such enormous popularity at Carrawburgh on Hadrian's Wall, and Sul Minerva, who watched over the healing waters of Bath, known to the Romans as "Aquae Sulis". The British deity Nodens, the traces of whose temple survive at Lydney in Gloucestershire, was likewise a god of healing – and the reverse, to judge from the curses scratched on lead and deposited at his shrine.

This shrine, surprisingly enough, was built in the later fourth century, when the multifarious minor gods of Roman Britain had long been under extreme pressure from the newcomers. Probably the first of these to arrive, during the second century, was the originally Persian god Mithras the Bullslayer, "the Lord of Light and Life" who was seen as locked in eternal battle with the powers of darkness. Especially popular with soldiers, he has left more evidence in Britain of his cult than any other Roman god, and the traveller can still view the remains of his temples at Carrawburgh and in London. His worshippers had to pass through terrifying ordeals before being admitted to the exclusive circle of initiates, usually by a rite of baptism in the blood of an animal: the richest devotees, indeed, lay in a ceremonial trench above which a bull was slaughtered, soaking them in its blood. Thereafter they joined a close and powerful freemasonry, sworn to aid each other in all worldy affairs and to honour Mithras above all other gods.

The worship of Mithras did not entirely exclude other deities, for his London temple also contained images of the Egyptian Serapis and perhaps of Bacchus, while his Carrawburgh shrine held a statue of Coventina. But the second of the newcomers would brook no rivals whatever, and when the first Christian missionaries arrived in Britain they were persecuted for refusing to observe even the formalised sham of emperor worship. In A.D. 312, however, Christianity itself became the official state religion not only of Britain but of the whole Empire: and though the old paganism was to linger on for another century or more, the death knell of the gods of Rome had been sounded.

See **Prehistoric Religion, Holy Wells and Sacred Springs, The First Christian Missionaries.**

BRINKBURN PRIORY

Northumberland
OS 81 NZ 116984

Set in lovely but little-frequented Coquetdale, the priory is some twenty-five miles north of Newcastle-upon-Tyne and four and a half miles south-east of attractive Rothbury, at the end of signposted minor road off the B6344. It can be reached from the main A1 by turning onto the A697 north of Morpeth, and then onto the B6344 three miles beyond Longhorsley.

Remote and idyllically set in a deep wooded valley, and almost encircled by a bend in the river Coquet, Brinkburn Priory's lofty monastic church stands complete and fully roofed, and until recently was in use for parish worship. It is not, however, entirely what it seems, for its roof and upper portions were rebuilt in 1858: yet the restoration was firmly based on surviving evidence, and provides the traveller with a rare opportunity to visit an isolated monastic church which is not merely a ruin, however picturesque. The priory to which it belonged was founded in 1135 for the canons of the Augustinian order, but never prospered greatly, doubtless because of its uncomfortable proximity to the troubled Anglo-Scottish border. Its church,

nevertheless, is a splendid example of the architecture of the latest twelfth and early thirteenth centuries, which is to say of the transition between the Norman and the Early English Gothic styles. Norman, for example, is the elaborately sculptured and round-arched north doorway: yet elsewhere the later style predominates, most impressively in the east front with its three tiers of characteristically Early English lancet windows, such as are repeated throughout the notably tall and narrow church. Beside it, in an almost surreal juxtaposition, is a part Georgian, part romantically castellated mansion, which incorporates fragments of the priory's monastic buildings.

See **Monasteries and Religious Houses.**

BRISTOL Avon

OS 172 ST 592723

Bristol is 115 miles west of London via the M4 motorway: and St Mary Redcliffe (which is open daily) stands prominently to the south of the city centre, by the inner ring road immediately east of the Avon bridge. Bristol also possesses several other fine medieval churches, mainly concentrated in the city centre area to the north-west of Redcliffe: much the most notable being the cathedral (originally St Augustine's Abbey church) on College Green. Almost immediately opposite the cathedral is the medieval Lord Mayor's Chapel, and nearby (for a complete contrast) is the restored Victorian ship the S.S. Great Britain, moored in the Floating Harbour.

Queen Elizabeth I called St Mary Redcliffe "the fairest goodliest, and most famous parish church in England", and her description can only be bettered by adding that it is also one of the very largest. Towering vast and impressive above the modern road system, indeed, it looks more like a cathedral – and that, no doubt, was how it was intended to appear. For the great medieval port of Bristol had no cathedral of its own – St Augustine's Abbey church not being promoted to that status until 1542 – and the wealthy Bristol merchants did their best to compensate by building their principal place of worship in as cathedral-like a manner as ever they could. The lavishness of their endowment is apparent as soon as the traveller approaches the main entrance, the showily hexagonal and fabulously ornate fourteenth century outer north porch, with its almost oriental-looking door frame: within were displayed holy relics, watched over by a priest from the encircling upper walkway while pilgrims filed in at one side door and out at the other. Beyond is the inner north porch (dating from c.1200 and thus the earliest part of the church) which once housed the shrine of Our Lady of Redcliffe: and beyond again the church itself sweeps eastward in a great vista of graceful columns and lofty arches, its roof vaults glowing with hundreds of gilded bosses.

Begun in the earlier fourteenth century, the main body of St Mary's was crowned in the mid-fifteenth by the great Perpendicular clerestory – literally a "clear storey" of huge six-light windows, flying-buttressed and pinnacled without and superimposed on the lower stages of the church like a smaller cross resting upon a larger one. Filling the whole

building with light, this clerestory was the gift of William Canynges, the greatest of all medieval Bristol merchants: but before visiting his tomb in the south transept there is much to see at the west end of the church, including St John's chapel with its American associations (a whalebone there is said to have been brought home by the Bristol-based Cabots); the armour and banners of William Penn's father, on the tower wall; and the pillar-font with its hovering gilded dove. Further east, in the south nave wall, are three distinctively arched recesses of c.1330; eastward again is the splendidly vaulted chancel – which has notable brasses under the carpets by its altar rail; and easternmost of all is the lower-roofed fifteenth century Lady Chapel, with its rather unfortunate glass.

Any visit to St Mary Redcliffe must also include the tombs of its greatest benefactor: William Canynges the younger, five times mayor of Bristol and twice its M.P., but at last a priest. The larger (but coarser) of his two monuments therefore shows him as a merchant prince, lying beside his wife above a tomb chest emblazoned with his arms and trademarks. Next to it, however, is a much finer alabaster effigy depicting him as a priest: for after his wife's death this remarkable man forsook business for holy orders, celebrating his first Mass in his own church in 1468 and dying in 1474 as Dean of Westbury. Behind it is an inscription listing his many merchant ships, and continuing:

"The Building's rare that here you may behold
To shrine his bones deserves a tomb of gold
The famous Fabrick that he here hath done
Shines in its sphere as glorious as the sun".

See **The Great Wool Churches.**

All Saints church at Brixworth has been called "perhaps the most imposing architectural memorial of the seventh century surviving north of the Alps": and though some scholars argue that it in fact belongs to a somewhat later period, there can be no doubt that it is by far the largest as well as the most stately and the most intriguing of all Anglo-Saxon churches. A monastery seems first to have been established here in about 675, on or near the site of some large ruined Roman building which provided the red tiles so prominent in the church's fabric: and it may be that the present church was begun either at that time, or slightly later, or else in about 750. Altered during the ninth or tenth century (perhaps after damage by Viking raiders) and again during the Norman and medieval periods (when the tower-top, spire, and south chapel were added) it nevertheless retains much of its original form and atmosphere, and well repays a detailed examination. A walk round the exterior, for example, reveals that this large church was once larger yet, being flanked at its western end by now-vanished aisles, whose tall arches have been partly filled in and partly converted into windows. It must thus have originally resembled a Christian Roman "basilica", a resemblance often attributed to the influence of St Wilfrid (d.709), a lover of all things Roman. A glance at the heads of the arches, however, demonstrates that the Saxon builders (though they re-used Roman tiles) had little experience of Roman building methods: for instead of arranging their tiles radially, they set them in a distinctly haphazard fashion at wildly varying angles, making up the deficiencies by lavish applications of mortar.

Supported as they are on solid blocks of walling rather than pillars, these great arches lend dignified strength rather than grace to Brixworth's high and spacious interior: an impression somewhat relieved by the more delicate triple window in the nave west wall, which once lit an upper chapel for the use of great men like the kings of Saxon Mercia. A much larger triple arch at the nave's east end, dividing it from the chancel or "presbytery", was long ago replaced by the present single opening: but the narrower Saxon "triumphal arch" beyond survives, leading into the semi-circular apse at the easternmost and thus most sacred part of the church. Beneath this apse – a Victorian rebuild on Saxon foundations – was apparently a semi-subterranean chapel containing some particularly holy relic, accessible to pilgrims via the sunken walkway or "ring crypt" visible from the churchyard.

Exactly what this sacred object was is uncertain, but it may well have been the human throat bone which came to light in 1809, concealed in a stone reliquary within the south chapel wall. Doubtless hidden at the Reformation, the bone was wrapped in paper which disintegrated immediately, and to whom it belonged can thus not be established beyond doubt: there is good reason to believe, however, that it is a relic of St Boniface, a famous Saxon preacher martyred in Holland in 755. It remains at Brixworth (where the reliquary can be seen in an iron cage near the pulpit) and is yet another reason for making a pilgrimage to this fascinating place of worship.
See **The Anglo Saxon Church, The Reformation.**

BRIXWORTH
Northamptonshire
OS 141 SP 747713
The small town of Brixworth is seven and a half miles north of Northampton, on the A508 Market Harborough road : it is also accessible from the M1, either via junction 16, the A45, and Northampton ; or via junction 18 (eleven miles west), the A428 through West Haddon, and minor roads through Ravensthorpe, Teeton and Spratton. The church is clearly visible (and signposted) from the town centre : it is generally open.

Below, the Saxon west door constructed with Roman tiles, and right, the towering spire of All Saints.

BROOKLAND Kent
OS 189 TQ 989258

Brookland church and village stand by the A259, five miles north-east of the historic and attractive Cinque Port of Rye and about the same distance west of New Romney, with its large and splendid church. To the north-east is Romney Marsh proper, with narrow dyke-bordered roads and lonely windswept churches.

Right, the north door, and far right, the detached timber-clad belfry. Below, the east end of the church showing the distinctly uneven set of its structure.

The most delightful and interesting of the notable Romney Marsh churches, St Augustine's at Brookland is best known for its detached timber belfry, three octagonal pyramids piled one on another and covered all over in wooden shingles, with massive beams inside to bear the weight of the bells. A steeple without a tower, it stands a few feet from the church, and was positioned thus either to lessen the effect of marshland gales or, more probably, to avoid adding an extra burden to a building which stands on uncertain foundations – as can be clearly seen by the pronounced lean of its interior arches. Both inside and out, indeed, the long low church is splendidly individual and eccentric: mostly medieval, part Georgian, and entirely untouched by tidy-minded Victorian restorers. Its furnishings include a fine set of

box pews, a two-decker pulpit and (uniquely) a "tithe pen" at the west end of the south aisle: there the portion of the parish's crops due to the vicar were weighed out and stored, and there too the Georgian church scales and measures remain, probably the only complete set still surviving. At the opposite end of the same aisle is a late medieval wall painting of St Thomas Becket's martyrdom, and in the thirteenth century chancel contemporary sedilia or priests' seating. The most outstanding of Brookland's many treasures, however, is its tiny Norman lead front, again unique in Britain. For it is decorated not only with the signs of the Zodiac but also with the Labours of the Months they represent, so that (for instance) Virgo is paired with August harvesting and Capricorn with killing the Christmas pig.

Canopied box pews in Ninekirks.

The huge but sparsely populated parish of Brougham, in the beautiful Eamont valley between the Pennines and the Lake District fells, bears the indelible mark of that truly remarkable woman Lady Anne Clifford (1590–1676). Dowager Countess of Dorset, Pembroke and Montgomery by marriage, and owner by inheritance of the great Clifford estates in Cumbria and West Yorkshire, this learned, imperious and charitable old lady had a passion for building and restoration: and though she was already well into her sixties when she returned here, she exercised it to the full at Brougham. For not only did she restore the ancient Norman castle (one of the six on her estates she reconstructed) and raise the still-pristine Countess Pillar by the main road, "for a memorial of her last parting in this place with her good and pious mother": she also built anew both the parish's places of worship.

The most ancient in origin of these stands quite alone in an unrivalled setting by the river Eamont, with the heights of Cross Fell away to the east. Known as "Ninekirks", which is to say "St Ninian's Kirk", it was traditionally founded in the late fourth century by the saint of Whithorn, who carved a cave-hermitage in the red sandstone cliffs by the Eamont ford. Here a settlement grew up, and

Ninekirks became Brougham's parish church, a status it retained even after the medieval community moved nearly two miles south-westwards to its present position. By Lady Anne's day, however, the isolated church was falling into ruin, and nothing now remains of it but an ancient altar slab and (under a trap-door in the chancel) an early medieval gravestone with cross and sword. All the rest was rebuilt by by Lady Anne in 1660 and (what is far more remarkable) remains almost as she knew it: a perfectly preserved north country rural church of the seventeenth century.

A long, low building in the modest Cumbrian tradition, Ninekirks is constructed of red sandstone, in the old-fashioned "Gothic Survival" style beloved of its historically-minded benefactress. Within, however, it is very much a Protestant place of worship, with panelled box pews (two of them canopied, for the aristocratic families from Brougham Castle and Hornby Hall); a workmanlike two-decker pulpit; and only a comparatively simple screen dividing nave from chancel. On the eastern wall, above the plain communion table and the "commandments board", are the builder's laurel-wreathed initials (A.P., for "Anne Pembroke"); and the octagonal stone font is also of her time, as is even the poor-box

BROUGHAM Cumbria
OS 90 NY 559299
The scattered parish of Brougham, one of the most picturesque and interesting in Cumbria, extends on both sides of the A66, being one and a half miles east of Penrith and some two and a half miles east of junction 40 of the M6 motorway. Its fine Norman castle (NY 537290) stands prominently south of the A66, as does Lady Anne's "Countess Pillar", about three-quarters of a mile east of the castle at NY 546289. Three-quarters of a mile east of the Pillar, a signposted track (beginning at NY 557289) leads north off the A66 towards Ninekirks: passing across fields and along the heights above the river, this track is not suitable for cars, but a delightful walk of about a mile along it brings the traveller to the lonely parish church (at NY 559299). St Wilfred's chapel (NY 527284) is half a mile south-west of the castle, on the B5262 immediately opposite the towering mock-Gothic walls of Brougham Hall and above Eamont Bridge: a few hundred yards away, by the bridge, are two prehistoric earthwork "henges", Arthur's Round Table (NY 523284) and Mayburgh Ring (NY 519285).

25

Above, the altar rail, communion table and commandments board. Right, the nave beyond the chancel screen.

by the door. The only tresspassers in this time-machine of an interior indeed, are the unobtrusive later monuments on the chancel walls, and the imitation "medieval" brasses in the sanctuary floor, laid down by a Victorian squire to prove an entirely bogus noble descent.

It was only for funerals, baptisms and great festivals that people of Brougham came to their remote parish church, leaving their horses in the now-ruined stable in its churchyard. At ordinary times, they attended service in St Wilfred's, their "chapel of ease" in the village: which was also rebuilt by Lady Anne, and which outwardly resembles Ninekirks. Its amazing interior, however, presents a violent contrast with the parish church's seventeenth century simplicity: for during the 1840s it was taken in hand by William Brougham (brother of the squire who laid the fake Ninekirks brasses) and jam-packed full of sumptuous medieval woodwork purchased from various European churches and castles. Canopied pews and carved or painted panels abound, so that it is virtually impossible to decide what is imported, what Victorian, and what original: but the richly carved screen at the west end may well be a survivor from Lady Anne's chapel – whose picturesque situation against a backdrop of Lake District mountains also makes it well worth a visit.

See **The First Christian Missionaries, The Prayer Book Church, Whithorn.**

Holy Wells and Sacred Springs

To come upon a spring suddenly gushing from a hill-side, or bubbling unexpectedly from the ground after heavy rain, can still be a moving and exciting experience: and for prehistoric man the mysterious appearance and inexplicable drying up of such springs must have seemed yet more wonderful. For him, too, as for countless later generations, natural water sources were not merely objects of wonder and beauty, but also the only available supplies of the greatest necessity of all life, be it plant, animal, or human. The springs themselves, indeed, were seen as living creatures, or the habitations of spirits who might give of their bounty or disastrously withold it: and when it was discovered that the water from certain sources also possessed curative powers, this can only have confirmed the belief in their supernatural origins. It is scarcely surprising, therefore, that the veneration of springs and wells, and the offering of gifts to the capricious deities who watched over and controlled them, were vital elements of pre-Christian religion. Evidence for such practices has been found all over Britain, among the most impressive being the huge hoard of Iron Age metalwork ritually deposited in Llyn Cerrig Bach on Anglesey and the vast quantity of coins and other objects cast into Coventina's Well at Carrawburgh. Among the latter was part of a human skull, and numbers of complete skulls found in wells or pools elsewhere lend credence to the view that the worship of water guardians was somehow connected with the Celtic cult of the severed head.

The Romans, who had well cults of their own, were careful to honour those of Britain, building a temple to Coventina and bathing in the medicinal waters of Buxton in Derbyshire, which they knew as "Aquae Arnemetiae", "the waters of she who dwells near the sacred grove". The curative hot springs of Bath likewise attracted both the ailing and the fashionable of Roman Britain, who worshipped their guardian goddess Sulis Minerva before immersing themselves in the impressive Roman bath complex still to be seen there. Many ancient holy wells and sacred springs, moreover, continued to be venerated after the establishment of Christianity, though they were then usually re-consecrated (at least in name) to more acceptable patrons: Arnemetia, for example, becoming "St Anne", and many pagan well goddesses becoming simply "Our Lady". Neither do the specifically Christian legends recounted to explain the miraculous appearance of a spring always successfully conceal its pagan past – for many of them, like the severed head stories about Hoylwell and St Urith's

well at Chittlehampton, are all too reminiscent of the Celtic association of skulls with sacred waters. In other cases, however, the Christian saints and hermits who established their dwellings near natural springs, using them both for drinking water and for baptisms, doubtless consecrated them by their presence: and this may well account for the veneration of holy wells at Clynnogfawr, Partrishow and Whitchurch Canonicorum.

Whatever the true nature of their origins, holy wells and sacred springs were closely connected with the shrines and pilgrimages of the middle ages, when virtually all pilgrimage centres (including Walsingham) boasted one or more of them. The Reformation (understandably viewing well cults as pagan and superstitious) severed their links with official religion – or at least attempted to do so: but only succeeded in altering the forms in which they were honoured. Right down to the present century, for example, people in northern and western areas of Britain hurried to draw "the cream of the well" – the first water it produced after dawn on certain festivals like New Year's Day or Ascension Day – which was thought to be especially good for complaints of the eyes or skin, or simply "lucky". The custom of decorating or "dressing" wells, moreover, still persists (or has been revived) in more than a score of villages in and around Derbyshire. There, on some fixed date during the summer months, panels beautifully and artistically inlaid with complex mosaic patterns of flower petals, bark and other natural materials are erected over the well or wells: generally these patterns depict Biblical subjects which, like the church services that often accompany well dressing ceremonies, serve to emphasise the determinedly Christian nature of the occasion. Elsewhere darker superstitions perhaps continue to prevail, and some sacred springs may even retain their original guardians: one at least, on the Welsh border, is certainly believed to be haunted by a being half man and half stag.

Yet by far the most widespread of the surviving methods of honouring holy wells and sacred springs is also the oldest practice of all: namely the custom of offering gifts to them. Few (it is to be hoped) now use human heads for this for this purpose, and it may be that not many now sincerely believe that a pin dropped into their waters will bring about the heart's desire. But Britain is still full of "wishing wells", and more often than not these wells contain good measure of coins thrown in "for luck": perhaps the traveller has even added to their number.

See **The Gods of Rome, Shrines and Pilgrimages**.

CANTERBURY Kent
St Martin's church
OS 179 TR 158577

The historic and hallowed city of Canterbury is some sixty-five miles south-east of London, via the A2 and M2. St Martin's stands on its eastern outskirts, at the foot of St Martin's Hill and immediately to the north of the A257 from Canterbury to the ancient and well-preserved Cinque Port of Sandwich, near the coast eleven miles to the east.

When St Augustine came as the first Christian missionary to Saxon Canterbury in A.D. 597, he is said to have found "an ancient church to the east of that city, built in honour of St Martin while the Romans yet occupied Britain." There worshipped Queen Bertha, the Frankish Christian wife of the pagan King Ethelbert of Kent: and from there, with Ethelbert's permission, Augustine and his forty monks began the work which soon afterwards bore fruit in the conversion of the king and the establishment of Christianity in southern England. Substantial remains of this momentous building survive as the chancel walls of the present parish church of St Martin, which are constructed mainly in Roman brick – a material used to a lesser extent in the walls of the much larger nave. Most scholars agree that this nave is an early seventh century addition, possibly built to provide room for the influx of monkish missionaries: and some declare that the chancel is only slightly earlier, perhaps representing a chapel built for Queen Bertha on the site (and from the materials) of the Roman church.

This, in itself, would make St Martin's the oldest Christian place of worship in England: but many authorities go further, asserting that the chancel is actually Roman work, probably raised soon after the death of St Martin in A.D. 397 and thus during the last years of Imperial rule in Britain. If so, it provides a unique link with Romano-British Christianity, long eclipsed by barbarian invasions but triumphantly revived by St Augustine from this hallowed spot.
See **The First Christian Missionaries, Iona, Whithorn.**

CANTERBURY Kent
Canterbury Cathedral
OS 179 TR 152578

The cathedral stands unmistakably at the centre of the ancient city, surrounded on all sides by medieval buildings which together form a group almost unrivalled anywhere else in Britain. Immediately to the north are the extensive and well-preserved monastic buildings of the Benedictine cathedral priory, including the cloister, chapter house, water tower, infirmary and treasury. Just to the east is a fine section of Canterbury's towering medieval city wall, and by passing through a door in this wall and crossing Broad Street the traveller reaches the ruins of St Augustine's Abbey, founded by the saint himself and rebuilt by the Normans. To the south-west of the cathedral, leaving the close by Christ Church Gateway, is the core of the medieval city. Turn right outside the gate for Palace Street, with its many timbered houses: or walk straight ahead down narrow Mercery Lane to reach the High Street, and then almost immediately left down Stour Street, with its charming Friary set in a market garden and (further on) the medieval Poor Priests' Hospital. Returning then to the High Street, a left turn brings the traveller first to the Eastbridge Hospital, then to St Peter's church, and finally to the splendid Westgate, one of the finest urban fortifications in England.

Canterbury Cathedral, the mother church of English Christianity and without doubt one of the most beautiful as well as the most atmospheric of British cathedrals, owes its pre-eminence to the success of St Augustine's mission to Saxon Kent in A.D. 597. The first church on the site – which, like nearby St Martin's, was apparently a restored Roman structure – was consecrated in about A.D. 602, with Augustine as its archbishop: he it was who appointed the subordinate bishops who helped spread Christianity throughout southern England, and since then the archbishops of Canterbury have remained the head not only of the English church but also of the Anglican communion throughout the world.

Nothing now remains of the Saxon church, and very little of its earliest Norman successor, begun by William the Conqueror's friend Archbishop Lanfranc in 1070. More survives, however, of the cathedral raised between 1096 and 1130 by Lanfranc's successor Anselm, including the exterior of the choir and the wonderful Norman crypt: while the greater part of the present building is linked either directly or indirectly to the second major event in the cathedral's history, the murder within its walls of Archbishop Thomas Becket in 1170. This remarkable man, the son of a minor London merchant but trained in his youth as a knight, rose largely by means of his own considerable talents to become Henry II's Chancellor and right hand man. In 1162 the king forced him (against his will) to accept the archbishopric of Canterbury, hoping thereby to increase his own influence over the Church: but instead Thomas resolutely defended ecclesiastical privileges against Henry's attacks, and for the next eight years bitter quarrels between the two erstwhile friends rocked all England. At last, during one of the king's notorious rages, he uttered the unguarded words which sent four knights hurrying to Canterbury: and in the confusion that followed Archbishop Thomas was slaughtered in the north transept of his own cathedral.

Always popular in life with the common people, the manner of Thomas's death turned him instantly into a holy martyr, and on the very day after his murder a cloth dipped in his blood is said to have cured a Canterbury woman of her paralysis. More miracles followed thick and fast, leading both to Becket's remarkably rapid official canonisation in 1173 and to an ever-increasing flow of pious sightseers: so that throughout the middle ages the cathedral remained not merely the most popular shrine in England, but also one of the most famous in western Europe. Monarchs, nobles and churchmen all flocked here, or at least paused to pay their respects when passing through the city on the ancient road from Dover to London: yet best-remembered of all the pilgrims are the thinly-fictionalised group of wayfarers immortalized by Geoffrey Chaucer's "Canterbury Tales", written between c.1380 and 1400.

For the late medieval as for the modern traveller, the first distant glimpse of the cathedral will have been provided by its great 250 foot "Bell Harry" central tower, begun in 1496 and largely paid for by the offerings of pilgrims. Not until the close has been entered through Christ Church Gate, with its Tudor heraldry, is the whole majestic length of the building revealed: and the traveller next passes through its west door into the nave, which was rebuilt on Norman foundations between 1391 and 1405, and is thus in the Perpendicular style. It is indeed doubly perpendicular, for though its master mason Henry Yevele was restricted as to length and width by the old foundations, there was no such limit as to height, and the nave columns

28

soar eighty feet up the splendid vault as clusters of uninterrupted verticals. The nave is, moreover, filled with clear light from the immensely tall and wide aisle windows (which occupy all the available space between the exterior buttresses) and from the clerestory windows above: and there is perhaps no building in England which better expresses the spirit of late Gothic architecture.

Having taken in this magnificent vista, the traveller should next follow in the footsteps of medieval pilgrims by passing along the north nave aisle, noticing on the wall at its east end the fine Elizabethan monument depicting the tragedies which overtook the Hales family, including a suicide and a burial at sea. This stands near the first of the three flights of stairs – from the nave up to the choir, from the choir up to the high altar area, and from the high altar up again to the Trinity Chapel – which are so memorable a feature of Canterbury's interior. Partly dictated by the building of the choir over an existing crypt, and partly designed to enhance the feeling of awe as pilgrims approached the martyr's shrine, these dramatic changes of level give the impression of "church piled on church, a new temple entered as soon as the first is ended".

After ascending the first stair, the pilgrim-traveller then immediately turns left to descend into what was (after the shrine itself) the most sacred place in the cathedral – the north transept or "Martyrdom" where St Thomas died on December the twenty-eighth 1170. Though it was rebuilt in the mid-fifteenth century, therefore, this transept retains its original Norman floor level, hence the descent: for the flagstones once stained by the martyr's blood were considered too holy to be moved, and the section of the wall against which his dying body fell was likewise preserved. This is now marked only by a simple inscription, but here once stood the Altar of the Sword's Point, displaying a fragment from one of the murderers' weapons: and here in recent years a pope and an archbishop of Canterbury have knelt together in prayer for Christian unity and reconciliation, as the traveller may also care to do in this hallowed place.

From the Martyrdom, too, the traveller can either pass (via a door in the west wall) into the Great Cloister of 1390–1411, with its wonderful collection of over eight hundred heraldic and pictorial roof bosses: or else descend into the Norman crypt, which is not only the earliest but, for many visitors, the most atmospheric part of the cathedral. Begun by Archbishop Anselm during the last years of the eleventh century, its treasures include a remarkable array of sculptured beasts on its column capitals and a complete set of twelfth century wall paintings in the side chapel of St Gabriel: while at its centre is the late medieval chapel of Our Lady in the Undercroft, where pilgrims once venerated a famous image of the Virgin as well as the hair shirt and drawers worn by St Thomas to mortify his flesh.

The majority of pilgrims, however, will have walked (or, if especially pious, crawled on their knees) from the Martyrdom up into the choir, and then up again into the Trinity Chapel, where the saint's shrine stood. This eastern end of the cathedral, indeed, was rebuilt specifically as a setting for the holy relics, after a fire which gutted the Norman choir in 1174: and its tall slender pillars, black Purbeck marble shafts, vaulted roof and (most distinctively of all) its pointed arches all proclaim the then entirely new Early Gothic style of architecture, which here appeared for the first time in an English cathedral. The jewel in this magnificent setting, the shrine itself, was torn out by Henry VIII: who not only nurtured a particular spite against the saint who had defied a king, but also coveted the riches showered on his relics during the centuries of pilgrimage. "Gold was the meanest thing to be seen there", reported an awed sixteenth century traveller, "for all shone and glittered with precious stones of an extraordinary size, some of them larger than a goose's egg" – the finest of all being the great "Regale of France", a fabulous ruby presented by the French king Louis VII. No less than twenty-six waggons, indeed, were needed to carry away all the treasure: and all that now remains to mark the site of the martyr's tomb is the thirteenth century marble pavement which surrounded it, worn by the feet of countless pilgrims.

Despite this loss, much remains to remind the modern Canterbury pilgrim that this was, for his medieval predecessors, the holiest place in all England. The windows of the Trinity Chapel, for example, contain some of the very finest stained glass in Europe, and depict in fascinating detail the many miracles wrought by St Thomas: while clustering round the shrine (as at Ely and St Albans) are the tombs of the great and powerful; including those of the Black Prince, decked with replicas of his shield and armour, and of King Henry IV, beautifullly portrayed in alabaster with a panel painting of the saint's death at his head. At the eastern end both the Trinity Chapel and of the whole cathedral, moreover, is the unique semi-circular extension called the Corona, which once housed the crown of Becket's skull, sheared off by his murderers' swords. Now, appropriately, it contains the Purbeck marble archbishop's throne known as St. Augustine's Chair: so that here are commemorated together the missionary who founded Canterbury Cathedral's greatness and the martyr whose death made it the noble and splendid place of worship it is today.

See **Ely, St Albans, The First Christian Missionaries, The Norman Church.**

CANTERBURY Kent
Eastbridge Hospital
OS 179 TR 147578

The hospital stands on the south side of Canterbury High Street, astride the bridge over the Stour and almost opposite the half-timbered "Canterbury Weavers".

This delightful little building, of special interest to travellers, is properly called the Hospital (or "hostel") of St Thomas the Martyr on Eastbridge; and was indeed intended as a place of rest as well as worship for some of the many pilgrims who flocked to the shrine of the murdered Archbishop Becket in nearby Canterbury Cathedral. Founded by Edward Fitz Odbold in 1180 (less than a decade after the saint's death) it was considerably enlarged during the fourteenth century, and thus existed in very much its present form when Chaucer wrote his famous "Canterbury Tales". Appropriately, it is entered directly from the city's main street, and immediately within is a tiny chapel, with a larger vaulted undercroft-dormitory beyond: there, between the pillars, stood beds for twelve poor pilgrims, who if in good health were only permitted to stay one night, in the care of a priest and a "respectable woman at least forty years old". She it was, doubtless, who served their food in the refectory hall on the upper storey, with its crown post roof and beautiful thirteenth century wall painting of Christ in Majesty: while the priest ministered to their spiritual needs in the adjacent upper chapel. Both these rooms are still used by the nine elderly people who now live permanently in the (private) cottages nearby: for though the hospital ceased to accommodate pilgrims after the destruction of the shrine at the Reformation, its charitable and hospitable functions continue.
See **Shrines and Pilgrimages, The Reformation.**

CARRAWBURGH
Northumberland
OS 87 NY 869713

Carrawburgh is set in bleak moorland thirty miles west of Newcastle-upon-Tyne and seven miles north-west of Hexham, via the A69, the A6079, and the B6318, which follows the line of Hadrian's Wall. It stands, indeed, virtually at the centre of this impressive Roman fortification, with notable remains all round. Four miles to the east via the B6318 is the better-preserved fort of Chesters (Cilurnum), whose museum displays the finds from Coventina's well: while four miles west on the same road is the most famous and complete of the Wall forts, Housesteads or Vercovicium, with well-displayed Chesterholm (or Vindolanda) about a mile to its south.

When the Romans added their fort of *Brocolitia* (now known as Carrawburgh) to Hadrian's Wall in about A.D. 130, they were trespassing on ground already sacred to a Celtic water goddess named Coventina, the site of whose holy well is still visible in a marshy hollow about a hundred yards west of the ramparts. In the characteristically eclectic Roman manner, they adopted the local deity as their own, and built round her well a square temple which has long since disappeared. When the well itself was dug out in 1876, however, it produced quite startling evidence of the devotion paid to the goddess by Roman and Britain alike: for it not only contained some 13,487 Roman coins, but also many offerings of objects such as bronze images of human heads and part of a human skull, as well as a number of stone altars. These altars (now displayed at Chesters Museum, four miles to the east) seem to have been hurriedly tumbled into the well, either when the shrine was attacked or perhaps as a last desperate offering to Coventina during a period of great danger. Their imagery demonstrates that the Romans imagined her either as a single goddess reclining on water weeds and pouring out her healing spring from a jar: or else (probably under the influence of the Britons, many of whose goddesses took triple form) as a trio of water nymphs. The other finds indicate that (again like other Celtic deities) she was associated with the widespread cult of the severed head.

Coventina – or the three Coventinas – did not, however, reign unchallenged at Carrawburgh. For in the early third century, at about the time when the fort was taken over by a Roman cohort from what is now Holland, a temple of Mithras was built some two hundred yards south-east of her well. Rediscovered in 1949, the temple was three times rebuilt during its period of use (once after destruction by raiding Picts in A.D. 297): and like its fellow in London was dedicated to the Persian sun god who became virtually the patron of the later Roman army and a dangerous rival to Christianity. Its final desecration at the beginning of the fourth century, indeed, was probably the work of the Christians whose religion had been adopted by the Emperor Constantine.

Now partially reconstructed, with replicas of some of its original fittings (the originals being exhibited in Newcastle-upon-Tyne's Museum of Antiquities) it was entered via a lobby with an "ordeal pit", and none but the initiates who had passed through this might penetrate into its interior. There, guarding a central space flanked by raised benches, stand statues of the god's two henchmen Cautes and Cautopates, respectively holding raised and lowered torches to represent the rising and setting sun. In the sanctuary at the far end (where Mithras himself would have been sculptured in the act of slaying the bull of darkness) are three altars, one showing the god as the Charioteer of the Sun: all three were erected by garrison commanders.

The worshippers of the Persian intruder, nevertheless, seem to have been anxious not to offend Carrawburgh's better-established patroness: and immediately south of the Mithraeum yet another shrine came to light as recently as 1957. Dedicated to "the Nymphs and the Spirit of the Place", it focused (like that of Coventina) on a well, and contained an altar set up by a Roman officer who apparently preferred the old deity to the new, or perhaps hoped to placate both. In the lobby of the Mithraeum itself, moreover, was a statue of a mother-goddess, most probably Coventina: and there is little doubt that the British goddess eventually triumphed over the interloper, for coins were still being offered at her well long after his temple had fallen to ruin.
See **The Gods of Rome, Holy Wells and Sacred Springs, London – Temple of Mithras.**

Ringed by a breathtaking panorama of Lakeland fells and overlooking a fertile wooded valley, Castlerigg stone circle has without doubt the most superb setting of all prehistoric places of worship in England. Named "the Carles" because it was once thought to be a gathering of Scandinavian warriors petrified for some wicked act, it may well be one of the earliest stone circles in Britain, dating perhaps from around 3100 B.C. in the Middle Stone Age. It consists of thirty-eight boulders in a flattened ring, with taller stones flanking the entrance (which faces due north) and a still loftier pillar set in the south-east radius. A curious arrangement of stones jutting into the circle from the east may be a later addi-

tion: but it aligns exactly on an earthen circle at the summit of Great Mell Fell, six miles away; while a line from the south-eastern pillar through a corner of the rectangle sights onto the point where the Midsummer sun would have set when the ring was built. Other alignments of specific stones with surrounding mountain tops have also been suggested: and it is at least possible that the circle was used by its calendarless builders to determine the dates of important seasonal festivals. Yet nothing can be certainly proven, and the mystery surrounding the Carles remains as strong as its atmosphere.
See **Prehistoric Religion.**

CASTLERIGG CARLES
Cumbria
OS 90 NY 292236
The circle is reached by a signposted lane, which turns south off the A66 one and a half miles east of Keswick and some fifteen miles west of junction 40 of the M6 motorway. All around is the unrivalled mountain landscape of the Lake District.

One of the grandest of the grand Perpendicular churches of mid-Norfolk, St Agnes's at Cawston was largely built (like its neighbour and rival at Salle) during the fifteenth century: and like Salle again it has an immensely tall tower, at 120 feet the third highest in Norfolk, whose west door is adorned with a "woodwose" (or wild man) and a dragon, the badges of the families that raised it. Oddly enough the tower lacks the usual crown of pinnacles and battlements, allegedly because the Salle men stole these for their own church: but this ommission is more than

made up for by the glorious angel roof over the nave, one of the very finest in East Anglia. On its projecting rows of "hammer beams", which support both vertical struts and reinforcing arched braces, stand stern archangels in scaly armour with outstretched wings: while near the chancel arch (with its faded painting) are the Virgin and St Agnes, the church's patroness. Scarcely less remarkable is the great fifteenth century painted screen across the chancel entrance, also an East Anglian speciality but more complete than most, and well restored after Reformation

CAWSTON Norfolk
OS 133 TG 134238
Cawston is some twelve miles north-west of Norwich, via the A140, the B1149, and the (signposted) B1145 west. St Agnes's tower dominates the village and the surrounding countryside: within sight, two miles to the west, is her neighbour and rival at Salle.

31

damage: among its twenty brighly-coloured saints are all twelve Apostles, including a bespectacled St Matthew; St Jerome with his pet lion (on the door); and, at the south end, a defaced figure of the popular but never canonised Master John Shorne, famous for conjuring the Devil into his boot.

Not so obvious, but equally worthy of notice, is the medieval "Plough Gallery" under the tower, so called from its carved inscription which begins "God spede the plow and send us ale corne enow" and mentions "Wat Goodale" – probably a jocular reference to the beer consumed by the medieval Cawston ploughmens' guild who erected it: their traditions are still kept up in this farming parish, and nearby stands the Norfolk plough blessed every January on Plough Sunday. By the door of this splendid church, moreover, is another unusual survival, an ancient iron poor box ingeniously designed so that coins cannot be extracted from it with a knife.

See **The Great Wool Churches, Salle.**

Left, St Agnes's glorious angel roof, and below, the painted fifteenth century screen which separates nave from chancel.

The first sign of Cerne Abbas from the main road is the famous Cerne Giant, a literally gigantic chalk-cut figure nearly 200 feet long, striding across the hill above the town. Wielding a knobbly 120 foot club, and equipped with a most impressive erect phallus some thirty feet in length, he is all too clearly associated with fertility: and it is surely no coincidence that maypole dancing (and very likely more practical fertility rites) used once to take place in the rectangular "Frying Pan" earthwork above his head. When the giant was made, who made him, and whom he represents, however, are all questions that cannot be definitely answered: though he has been variously "identified" as a Celtic god, the symbol of a Civil War "clubmen's" revolt, and even an extra-terrestrial. A more plausible current theory suggests that he may be a Romano-British figure of Hercules, cut perhaps during the reign of the mad Emperor Commodus (A.D. 180–93), who believed himself to be a reincarnation of that hero; while a tradition dating from at least the thirteenth century (and still current in 1764) declares that his name was Helith, Helis or Heil, and that he was still being worshipped hereabouts when St Augustine converted the local Saxons and founded Cerne Abbey.

How the pagan giant escaped destruction (or at least emasculation) by the abbey's Benedictine monks is even more of a puzzle: yet he has certainly outlasted both them and most of their monastic buildings, though the magnificently carved porch of the abbot's hall (dating from 1509) is well worth seeking out at the end of Cerne's picturesque Abbey Street. Nearby is the fine parish church of St Mary, a largely late medieval building whose noble west tower is adorned by a statue of the Virgin, with a pair of fat-cheeked pipers above her head: its light and spacious interior has an unusual stone screen across its thirteenth century chancel, within which are wall-paintings of the life and martyrdom of St John the Baptist.
See **The Gods of Rome, Prehistoric Religion.**

CERNE ABBAS Dorset
OS 194 ST 667016
Cerne Abbas is just off the A352, roughly equidistant between Sherborne and Dorchester: the giant is best seen from the viewing area by the main road, near the turning to the outstandingly attractive little town. The church is in the town centre, and from its tower end runs Abbey Street, at whose far end are the monastic remains (generally open to the public) in the gardens of Abbey Farm. There is also much else to see in this picturesque area; including Sherborne Abbey (the finest church in Dorset); the great Iron Age hillfort of Maiden Castle, south of Dorchester; and Abbotsbury and Winterbourne Abbas, respectively to the south-west and west of Dorchester.

A medieval church with Norman features – notably the slender round-headed arch behind the pulpit – and an imposing knightly monument of c.1390 in the Lady Chapel; St. Mary Magdalene's at Chewton Mendip is best known for its glorious tower. Distinguished even in a county famous for its towers, and one of the highest in Somerset, this was completed during the 1540s, and thus at the very end of the middle ages. It is built of silver-grey Doulting stone, and on each face has two pairs of tall traceried windows, the lower pair blank and the upper with perforated openings to let out the sound of the bells: while overtopping all is a crown of pinnacles and turrets linked by delicately pierced battlements. On its western face are fine though time-worn sculptures of Christ in Glory flanked by eight flying angels, some censing Him and others bearing the instruments of His Passion.

CHEWTON MENDIP Somerset
OS 182 ST 597532
Chewton Mendip stands on the northern slopes of the Mendip hills, and on the A39 five and a half miles north of the beautiful cathedral city of Wells. Some five miles north are Stanton Drew stone circles, and nine miles west (through the Mendips) is picturesque Cheddar Gorge.

The splendid tapering tower of St Hieritha's church, one of the finest and tallest in Devon, overlooks the little square in the middle of Chittlehampton – "the farmstead of the dwellers in the hollow" – and in a niche on its south face is a modern statue of its patroness, to whom no other place of worship anywhere is dedicated. Within the fifteenth century church she appears again, crudely carved with a book and the palm of martyrdom, alongside four sainted philosophers on the medieval pulpit: and she herself may still lie buried beneath the arched shrine-chamber to the north of the chancel, where once her revered image stood by a pillar.

Though she is said to have wrought many miracles, and certainly attracted numerous pilgrims to her church, Chittlehampton's Hieritha – also called St Urith – is an obscure figure. According to a fifteenth century hymn, however, she was a maiden devoted to a religious life, who after incurring her stepmother's jealously was murdered in a village hayfield by the scythes of mowers: where she fell a spring burst forth in token of her purity – its site can still be seen to the east of the village – and the dry earth blossomed with flowers. Curiously enough, precisely the same story is told of St Sidwell (or Sithewell) of Exeter, some thirty miles to the south-east: but whether Sidwell was therefore really Hieritha, or Hieritha actually Sidwell – of whether both of them were perhaps local water-goddesses baptised into the ranks of Christian saints – can now only be a matter for speculation.
See **Holy Wells and Sacred Springs, Shrines and Pilgrimages, Whitchurch Canonicorum.**

CHITTLEHAMPTON Devon
OS 180 SS 636256
Chittlehampton is set in pretty countryside some seven miles south-east of Barnstaple, via the A377 south and the B3227 eastwards towards South Molton: Tavistock is some six miles to the north-west, via the A377 and a minor road north of Chapelton.

The First Christian Missionaries

We shall probably never know precisely when Christiantiy first came to Britain, though romantic legend insists that the poineer missionaries – led, it is said, by Joseph of Arimathea, in whose tomb Jesus was laid – arrived not long after Christ's death. More reliably, a Roman writer living as far away as north Africa reported the existence of British Christians in about A.D. 200, and it was probably at about that time that the first recorded British martyrs died at St Albans. Archaeology likewise provides some evidence of Christians worshipping in secret well before the Emperor Constantine accepted their faith as the official religion of the Roman Empire in A.D. 312, by which period there was plainly a well-established Romano-British church, with bishoprics at London, York and perhaps Lincoln.

These fourth century Christians apparently felt confident enough to attack the temples of their pagan rivals at London and Carrawburgh; and what little we know of them suggests that they were an independent-minded and decidedly egalitarian group, much influenced by the levelling doctrines of St Martin, to whom early churches at Canterbury and Whithorn were dedicated. This tendency towards individualism must have been increased by Britain's isolation after the collapse of Imperial power here in A.D. 410, and seems to have been exported by the British missionaries who carried the faith of Christ into the Celtic lands which had never known Roman rule. Among these were St Ninian of Whithorn and St Patrick, the Britons who respectively evangelised south-western Scotland and Ireland.

The Church in the southern part of Britain, however, suffered a catastrophic blow from the invasion of the pagan Anglo-Saxons, who by about 550 had conquered most of what is now England, effectively destroying Christiantity there. If a few pockets of faith survived (as church buildings certainly survived at Canterbury and elsewhere) they apparently made little impression on the fierce worshippers of Woden and Thor. It was a different story in the Celtic lands to the west, which the Saxons were slow to penetrate, or never penetrated at all. For in Cornwall, Cumbria, and especially in Wales, the fifth and sixth centuries were a golden "Age of the Saints", when monasteries and churches sprang up everywhere under the direction of famous holy men like St David, St Beuno of Clynnogfawr and St Brynach of Nevern, and when lesser-known but locally-renowned hermits (perhaps including St Issui of Partrishow) spread the Gospel from their cells beside ancient holy wells in remote valleys. At this time, too, the seaways between Ireland, Wales and Cornwall were crowded with coracles and

(at least according to legend) with millstones and miraculously-expanding leaves, each bearing a Celtic saint on some missionary journey to his or her fellow-Britons.

Not surprisingly, these western British Christians were at first less anxious to evangelise their pagan English neighbours, regarding the race which had stolen their lands and slaughtered their kin as scarcely worthy of salvation. It was from further-off Ireland, therefore, that the strongest Celtic missionary impulse came, headed by figures like the great Columba of Iona, whose tireless preaching and spectacular miracles converted the heathen Picts and whose influence had begun to pervade English Northumbria by the time of his death in 597. In that year, moreover, Christianity mounted an attack from a new direction, when St Augustine landed on the extreme southeastern tip of England and established his missionary base at Canterbury. He had come from Rome, where the sainted Pope Gregory is said to have encountered a party of fair-haired captive English boys in the slave market and (remarking that they resembled "not Angles but angels") determined to win their native land for Christ. Exploiting the toehold afforded by the Saxon king of Kent's marriage to a Christian Frankish princess, the Pope despatched Augustine to the Kentish court, where he was well received and (after converting the king) began to spread Christianity according to the doctrines of the Church of Rome.

At first, however, some of the Anglo-Saxons were inclined to accept Christ as merely an addition to the pantheon of pagan gods they already worshipped: King Raedwald of East Anglia, for instance, simply erected an image of Him alongside those of Woden and Thor in his royal temple. This was clearly unsatisfactory, but Pope Gregory wisely realised that the conversion of the English heathens could only be achieved by proceeding cautiously, using persuasion rather than force. In a letter written to Augustine in 601, therefore, he advised the missionary not to destroy pagan temples, but rather to rid them of their idols, exorcise them with holy water, and set up Christian altars within them: the notoriously conservative Saxons could thus continue to use their accustomed places of worship, but henceforth they would venerate Christ there. Nor was Augustine to forbid the customary ritual slaughter of oxen, and the gargantuan feasts that followed. Instead of sacrificing the beasts to the old pagan dieties, however, the converted Saxons were to thank the true God for the food He provided, and to feast in honour of some Christian festival or saint's day, preferably that which coincided most closely with the date of a pagan seasonal observance. Rather than honouring the spring festival of the dawn goddess Eostra, for instance, the converts were to celebrate the Resurrection of Christ (which they obstinately continued to call "Easter"): And instead of offering sacrifices to the dead at the beginning of November, they were then to keep the Christian commemoration of All Saints' Day. On the whole these gradualist measures seemed to have worked, though a century after Augustine's time laws were still being passed against "sacrificing to demons": while to this day Englishmen still retain the memory of the heathen Saxon taboo against eating horsemeat.

Augustine had to deal, moreover, not only with the pagan Saxons, but also with the long established Celtic Christians of Wales and the west: and here he was less than successful. Failing to appreciate the extent of the distrust between Briton and Saxon, Pope Gregory had given his missionary authority over all British Christians – and authority which the Celtic bishops were understandably not prepared to admit, even after Augustine had demonstrated his power by miraculously curing a blind man in their presence. Perhaps because the man cured was a Saxon, the Britons refused to be impressed, and their suspicions of the newcomer were confirmed when Augustine discourteously failed to rise from his chair to greet their representations: neither would they accept his bald declaration that the customs of the newly-imported brand of Roman Christianity were superior to their own time honoured practice.

This Roman style of Christianity was, of course, also that embraced by most of the nations of western Europe: but in England it was at first a sickly growth, insecure even in its Kentish stronghold and unable to maintain its outpost in Northumbria, whence St Paulinus's followers were expelled by a pagan invasion in 632. The initiative thereafter passed back to the Celtic Church, for the Christian kings who reconquered Northumbria had been baptised on Iona, and from Iona came the monks who established a base on Lindisfarne and achieved notable successes in converting the northern English. During the period of Northumbrian ascendancy which followed, moreover, Celtic or Celtic-eduacated missionaries spread the faith into the English midlands and even as far south as Essex, while upholders of the Roman practice expanded their influence from Kent into the west country and East Anglia.

A clash between the two forms of Christianity – between Iona and Lindisfarne on the one hand and Rome and Canterbury on the other – had therefore become inevitable by the middle of the seventh cen-

tury. The Celtic Church, inheritor of the independent and egalitarian traditions of the Romano-British Christians and long cut off from Europe, was essentially a body of individuals, revering island-dwelling abbots rather than bishops and suspicious of rigid hierarchies or centralising authority. The Roman Church, conversely, emphasised the importance of just such a system of authority, descending from the Pope via a network of bishops to the humblest priest and the least of his flock. It was also quite certain of its unassailable rectitude, refusing to compromise with its Celtic rivals or even to acknowledge the validity of their ancient customs, which it regarded as hopelessly outdated if not dangerously heretical. These, then, were the real points at issue: but matters came to a head over a lesser dispute about the correct date for observing Easter, which was seriously disrupting the home life of the Northumbrian King Oswy and his Kentish wife – a follower of the Roman practice who was thus still fasting for Lent while her "Celtic" husband celebrated the feast. In 664, therefore, King Oswy summoned the leaders of both parties to a debate at Whitby, and the result was perhaps inevitable. For the advocates of Rome rightly claimed to represent the majority of European Christians, and not merely those of a few remote islands: and to be the heirs, not merely of St Columba, but of St Peter who held the keys of Heaven. Against such a doorkeeper, as Oswy remarked, there could be no disputing: and from then on until the Reformation the English church was to be united under the authority of Rome and the primacy of St Augustine's archbishopric of Canterbury.

Elsewhere in Britain, the Celtic traditions of the first Christian missionaries persisted longer. In Scotland, for example, the Celtic monks called "Culdees" or "servants of God" (whose monasteries included Abernethy and St Andrews) remained a dominant influence until the twelfth century, when Queen Margaret and her Anglicised royal descendants led their northern realm into the Roman fold. While in parts of Wales the old ways lingered on for a further hundred years, until Edward I completed his conquest of the Welsh principalities during the 1290s. Throughout the long history of British Christianity, moreover, the shrines of the first missionaries have continued to be honoured in one form or another: and at St Albans or Whithorn, at Iona, Lindisfarne or Canterbury, the modern traveller can still stand in places hallowed by over twelve centuries of continuous Christian worship.

See **The Anglo-Saxon Church, Monasteries and Religious Houses, Shrines and Pilgrimages.**

CLEY-NEXT-THE-SEA Norfolk
OS 133 TG 048432

Cley (usually pronounced "cly") is some twenty-five miles north of Norwich, and nine miles west of Cromer via the A149: it stands "next the sea" in a part of Norfolk equally famous for its scenic beauty and its fine churches. St Margaret's is on the southern edge of the village, by the road to Holt. A mile or so east is Blakeney, with its medieval guildhall and distinctive beacon-towered church: and within ten miles to the south-east are Binham Priory, Little Snoring, and the amazing pilgrimage centre of Walsingham.

A large, odd, and infinitely engaging church, St Margaret's dates principally from Cley's great days as a late medieval seaport, before the Glaven estuary silted up. The stumpy tower and the little chancel are admittedly earlier, of the thirteenth century, and there was probably a plan to rebuild them: but it never materialised, and now they are dwarfed by the mighty nave with its oversailing clerestory, lit by the alternating pointed and star-shaped windows which are one of the church's many distinctive features. These and the transepts were possibly designed by John Ramsey, Master Mason of Norwich Cathedral, and date from the earlier fourteenth century: while the aisles and the sumptuous two-storeyed porch (with its startling, almost Arabic, battlements) were built about a hundred years later, not long after the time when Cley's piratical mariners seized Prince James of Scotland's ship and carried him prisoner to King Henry IV. By the end of Queen Elizabeth's reign, however, the seaport's glory had departed, and its church's transepts were abandoned for want of use, falling into the ruin which adds another element to the strangeness of St Margaret's exterior.

Nor is its interior any less worthy of close inspection. There, above the nave arches, elaborate and still coloured niches for saint's images rest on a series of delightful carved figures, including a piping minstrel, a lion, St George wrestling with the Dragon and an imp with glass eyes – not to mention the rudely gesticulating fellow in the south aisle, above the organ. Lower down are a fine collection of fifteenth century bench ends, also carved with grotesques and fabulous beasts: while at the west end the font is – typically of this part of East Anglia – sculptured with representations of the Church's Seven Sacraments, from baptism via a fine marriage scene to the last rites for a dying man in bed. Set about the floors, moreover, are many fine medieval brasses, the most notable concealed beneath the blue mat behind the organ. This depicts John Symondes (d.1511) and his wife as corpses in shrouds, a reminder of mortality reinforced by upside-down scrolls inscribed "Now thus", arranged (like the names of the row of children below) so that the traveller can read them without irreverently turning his back on the altar – yet another of the individual touches which make a visit to Cley so memorable.

The font in St Margaret's decorated with representations of the Seven Sacrements.

Left, the north front, and above, the north porch from within the church.

Probably the largest and finest late medieval church in north-west Wales, St Beuno's at Clynnogfawr was built between 1480 and 1530 in a lavish Perpendicular style, with a sturdy tower, a two-storeyed porch, a particularly wide and splendidly-roofed nave, and (beyond the restored chancel screen) medieval choir stalls lit by a noble east window. It owes its grandeur – exceptional in this region of humble places of worship – to its situation on the main pilgrim route to the holy island of Bardsey, off the top of the Lleyn peninsula; and to the fact that it possessed a famous shrine of its own – that of St Beuno, special patron of Gwynedd. Traditionally the uncle of St Winefride of Holywell, this early seventh century evangelist founded a monastery here at Clynnog – alias "celynnog", "the hamlet of holly trees" – and here he probably lay buried beneath the Eglwys y Bedd ("church of the grave"), now a separate

chapel accessible via a vaulted passage from the present church tower. To his tomb flocked both passing travellers and the farmers and mountain herdsmen of Snowdonia, who until at least the eighteenth century offered their powerful protector an annual money tribute, which they placed in the "Cyff Beuno", a medieval chest hollowed from a single mighty baulk of timber. This is still to be seen in the church, as is St Beuno's Stone and a rather less sanctified relic – the "dog tongs" used to capture and expel stray hounds whose yapping disturbed Georgian services. Some half a mile south of the church, moreover, is a fine example of a holy well with steps leading down into it, likewise dedicated to St Beuno and said to possess the power of curing diseases in children.
See **Holywell, Holy Wells and Sacred Springs, Shrines and Pilgrimages.**

CLYNNOGFAWR Gwynedd
OS 115 SH 414498
Clynnogfawr (pronounced approximately "clunnogvower") is nine miles south-west of Caernarfon, with its famous castle: and stands on the A499 to Pwllheli and the outstandingly attractive coastline of the Lleyn peninsula. The church is in the small village, and the holy well is about half a mile to the south, by the main road at OS 413494: to the south and east are spectacular mountain ranges.

As is clear from its engagingly varied exterior, St Nicholas's at Compton includes elements of many periods – a Saxon tower with a fourteenth century spire, windows in several styles of Gothic, and Victorian tiled dormers in its roof. Essentially, however, it is a Norman church; and from the late Norman period (that is, from c.1180) originates its most striking and indeed now unique feature, its two-storey sanctuary. This was constructed by building a stone ceiling part way up an existing chancel, thus dividing it horizontally into a vaulted tower chamber for the principal

altar and an open fronted upper room (still with its original guard rail, among the oldest pieces of church woodwork in Britain) whose precise purpose remains a mystery. It is possible that this upper chamber was installed as the private chapel of a local manor house: but perhaps more likely that it was built to house some specially holy relic, a magnet for wayfarers passing along the nearby Pilgrims' Way on the Hog's Back ridge above Compton. Certainly its construction appears to coincide with the first rush of pilgrims to the tomb of the martyred St Thomas Becket at

COMPTON Surrey
OS 186 SU 955470
Compton village is two and a half miles south-west of Guildford (which has a fine Norman keep and an interesting museum) on the B3000, which runs between the A3100 to the east and the main A3 to the west: the church is set back from the village centre, in a wooded churchyard. Less than a mile to the north are some fine stretches of the North Downs Way/ Pilgrims Way footpath.

Canterbury: and there is other evidence that Compton's chancel once enshrined some object of unusual sanctity. Low down in its north wall is a square window, perhaps designed to allow a hermit in a cell outside to keep watch on the interior: while the stairway to the upper chapel passes through what is apparently another hermit's cell or watching chamber, equipped with a window looking onto the altar and with an ancient board supposedly worn smooth by the elbows of praying recluses.

While speculating on the true explanation for its enigmatic upper room, there is much else to see in the church: including a Norman font; recently-revealed twelfth century wall painting above the chancel arch; a little thirteenth century Virgin and Child in the east window; and not least the Norman knight roughly scratched on the wall near the pulpit steps, perhaps by some earlier traveller to Compton.
See **The Norman Church, Shrines and Pilgrimages.**

CULLOMPTON Devon
OS 192 ST 022072
Cullompton is twelve and a half miles north-east of the attractive cathedral city of Exeter, and lies immediately west of junction 28 of the M5 motorway.

Above, the brilliantly coloured west side of the rood screen. Right, the massive carved base of the rood is stored at the west end of the Lane aisle.

A large and truly sumptuous building, with outstanding examples of all the features which make the late medieval churches of Devon so famous, St Andrew's at Cullompton is not to be missed by any seeker after places of worship in Devon. Built in a raspberries-and-cream combination of red-pink sandstone with carved Beer stone trimmings, it presents first its great west tower, constructed in 1545–9 – which is to say at the height of the Reformation upheavals, so that the sculptured Crucifixion on its west face must have been defaced almost as soon as it was erected. The second impression is of great width, caused by the fact that the

church has not one but two south aisles, the outermost built in 1526 by John Lane, a wealthy Cullompton merchant who was determined to outdo similar additions to the rival parish churches of Tiverton and Ottery St Mary, and equally determined that his generosity should not be forgotten. The exterior of the Lane aisle therefore has a long inscription (placed low down for easy reading but now much worn) recording his benefaction and begging visitors to pray for his soul: while above the windows are his initials and trademarks and on the buttresses are a fine fleet of his merchant ships, those on the second and fifth buttresses from the west

being particularly well preserved.

All this richness, however, is scarcely an adequate preparation for Cullompton's interior, whose white walls and finely-carved nave pillars point up two great blocks of colour – the wonderful barrel-roof, which runs the whole length of the church, and the multicoloured and gilded rood screen which cuts right across its east end. Flanked by rows of golden angels and carried on traceried double arches, the roof has no less than 144 panels, each cross-braced with the saltire of St Andrew, the church's patron: while to the east of the rood screen are two more fine pieces of woodcarving, the "parclose" screens dividing off the chapels on either side of the chancel. These last are unpainted, but the main screen – whose west side has been re-tinted – is as brilliantly coloured as all such rood screens once were: and its effect must

have been still more dramatic before the Reformation, when it was surmounted by the "rood" itself, the mighty Crucifix whose base – grimly representing the skull-strewn hill of Golgotha, and unique in Britain – is preserved at the back of the Lane aisle.

This outer south aisle is the most ornately decorated part of the whole church, though here the effect depends on sculpture rather than colour. Each of the piers dividing it from the inner aisle, for example, has a buttress inlaid with figures under canopies: and its gloriously fan-vaulted roof is flanked and bossed with a heavenly choir of angels, each bearing a shield with an emblem either of Christ's Passion or of the cloth trade, with John Lane's merchant's mark significantly predominating.

See **The Great Wool Churches, The Reformation.**

The fan-vaulted roof of the Lane aisle.

The Anglo-Saxon Church

When the Anglo-Saxons – the shorthand title of the Angles, Saxons, Jutes, Frisians and other Germanic peoples – conquered and settled England in the fifth and sixth centuries, they were still an entirely pagan race. Comparatively little is known in detail of their beliefs, but their principal deities (whose names are remembered in the days of the week) were clearly Tiw the war god; Woden the cunning magician and chief of the gods; Thor the blustering wielder of thunder and lightning; and the fertility goddess Frey. It is evident, too, that Anglo-Saxon paganism was a somewhat bleak affair, holding out little hope even to the heroes whose death in battle earned them a place in the feast hall of Valhalla: for even they were destined (along with the gods themselves) to be eventually overwhelmed by the forces of winter and chaos. Thus, in a famous story recorded by the historian Bede, a heathen Saxon nobleman compared the life of a man to a sparrow flying through a brightly-lit hall, from darkness to darkness. Of what came before or after earthly existence, his beliefs could tell him nothing: and he therefore advised his king to adopt the Christian faith, which offered both knowledge and the hope of salvation.

On the whole, then, the Anglo-Saxons accepted conversion fairly readily: and within less than a century after St Augustine's arrival in 597, England was at least nominally a Christian land. Its earliest churches (as at Canterbury) were apparently housed in reconstructed Roman buildings (as at Brixworth) based on Roman models, sometimes rather ineptly. As missionaries moved into new territory, however, they might first mark their places of worship by erecting a "standing cross", like that which still remains at Ruthwell. This might later be replaced by a "minster", or mother church for a large area – often a sizeable building like Brixworth or Stow-in-Lindsey, but sometimes surprisingly small, like St Gregory's Minster: and this, in turn, would generally develop a network of smaller satellite churches in the surrounding countryside. Many of these lesser churches, the ancestors of the later parish church, were built by local landowners to serve virtually as private chapels. Many of them (like the sole surviving example at Greensted) were at first constructed of wood, only being rebuilt as simple stone structures at a considerably later date. The fact that the Saxons possessed no native tradition of building in stone, indeed, is evident both from the somewhat chaotic layouts of churches like Bosham and from the often clumsy masonry work at Brixworth and elsewhere.

Yet Saxon churches – which are characteristically tall and narrow in plan – can be exceedingly impressive in their monolithic simplicity: and many of the later examples possessed towers so sturdy that they have survived the rebuilding of the main body of the church during the later middle ages. Generally square or rectangular, but sometimes round (particularly in East Anglia, as at Little Snoring) these towers are thought to have originally been crowned by timber belfries or upper works, which were nearly always reconstructed in stone at a subsequent date: a remarkable Saxon "Rhenish helm" spire, nevertheless, is still to be seen at Sompting.

Deerhurst, like many of the greater Saxon churches, was attached to a monastery, a type of institution both numerous and important in Anglo-Saxon England. Some of the oldest monasteries (such as Lindisfarne) had originally been settled by Celtic monks, and others adhered to Benedictine conventions: but the typical early Saxon religious house was an "independent" monastery, following an individual rule laid down by the founder – or the foundress, since many of the most famous houses were established by royal princesses turned abbess, among them St Etheldreda of Ely and St Sexburga of Minster-in-Sheppey. Very often, too, these formidable ladies ruled monks as well as nuns, for the "double monastery" of both men and women was a characteristic feature of Anglo-Saxon monasticism, and wherever it occurred was invariably under the authority of an abbess.

The church at Bradwell-on-Sea is some fifty years later than the other Kentish churches. Situated close to the advancing sea, it was used as a barn until 1920. The nave has been reconstructed and restored, and the simple, white-washed walls starkly echo the austerity of the seventh-century Anglo-Saxon places of worship. The remains of the apsidal chapel are almost certainly those built in 653 by Saint Cedd, bishop of the East Saxons. He probably favoured a rectangular east end, in keeping with Celtic tradition. Although he was English by birth, Cedd's training had been essentially Celtic, and it continued to influence him throughout his life. He constantly referred to Lindisfarne, and it was the Irish cleric, Finan, who, together with two other Irish bishops, consecrated him bishop of the East Saxons. He had no fixed seat, and his life was consequently spent, like that of the Irish missionaries, in travel and in residing in monasteries which he himself had consecrated. Bradwell-on-Sea stands as a remarkable memorial to Saint Cedd's mission, built in the Roman fort of *Othona*, at the northern end of the promontory between the rivers Crouch and Blackwater. The site was typically Celtic in its austerity, matching well that chosen by the Irish Fursa on the Suffolk coast a generation earlier. Later in life, Saint Cedd continued to visit his spiritual home, Northumbria, and, having established a friendship with one of the under-kings of Deira (north-east England), he obtained a site for his monastery at Lastingham, deep in the Yorkshire moors. He fasted throughout Lent in order to purify the site, an austerity which belonged essentially to the Celtic Church which so influenced his misson.

Veneration of relics was a major feature of Anglo-Saxon worship. Churches were sometimes specially re-built with ring-cists to exhibit relics, while the translation of a saint to a new resting-place was an occasion for grand ceremonies, and served to attract more pilgrims to the church. Some of the biggest collectors of relics were the great cathedrals, Canterbury, Winchester, Durham, London, amongst others. Relics frequently changed hands, London, for example, losing the remains of Saint Alphege to Canterbury. Some of the great centres for relics would seem to have been the churches associated with the tenth century monastic revival. Glastonbury, for example, acquired a great number of relics from North Britain and Ireland. The popular Irish saint, Brigit (Brigid, Bride), is alleged to have been buried there, and a necklace belonging to her is on view in the museum. On the whole, relics have a southern and central distribution, corresponding to Wessex and Mercia. East-Anglia was badly-affected by the Viking incursions and may never have fully-recovered. Northumbria, with the exception of Durham, lost many relics to the south in the tenth century.

The position of the altar in Anglo-Saxon churches, is also a question which separates the Saxon Church from the later churches where the altar was normally positioned against the east wall. In the Saxon Church it was free-standing and the priest celebrated the Eucharist standing behind it, and facing the congregation. The semi-circular apses of the Anglo-Saxon period frequently contained seats where the priests could sit and face the congregations. The recently-excavated Anglo-Saxon church at Repton has provided much new information. The relics of Saint Wystan were once housed in its splendid pillared crypt. Excavations at Saint Albans have also revealed traces of the apse of a major Anglo-Saxon church, comparable with Winchester, where the Old Minster was sited, not underneath the present cathedral, but close beside it.

Another major Anglo-Saxon church excavation has taken place within the last year or so at Saint Oswald's, Gloucester. This church was founded in the late ninth century by the Mercian Aethelfleda, who was known as 'Lady of the Mercians', after the death of her husband, Aethelred, King of Mercia. In 909, the remains of Saint Oswald of Northumbria were brought here from Bardney in Lincolnshire. The structure declined in the Middle ages, and, today, only a single wall remains standing. But a great crypt, twenty seven feet square, has been discovered at the east end of the building. It may, perhaps, have been constructed as a shrine to Oswald, where pilgrims could venerate the body, or, alternatively, it could have been the mausoleum of the queen herself. Archaeology is revealing that, far from being a simpler vesion of later churches, Anglo-Saxon churches and church ritual were designed for worship quite different from that with which we ourselves are familiar. In order to understand the peculiarities of the structures themselves, we have to appreciate the nature of the ritual enacted within them.

The large number of Saxon royal saints (kings as well as abbesses) underlines another special characteristic of the old English Church, namely its close connections with the monarchy. For the rulers both of the early Saxon regional kingdoms and later of the whole English nation saw themselves not only as the sworn protectors of the Church but also as effectively its high priests – a role reflected in the quasi-priestly vestments still worn by British monarchs during their coronation ceremonies. This excellent relationship with the state, combined with comparatively peaceful conditions, resulted in a golden age for the English Church during the eighth century: when it exercised considerable influence on European learning and culture, producing great works of art like the Lindisfarne Gospels as well as eminent historians like Bede (673–735) and scholars like Alcuin (735–804).

At the end of that century, however, the first portents of disaster had appeared on the horizon with the Viking raid on Lindisfarne: and by time Alfred ascended the throne of Wessex in 871 scarcely a church or monastery in England survived undamaged, while learning had so greatly declined that it was hard to find a priest who understood even the simplest Latin. Only the great King Alfred's victories over the Danes, in fact, prevented the total submergence of the Anglo-Saxon Church: and though his and his successors' subsequent patronage of scholarship and church-building did much to ameliorate the shattering blow it had suffered, it was never to re-attain its former glories. In the period before the Norman Conquest, nevertheless, it experienced a notable revival, encouraged by the tenth century monastic reforms of St Dunstan and supported by kings like Edgar, Cnut and the saintly Edward the Confessor. To this period belong a number of fine surviving churches, including Stow-in-Lindsey and the rebuilt St Gregory's Minster. Until the very end of its existence, moreover, the Anglo-Saxon church was to maintain the close connection with the crown, the leadership in learning and culture, and the individual customs and practices born of its long and honourable history. Yet these very characteristics were viewed as evidence of its decadence and insularity by the invading Normans, who within three decades of 1066 had completed the sweeping changes which transformed the Anglo-Saxon into The Norman Church.

See **The First Christian Missionaries, The Norman Church, Shrines and Pilgrimages.**

DEERHURST Gloucestershire
OS 150 SO 870299

Deerhurst is seven miles north of the cathedral city of Gloucester and three miles south-west of Tewkesbury (with its splendid medieval abbey church) via the A38, the B4213, and a minor road: the nearest access from the M5 is via junction 9, immediately east of Tewkesbury. The church dominates the small Severn-side village, and Odda's Chapel is some two hundred yards south-west of the churchyard gate, clearly signposted.

A single Anglo-Saxon church in a small village is unusual enough, but Deerhurst posseses two such churches, a testimony to the fact that here stood the ecclesiastical capital of Hwicce, the Saxon kingdom centred on the lower Severn valley. Much the largest, once the premier monastery of Hwicce and now the parish church of St Mary, appears from a distance as a tall rectangular building lit by medieval windows, with a substantial west tower. Closer inspection, however, reveals a bewildering array of some thirty Anglo-Saxon doors and windows, demonstrating that the church dates essentially from the eighth to tenth centuries, and was a very complex building indeed. The round-headed arch above the west door and its snarling beast-head guardian, for example, originally led to a third-storey Saxon chapel, lit by the amazing double gabled window which can be seen by passing through the three successive doorways into the church, noticing in the process more beast heads and the mutilated eighth century Virgin and Child above the middle door. High up in the interior west wall is the famous triangular headed window, the finest and most elaborate in any Saxon church and of such distinctive design that (probably mistaken) attempts have been made to derive it from Roman or even Abyssinian sources.

At the opposite end of the church (beyond the pews arranged round three sides of the communion table, an unusual commendable survival of post-Reformation Protestant practice) is a great blocked archway, which once led to the polygonal Saxon apse whose remains can be seen outside the eastern wall: they incorporate another of Deerhurst's treasures, a sculptured tenth century angel with wide, staring eyes. Nor does even this exhaust the church's riches, for St Mary's also posseses a fine Saxon font, medieval stained glass and (at the east end of the medieval north aisle) a splendid and unique brass: it commemorates the royal judge Sir John Cassy (d.1440) and his wife Alice, beneath whose feet is a dog labelled "Terri", the only surviving example of a medieval pet named on a monument.

Odda's Chapel, Deerhurst's second Saxon church, is a very much simpler place of worship – so simple, indeed, that it was not rediscovered until 1885, doing duty as the kitchen and living rooms of the farmhouse later built into it. Dedicated by Edward the Confessor's friend Earl Odda ten years before the Norman Conquest, it is now on display as one of the most complete surviving late Saxon chapels.

See **The Anglo-Saxon Church, Monasteries and Religious Houses.**

DIDDINGTON Cambridgeshire
OS 153 TL 191659

The little church stands almost immediately east of the main A1, some two miles south of its junction with the A604 to Huntington and three miles north of its junction with the A45 at Eaton Socon: it is reached by taking the signposted road to Diddington, and then turning left at once through a gate. About a mile to the north (also on the A1) is Buckden, with its fifteenth century fortified bishop's palace.

Within sight and sound of the busy A1, yet charmingly rural, St Lawrence's at Diddington well exemplifies the mixture of styles and variety of contents which make up the typical English country church. A building of several periods, its most immediately noticeably features are its neat tower and attractive porch of orange brick, a material just becoming common when they raised in the early Tudor period. Brick, too, has been used to repair the east end of the church, which is otherwise Early English Gothic of the thirteenth century, as are the pillars and arches of the nave. The south chapel, however, is in the later Perpendicular style: probably built for the local Tayllard family in about 1505, it contains most of the church's treasures. Here, for instance, are the monumental brasses of William Tayllard (d.1505) and his heraldically mantled wife, flanked by figures of saints: while the fifteenth century stained glass window above the squire's pew vividly depicts St Katharine with her wheel, the Resurrection, and St Margaret with her dragon. The adjacent window, by contrast, is full of yellow-tinted glass brought from Holland: and between the two, above an ancient chest, is the touching memorial to a Georgian servant "who endeavouring with uncommon Fidelity to Save his master ... was unfortunately drownded with him in the Ouze".

DISSERTH Powys
OS 147 SO 035584

Disserth (the church, a farm, and the unfortunate caravan site) is three miles south-west of the Victorian spa town of Llandrindod Wells, via the A483 and a minor road turning west at Howey towards Newbridge-on-Wye. The unspoilt surrounding countryside contains several other churches worth visiting, notably Aberedw (SO 080473) south-east of Builth Wells on the B4567; and Cefnllys (SO 085615) at the foot of a fortress-crowned hill immediately east of Llandrindod Wells.

"Diserth" is the Welsh word for a desert or remote place, and it is this continuing seclusion (now alas disturbed by caravans) that has allowed it to retain its delightfully unchanged character. Set on the bank of the lovely river Ithon, it stands in an almost circular churchyard – a sure sign of an early Celtic foundation, perhaps by its patron St Cewydd, an obscure holy man known (appropriately enough in this damp region) as "Cewydd y Glaw" or "Cewydd of the Rain". The present building is essentially medieval, a typically simple Welsh church consisting of a long, low nave and chancel in one, whitewashed and almost farm-like: with a hefty thick-walled west tower, doubtless used as a refuge in times of trouble. But what makes Disserth unforgettable is its interior, which remains that of an eighteenth century Welsh rural church, untouched by Victorian "restorers". Splendidly roofed in timber and lit by unusual wood-framed windows, it is crowded with box pews, many of them dated (between 1666 and 1722) and labelled with the name of the farm to which it belonged. Two such pews even invade the sanctuary to flank the altar: and above them all rises the three-decker pulpit – from which, it is said, the eighteenth century Parson Jones once conjured the troublesome spirit of a dishonest tradesman into a silver snuff-box.

See **The Prayer Book Church.**

Western and eastern ends of the delightfully unrestored nave and chancel at Disserth.

DUNDRENNAN ABBEY
Dumfries and Galloway
OS 84 NX 748474

One of the most beautifully sited monasteries in Scotland, Dundrennan stands by the A711 five miles south-east of the attractive port of Kirkcudbright ("kirkubree"), with its sixteenth century Maclellan's Castle. Less than a mile to the south is the picturesque Solway Firth coastline: and to the north, beyond Castle Douglas town and the grim fortress of Threave, is the wild Galloway hill country.

Below, the substantial abbey ruins, and right, the effigy of the assassinated abbot of Dundrennan.

Set in one of those secluded and wooded valleys so eagerly sought after by the wilderness-loving Cistercians, Dundrennan was founded in 1142, probably by King David I and his friend Fergus, Lord of Galloway. Its first "white monks" came from that great power-house of the Cistercian order, Rievaulx in Yorkshire: and like its mother abbey Dundrennan soon prospered as a centre of wool production, sending Galloway fleeces to England and Ireland from its own port of Abbey Burnfoot on the nearby Solway Firth. This property is reflected in the substantial remains of its fine cross-shaped church, whose transepts – the "arms" of the cross – survive to their full height, combining round-topped Norman windows with pointed Gothic structural arches in a manner characteristic of the mid twelfth century period of transition between these two architectural styles. A later and far more decorative phase of Gothic appears in the adjacent entrance face of the chapter house, with its fancifully-cusped doorway and flanking pairs of windows: within this room the monks met daily to hear a chapter of their monastic rule read out and on occasion to discuss the abbey's business, and here too distinguished abbots were often buried (four of their tomb slabs are set into the floor) so that their good example and wise advice might endure after death.

At least one abbot of Dundrennan, however, apparently died in violent and sensational circumstances. His unidentified (but seemingly sixteenth century) effigy, now set into a recess by the west door of the church, shows him with a dagger plunged into his breast: while beneath his feet he tramples a half-naked figure – presumably his assassin – whose innards spill from a gaping wound in its stomach.

See **Abbey Dore, Melrose Abbey,**

EDENHAM Lincolnshire
OS 130 TF 062219

The church stands by the A151, three miles west of Bourne and seven miles east of the main A1: the huge mansion of Grimsthorpe Castle, two miles west, is not open to the public but is clearly visible from the road. The surrounding countryside, though little visited, is attractive: whilst to the east, beyond Bourne (traditionally the home of the hero Hereward the Wake) are the wide expanses of the Fens.

Set in the pleasant rolling countryside of south-west Lincolnshire, St Michael's at Edenham has a fine late-medieval tower and a splendidly carved south porch: while within are graceful clustered columns and arches in the first or Early English style of Gothic; an unusual and well-preserved Norman Font; and much else of interest. It is chiefly notable, however, as an example of an "estate church", the burial place and almost the private chapel of the aristocratic family of Bertie, Lords Willoughby and Dukes of Ancaster: whose great mansion of Grimsthorpe Castle stands some two miles to the west. The effigies of their predecessors, all dating from the fourteenth century, lie under or near the tower, and are much worn by their sojourn in the churchyard, where they were exiled to make room for the Bertie monuments which throng the east end. The earliest of these (in the large "lord's pew" by the pulpit) is to a Bertie who fell during the Civil War, and is hung about with military accoutrements and topped by a pair of carved cannon: while in the chancel are a whole series of Georgian aristocrats frozen in marble, including seven lesser relations represented by busts and a noble baby borne up by angels. Even the church's blue carpet is aristocratic, or rather royal: for it was used in Westminster Abbey during the Coronation of George VI, and presented by the Lord Ancaster who served as Lord Great Chamberlain of England on that occasion.

The famous medieval crown spire of St Giles's High Kirk – often wrongly called a cathedral, a status it only possessed for two brief periods in the seventeenth century – is one of Edinburgh's best-known landmarks. It is, moreover, virtually the only part of the medieval church to survive unaltered, for during its long life at the storm-centre of Scots politics St Giles's has suffered so many changes that its architectural history is difficult indeed to disentangle, and it is now principally visited for its many associations. Edinburgh's only parish church throughout the middle ages, its core dates mainly from the late fourteenth to early sixteenth centuries, during which time so many side chapels were added to the originally cruciform building that it assumed its present rectangular shape. Its most prized possession was a famous image of St Giles, annually regilded at the town's expense and carried with great ceremony about the streets on his feast day. By 1557, however, the sternly Calvinist form of Protestantism preached by John Knox had taken hold on Edinburgh, and instead of parading the effigy, the crowd threw it into the nearby Nor' Loch, afterwards pulling it out and burning it.

This event signalled the beginning of St Giles's greatest viscissitudes. Swept clean of "Popish" images and furnishings by a triumphant Knox in 1560, it was internally divided into three separate Presbyterian kirks in 1581. In 1633, however, it became one again, as the cathedral of the unpopular new Edinburgh bishopric established by Charles I: but the first service held there according to the Anglican Book of Common Prayer was disrupted when an outraged local market woman named Jenny Geddes hurled her stool at the preacher's head; an action which eventually led to the signing of the National Covenant in defence of Scots Presbyterianism – and, indirectly, to the Civil Wars between King, Parliament and Scots. Divided

again, in 1639, a cathedral once more between 1661 and 1689, and yet again divided after the final victory of Presbyterianism, St Giles's was by the later Georgian period serving as four kirks, an assembly hall, a police station and a fire-engine house. Between 1829 and 1833 the exterior was entirely revamped, and given its present rather dour cladding of polished stone: but not until fifty years later was the restored interior finally freed of its partition walls, with the avowed intention of creating here "the Westminster Abbey of Scotland".

It is to the late Victorian period, then, that many of the High Kirk's current furnishings and monuments belong. Notable among them is the tomb of the famous Montrose, the commander of the Royalist forces during the Civil War, who was buried here after being executed by the Presbyterians in 1650. This is in the Chepman Aisle, to the south of the chancel, while across the church is commemorated his great adversary the Marquis of Argyll, the Presbyterian leader who was himself put to death when the Scots political see-saw tilted against him in 1661. Perhaps the most striking feature of the whole building, nevertheless, is the Thistle Chapel added to its south-east corner in 1911, to accommodate the chivalric ceremonial of the Order of the Thistle, Scotland's equivalent of the English Order of the Garter. Designed by Sir Robert Lorimer, the small but lofty chapel has an amazingly sumptuous vaulted ceiling, coated with elaborate roof-bosses: round its walls, surmounted by their swords and heraldic helms and by lushly carved canopies, are the stalls of the order's knights, with the sovereign's stall at the west end. All this richness presents a curiously ironic counterpoint to St Giles's stern traditions, and one wonders what John Knox would have made of it.

See **The Reformation.**

EDINBURGH Lothian
OS 66 NT 287735
Edinburgh, the capital of Scotland and without doubt its most beautiful and interesting city, is 378 miles north of London. The High Kirk of St Giles stands at its very heart, near the gates of the great castle on its towering rock, and by the Royal Mile which leads from the castle westward to Holyroodhouse and its ruined abbey. A short walk down the hill to the north brings the traveller to the famous thoroughfare of Princes Street, and thereafter to the Georgian New Town: while to the east is the Grassmarket and (on Candlemaker Row) the Greyfriars Kirk, whose churchyard contains the monuments of many renowned Scots.

Best known for its picturesque site above the wooded gorge of the river Tees, Egglestone Abbey is a good example of a small religious house, and provides telling evidence of the fate of such establishments after the Reformation. It was founded in 1196 for the "white canons" of the Premonstratensian order, but was never very prosperous, partly due to repeated Scottish raids: so its church (rebuilt between *c.*1250 and *c.*1300) was a comparatively modest one, today chiefly remarkable for its strange vertical-barred east window, perhaps the product of seventeenth century repairs. Of the church's central portion, however, scarcely anything now remains, apparently because the tower it supported was demolished in order to afford a better view from the manor house built after the dissolution by the site's new owner. As

so often happened, this largely Elizabethan mansion was adapted from parts of the monastic buildings, in this case the canons' dormitory and refectory – which became the house's great hall, with a suitably enlarged fireplace. Beyond it to the north is a well preserved rere-dorter (or monastic toilet) with lavatory seats on two levels: they emptied into a drain within the thickness of the wall, which was flushed by a channel cut from a nearby beck. This efficient arrangement underlines the general monastic concern with sanitation: and it is even possible that the availability of running water was the reason why the canons' cloister was built on the northern rather than (as was usual) the more sheltered southern side of the church.

See **Monasteries and Religious Houses, The Reformation.**

EGGLESTONE ABBEY
Durham
OS 92 NZ 062151
The abbey is about a mile south of Barnard Castle (which has a fine medieval fortress and the notable Bowes Museum, housed in a French-style chateau) via a signposted minor road off the B6277. It may be reached from the main A1 via the A66, which continues west over the Pennine moors to Brougham.

The Norman Church

The Norman Conquest of 1066–70 brought sweeping changes to England, and not the least of them was the complete transformation of the English Church. The Anglo-Saxon Church was (at least in the highly prejudiced Norman view) a backward, eccentric and even corrupt institution, sorely in need of reform along the latest European lines: almost its only merit, indeed, was its tradition of unquestioning obedience to the monarch. Exploiting this tradition, William the Conqueror and his friend Lanfranc (appointed archbishop of Canterbury in 1070) undertook a thoroughgoing re-organisation and Normanisation of the English Church, so that within a decade of the Battle of Hastings only one Anglo-Saxon bishop remained in office, while most of the greater monasteries had been provided with Norman abbots. These great Norman clerics frequently had scant patience with Anglo-Saxon ecclesiastical customs, some of them even going so far as to destroy the relics of English saints: and little regard for the Saxon churches and cathedrals they had inherited, which they set about rebuilding as quickly as possible. Scarcely a trace of Anglo-Saxon work, indeed, now survives in any English cathedral. Between 1066 and 1200, moreover, the number of monasteries and religious houses in England more than quadrupled, nearly all the new houses being founded by Norman landowners and many of them (especially at first) being settled by monks from Normandy or elsewhere in France. Both landowners and monks likewise sponsored a wholesale reconstruction of English parish churches.

All these factors combined to produce, during the century and a half following the Norman Conquest, a campaign of church-building on a scale previously unexampled in Britain, and the like of which would not be seen again until the Victorian Gothic Revival. The modern traveller, indeed, need rarely journey very far to find a church which, if not wholly or substantially Norman, contains at least some reminder of this great period of rebuilding. Nor is it easy to mistake the evidence when it occurs for Norman architecture is highly distinctive. Its principal hallmarks are the round-headed arches that appear everywhere in Norman churches – over windows and doors, as carved decoration, and most strikingly at the entrance to the chancel, or in the great arcades between nave and aisles; where, in major buildings like Ely Cathedral or Wymondham Abbey, they rise in double or triple tiers. The massive round pillars on which such arches rest are likewise a typically Norman feature: and help to produce the impression of fortress-like solidity so characteristic not only of great Norman churches like St Albans, but also of much smaller places of worship like the noble chapel of St John in the Tower of London.

This impression is strongest where (as in early Norman churches like the last-mentioned, and in a few later examples like Kirkwall Cathedral) carved decoration is kept to a severe minimum: though in such cases the austerity of the architecture must frequently have been relieved by wall paintings like the fine surviving series at Kempley. As the Norman period progressed, however, sculptural embellishment became increasingly popular and elaborate. Often (as at Lindisfarne Priory and in the sumptuous Prior's Door at Ely) it focussed on doorways, which may be flanked by rows of five or six columns, and topped by the same number of concentric round arches carved with the favourite Norman zigzag pattern or encrusted with animal heads. Wall decoration frequently took the form of "blank arcading" – rows of round arches carved in low relief, and sometimes intersecting each other like trellis work: while within the church the chancel arch is generally richly ornamented – as at Compton, with its remarkable and mysterious two-storeyed sanctuary. Perhaps the most delightful examples of later Norman sculpture, however, are to be found on the "capitals" or heads of pillars, with their elaborate foliage patterns or fantastic beasts locked in combat: these appear most magnificently in the crypt of Canterbury Cathedral, built in the first decades of the twelfth century and the largest and finest of all Norman crypts.

By mounting into the superb choir above that crypt, moreover, the traveller can witness how the latest development of Norman architecture merged into the Gothic style which was to hold sway during the remainder of the middle ages. Raised during the 1180s, the Canterbury choir is still equipped with mighty pillars, but these are far taller and more slender than the squat piers of immediately post-Conquest churches. Clusters of soaring shafts add a grace unknown in the monolithic early Norman churches; and, most telling of all, the main arches are no longer round and Norman, but pointed Gothic. This 'transitional Norman' architecture, seen also at Brinkburn Priory and London's Temple Church, has a distinctive beauty of its own: but some travellers may prefer the uncompromisingly austere style of the earlier period, when the Normans were still impressing their personality on conquered England with churches built like fortresses.

The extensive ruins of Elgin Cathedral, pleasantly set in parkland by the river Lossie, demonstrate that here stood the very grandest and most beautiful of Scotland's great medieval churches, called in 1390 "the ornament of the realm, the glory of the kingdom, the delight of foreigners and strangers." Begun before 1224, and extensively enlarged after the first of a series of calamitous fires in 1270, it includes a number of features rare anywhere in Scotland, and all the more surprising in this comparatively remote situation, far to the north of the centres of power. It has, for example, a fine octagonal chapter house; and originally possessed three great towers, of which only the western pair still survive: while the nave was flanked not by single but by double aisles, the outermost each containing five chapels. The greatest surviving glory of Elgin, nevertheless, is the magnificent east front, with its ten tall lancet windows arranged in two tiers, flanked by massive octagonal buttresses and topped by a rose window: undoubtedly one of the best examples of early Gothic architecture anywhere in Britain.

The cathedral's beauty, however, did not preserve it from disaster and eventual ruin, mainly brought about by the hand of man. In 1390 it was burnt, along with the whole town of Elgin, by "wyld wykked Heland-men" under the notorious Wolf of Badenoch, the unruly prince whom its bishop had dared to excommunicate. Thereafter it was extensively repaired, but in 1567, following the Reformation, it was deliberately unroofed so that the lead might be sold: and in 1640 the decaying interior was ransacked by fanatical Covenanters, while fifteen years later Cromwellian troopers used the windows for target practice. Finally, in 1711, the central tower collapsed, demolishing the middle of the building, which then became a rubbish dump and stone quarry. Only in 1825 did the authorities at last appoint a paid "keeper of the ruins", a cobbler named John Shanks: by the time he died at the age of 83, this splendid character claimed to have carted from the interior some 3000 barrowloads of rubble, and the preservation of the cathedral's remains was assured.
See **The Reformation.**

ELGIN Grampian
OS 28 NJ 221632
The attractive burgh of Elgin stands near the north-east coast of Scotland and the A96, some thirty-seven miles east-north-east of Inverness: apart from the cathedral (on the east side of the town in Cooper Park) it contains many notable buildings, including the so-called "Bishop's House" (in fact the fortified residence of a canon) immediately west of the cathedral. Six miles to the south-west, via the B9010 and a minor road, is the restored medieval priory of Pluscarden, now once again occupied by monks and generally open to the public.

ELSTOW Bedfordshire
OS 153 TL 049474
Elstow is immediately south of Bedford, off the A6 road to Luton: and some eight miles north-east of junction 13 of the M1 motorway, via the A421 (which passes through Marston Moretaine). The church is at the centre of the attractive village, and looks across the village green towards the Moot Hall of c.1500, now a Bunyan museum (open afternoons Tuesday–Sunday, from April until October): it is usually open in summer, but if it is locked the addresses of key-holders are given on the notice by the churchyard gate.

The detached bell-tower at Elstow.

Now a truncated but a strikingly lofty building with an attractive detached bell-tower – a later and less massive version of the tower at nearby Marston Moretaine – the church of St Mary and St Helena was once the western end of a great Benedictine nunnery church. The remainder of the nuns' church was demolished after the Reformation, when the present east wall was built: and later still part of the monastic cloister was incorporated into the adjacent but now ruined Jacobean mansion, while the nuns' parlour became the parish vestry. This impressively vaulted room is accessible from within the Norman and

47

Above, the vaulted parish vestry was once the nuns' parlour. Right, the Bunyan window in the east wall of the south aisle.

thirteenth century church, via a door at the west end of the south aisle: in the same aisle is the only surviving brass to a Benedictine abbess (Dame Elizabeth Herwy d.1527), bearing her staff of office.

The reason why most travellers come to Elstow, however, is proclaimed by the Victorian stained glass window east of the abbess's brass: a window commemorating the incomparable John Bunyan, author of the "Pilgrim's Progress". He was indeed born and baptised here, but that he should now be honoured within this church is somewhat ironic: for the Puritan Bunyan came to regard most established churches as works of the Devil, and is believed to have had Elstow's in mind when he wrote of "the Castle of Beelzebub", from which Christian escaped to begin his pilgrimage to salvation.

See **Marston Moretaine.**

The most distinctive and some would say the most beautiful of English cathedrals, Ely owes its origins to St Etheldreda, the most famous and formidable of Anglo-Saxon female saints. Born a daughter of the East Anglian royal house, she was the wife in succession of a prince of the Fenland and a king of Northumbria – though in name only, for she was vowed to perpetual virginity: and in 673 the pressures of this situation caused her to take refuge in the inaccessible "eel island" amid the trackless fens, where she established a monastery and ruled as abbess until her death in 679. Thereafter the renown of the royal saint and her abbey – sacked by the Vikings in 869, but refounded for Benedictine monks a century later – grew apace, so that by the Norman Conquest it was among the largest and richest in England. At that time, however, its strategic position made it an ideal centre for the desperate anti-Norman resistance led by Hereward the Wake, a resistance which cost Ely a heavy price in lands and treasure confiscated by William the Conqueror. Yet even that stern monarch stood in awe of the abbey's saintly patroness, and it is said that he dared only throw a piece of gold onto her shrine from a safe distance, hoping thereby to avert her wrath.

It was the Normans, nevertheless, who were responsible for many of the finest features of the present great church, which was begun in 1081 by the Conqueror's kinsman Abbot Simeon and (having been raised to cathedral status in 1109) completed in its original form by 1189. Of around this last date is the splendid west front by which the cathedral is entered, though this was later altered by the addition of a Gothic Galilee porch (distinguishable by its pointed arches and windows), the heightening of its central tower, and the collapse of one of its twin-turreted flanking transepts. Far more distinctively Norman is the truly magnificent sweep of triple-tiered arches – clerestory on gallery on arcade – which makes Ely's lengthy nave one of the most breathtaking architectural experiences in Britain, and which leads the eye into a vista extending virtually uninterrupted to the distant eastern end of the cathedral. Most unusual in a great medieval church, this prospect exists only because of the eighteenth century destruction of the stone Norman screen which (as in most other cathedrals) divided the nave from the choir beyond. In the nave, too, is Ely's only remaining link with St Etheldreda's time, the base of a memorial cross to her steward Ovin; while a nearby door in the south aisle wall brings the traveller to the cathedral's finest Norman survival, the beautifully and ornately carved "Prior's Door" which led into the church from the now-vanished monastic cloister.

But the greatest glory of Ely (and indeed probably the most impressive achievement of medieval architctural engineering anywhere in Europe) is the great central octagon: the

brilliant solution to the problems caused by the collapse of the Norman central tower, which fell "with a roar like thunder" on February the twelfth 1322, taking with it much of the choir and damaging the transepts. Instead of replacing it with a conventional new tower, the cathedral sacrist Alan of Walsingham ("a man eminently skilled in architecture") hit on the revolutionary notion of spanning the seventy-two foot gap with a massive octagonal "lantern", thus obtaining the maximum well-lit space for the services which took place beneath. In order to do so, he first raised eight soaring stone pillars: each of these features a canopied niche resting on corbels depicting scenes from St Etheldreda's life; while by the north-western and south-eastern arches are portrait-heads of Alan himself, his master mason, and the contemporary prior and bishop of Ely. On these pillars rest sixteen tremendous inward-canted timber struts – concealed by wooden vaulting – which are arranged as eight triangles supporting the lantern itself, a lead-covered timber octagon with corner posts each constructed from a single ten-ton oak tree. Between these last are the windows which fill the space below with light, and at the centre of the lantern's ceiling, 150 feet above ground, is a fine contemporary carving of Christ in Glory. Above this again, moreover, is a chamber which originally housed six mighty bells, the timber joints being designed to open and close with the vibrations caused by their ringing: and though the whole amazing roof structure weighs over four hundred tons, it is so perfectly engineered that it has stood for more than six centuries without ever needing major alteration.

The eastern parts of the cathedral, though less dramatic, are equally worthy of close inspection. Immediately beyond the octagon is the choir, built in the Decorated style of Gothic to replace that crushed by the falling tower: and beyond again is the Early English presbytery, completed in 1232 to house not only the shrine of St Etheldreda (whose position is marked by a floor slab) but also those of her saintly relations Sexburga, Withburga and Ermenhilda. Round this galaxy of holy virgins clustered – as at Canterbury and St Albans – the tombs of those important enough to be buried close to the wonder-working relics, and both choir aisles abound in notable monuments. In the south aisle (to name but a few) are the fine Elizabethan brasses of Bishop Goodrich and Dean Tyndale, and the canopied tombs of Bishop William of Louth and of John Tiptoft, Earl of Worcester, an austere-faced coronetted figure lying between two wives. While in the north aisle are many bishops, including at the west end Bishop Nigel (d.1133) – commemorated by a black marble slab, which shows him carried up to heaven in a sheet – and (midway along) Bishop Redman, who died in 1505 and whose tomb is surmounted by quite remarkably rich Perpendicular canopy-work.

ELY Cambridgeshire
OS 143 TL 541802
Ely is some sixty-five miles north of London and fifteen miles north-east of Cambridge, via the A10. Its cathedral is visible for many miles across the flat surrounding Fenlands, and totally dominates the little city: among its many other attractions is a most interesting museum of stained glass (closed in winter), which is housed in the gallery of the Norman nave. Many of the villages round about also possess splendid churches, most notably that of Isleham (eight miles south-east): while six miles to the south, near Soham, is the National Trust's reserve at Wicken Fen, which preserves a tract of undrained fenland as it would have appeared in the days of Etheldreda and Hereward.

The lantern of Ely Cathedral.

Even this, however, pales beside the almost over-ornate decoration of the two chantry chapels of early Tudor bishops, which flank the extreme eastern end of the cathedral and are in some ways its most extraordinary features. Carved from the soft local stone called clunch, their pinnacled and cannopied screens resemble feats of cake-icing rather than of sculpture, and their interiors are no less sumptuous: that of Bishop Allcock (to the north) is everywhere embellished by his punning badge of a cockerel; while that of Bishop West (d.1534) has a lavish painted and panelled ceiling, a precursor of the Renaissance fashions to come.

Altogether more restrained is the Lady Chapel: which, unusually, stands almost detached from the cathedral, to the east of the north transept. It is, however, emphatically not to be missed, for it is among the finest Decorated buildings in England, begun in 1321 and (surprisingly enough) continued while work on the great octagon was simultaneously in progress. Lofty and full of light, with a daring single-span stone roof adorned with many carved bosses, it rounds off most appropriately a visit to this magnificent cathedral.

See **The Anglo-Saxon Church, Canterbury, St Albans, Shrines and Pilgrimages.**

Monasteries and Religious Houses

The monasteries and religious houses whose remains survive all over Britain testify to the strength of a movement of tremendous importance in the history of Christianity. Its mainspring was the desire to abandon the world and seek God through a rigorous system of prayer, meditation, and penance, which first appeared among the Christians of the later Roman Empire. In Egypt, especially, large numbers of both men and women withdrew into the desert to live the solitary life of hermits, and the word "monk" is indeed derived from "monos", the Greek for "one who dwells alone". Before long, however, many of these hermits began gathering into loose communities under the direction of an abbot (meaning "father"), sometimes following a common rule. From Egypt the monastic movement spread across Europe to take root in Britain and Ireland, many of whose first Christian missionaries were themselves monks. The earliest British monasteries bore little resemblance to the great institutions of the middle ages, with their rigidly ordered buildings grouped round a single church. For among the Celtic Christians the ancient tradition of hermit communities persisted long, and monasteries like Iona would originally have consisted of many small individual "cells" of woven wattles or rough stone, with perhaps three or four churches and chapels scattered among them, all surrounded by a defensive earthwork bank.

This tradition of communal individualism was carried over into the Anglo-Saxon Church by the Celtic monks who first colonised Lindisfarne, and many early Anglo-Saxon monasteries were independent institutions, founded by some pious lay person who had retired from the world and attracted others to follow his or her example. Often they were "double houses" for both men and women, invariably ruled by an abbess. Such independent Saxon monasteries generally adhered to their own rule, more or less rigid as their various founders had decreed: but alongside them existed an increasing number of houses observing some version of the rule devised in sixth century Italy by St Benedict of Nursia. "Benedictine" influence grew yet stronger with the monastic revival which followed the disastrous Viking invasions, when St Dunstan strove to subordinate independent monasteries to a uniform system of observances: while at the Norman Conquest most English monasteries became part of the Benedictine "order", the great European family of monks following the same rule. In Scotland and Wales the ancient Celtic forms of monasticism were to linger on (as at Abernethy) for two more centuries, but there too the centralised orders of monks and canons eventually triumphed.

The Benedictine rule – upon which those of many later orders were also based – regulated every moment of the monk's life, decreeing first of all that he must keep until death his vows of personal poverty, chastity, and obedience to his abbot. Beyond this, his principal duty was to praise God by reciting, in common with his brethren, seven services every twenty-four hours. The first of these ("Vigils") took place at the dead of night, and was followed, after a period of meditation, by the service of "Lauds" at first light and a third service called "Prime" at sunrise. About three hours later (after a period of work) came "Terce", and on Sundays or holy days Mass would be celebrated between this and the service of "Nones" at noon: thereafter the monk was allowed a two hour rest before rising for work or meditation and the evening service of "Vespers". This was followed by the one meal of the day, eaten with his brethren in the refectory while one of their number read from a holy book, and by the dusk service of "Compline", whereafter the monk retired for a few hours sleep before beginning the whole round again.

The rigidly ordered nature of the monk's life is also reflected in the arrangement of buildings within the monastery: which, apart from comparatively minor variations between order and order or dictated by local geography, differs little wherever in Britain it is sited. Much the most important building, of course, was the monastic church, nearly always cruciform and frequently of great magnificence, especially in the larger houses. The nave at its west end might be used (particularly in Cistercian monasteries) to accommodate the inferior grade of monks called "lay brothers", or (as at Wymondham) employed by the local people as a parish church, a situation which not infrequently gave rise to disputes between monks and parishioners. To the east, beyond a rood-screen and a second screen called the pulpitum, was the choir where the monks sang or recited their services, gaining access to it during the hours of darkness via a "night stair" leading directly from their sleeping quarters. The choir's focus was the high altar on its raised dais: and behind this, in larger monastic churches like Abbey Dore, was a passage called the ambulatory, which linked the aisles on either side of the choir and allowed the monks to process round the eastern end of the church – where might likewise be situated a number of small chapels, in which monks who were also priests said their daily Masses.

Generally the church formed the northern side of the monks' cloister – the "enclosure" wherein they lived and worked – thus sheltering it from cold winds but allowing the southern sunshine to warm its central courtyard or "cloister garth". This was surrounded by a covered walkway where the monks took exercise, and which they also used for activities requiring strong light, such as study or the writing and illumination of manuscripts. Round the other three sides of the courtyard were arranged the monastic living quarters. On the east side, beginning at the transept of the church, was a corridor sometimes used as a library: and then came the often richly decorated chapter house, where the community generally met daily to transact the business of the monastery, and where the tombs of specially revered abbots might be situated. The upper storey of the eastern range, meanwhile, was usually occupied by the monks' dormitory; with its attached "rere-dorter" or multiple toilet, frequently positioned (as at Egglestone Abbey) above a drain ingeniously flushed by a diverted stream.

South of the courtyard was the range including the refectory, with its pulpit for mealtime readings and sometimes a "lavatorium" or washing-place outside its door: and here too were the kitchen and (in many monasteries) the "warming house", the only other place within the cloister where a fire was allowed. Uses of the western range varied considerably. In Cistercian monasteries (like Melrose) it was generally used to accommodate the lay brothers, but elsewhere it might house the abbot's lodgings – though in the later days of monasticism these were more often in a separate building outside the cloister. Outside the cloister, too, was the monastery's infirmary, used by sick monks and those convalescing after their periodic medicinal blood letting: while elsewhere in the monastic precinct were such buildings as stables, mills, a guest-house and (especially in the monasteries of the sheep-farming Cistercians) barns for the house's produce.

These Cistercians belonged to one of the several offshoots of the Benedictine order which sprang up from the eleventh century onwards. While the Cluniacs, another such new order, concentrated on elaborate religious ceremonial, the Cistercians emphasised the importance of austerity and hard manual labour, and generally chose to found their houses in wild and remote countryside far from the haunts of men – a policy which has bequeathed some of the most beautifully sited monastic ruins in Britian, including Dundrennan and Melrose. Often, to, Cistercian monasteries were particularly large and splendid, for these "white monks" – so called because, unlike the black-cowled Benedictines, they wore white habits – developed into wealthy and highly successful farmers. Very different, and far less numerous than either Benedictines or Cistercians, were the Carthusian monks: whose well preserved Mount Grace Priory graphically demonstrates how they rejected both worldly wealth and communal activity to follow the ancient tradition of living as hermits within their monastery.

By no means all British religious houses, however, were occupied by monks. Equally numerous were the abbeys and priories of the canons regular, though many of these (like Brinkburn Priory and Egglestone Abbey) were comparatively small. Canons – the two principle orders being the Augustinians and Premonstratensians – differed from monks principally in that they were invariably ordained priests, and followed a somewhat less strict rule which enabled them both to perform parish work and to serve such institutions as the hospital attached to St Bartholomew the Great in London. Yet more heavily engaged in the worldly front line were the four orders of friars, whose name derives from the French for "brothers" and whose vows obliged them to live entirely by begging and to minister to the poorest of the poor: for this reason their houses were usually in towns, and few traces of them have therefore survived. The military or crusading orders of the Knights Templars and Knights Hospitallers, however, are still respectively commemorated by the Temple Church in London and by Torphichen preceptory. The nunnery churches at Minster-in-Sheppey and St Helen's Bishopgate in London, meanwhile, serve as a reminder that most religious orders had their branches for women: and though medieval nunneries had declined greatly in status since their Anglo-Saxon heyday, they continued to play an important part in the religious life of Britain.

The high water monk of monasticism in Britain was probably the twelfth and thirteenth centuries. Thereafter (with the notable exception of the Carthusians) the religious orders went into a very gradual decline, which accelerated as the middle ages drew to a close. The reasons for this are complex, but an increasing lack of lay interest was among them: few new houses were founded after the fourteenth century, and those that existed declined in income as the emphasis of popular piety shifted to the parish church. Recruitment into the orders likewise fell away drastically: and these factors combined to produce, not the wholesale debauchery so often depicted by historical novelists, but a feeling of demoralisation and a distinct weakening of discipline, especially in the smaller houses. Some of the larger monasteries like St Albans, conversely, had become little more than property-owning corporations, while many Scottish houses had fallen into the hands of lay noblemen known as "commendators". It may be, indeed, that monasteries and religious houses had already outlived their usefulness when Henry VIII, greedy for their estates, dissolved them at the Reformation. Yet during their great days they had contributed much to the survival of culture and learning, shining out as bastions of order and civilisation in an otherwise chaotic and violent world: and even in their ruin they have bequeathed to the traveller a rich heritage of interest and beauty.

See **The First Christian Missionaries, The Anglo-Saxon Church, The Reformation.**

The unique fifteenth century grouping of church, almshouses and school at Ewelme – all still in full use – is perhaps the most graphic surviving reminder of the medieval belief that lavish charity could purchase the donors a place in Heaven; or at least help to expiate their sins, and so shorten their punishment in Purgatory. The hopeful founders here were the formidable Alice Chaucer, lady of the manor and grand-daughter of the famous poet; and her husband William de la Pole, Earl of Suffolk, a powerful but violently unpopular politician who was eventually to be lynched by sailors. Work began first, in 1432, on the church of St Mary. Replacing an earlier parish church (whose rather insignificant tower still stands, quite outclassed by the grandiose new fabric) this is a fine spacious building, noticeably reminiscent of the great churches of de la Pole's native East Anglia. It has a Suffolk-style pinnacled font cover, soaring over ten feet high; delicate wooden screens dividing off the nave, chancel, and flanking chapels; and a splendid angel-carved roof over the south of St John's chapel.

This chapel, with its contemporary stained glass and walls painted with the "IHS" monogram of Christ, is in fact the most sumptuous part of St Mary's. Since 1437 it has served as the chapel of the almshouses

Alice and William established immediately south of the church for thirteen poor men and two priests – one of whom was to teach the village children in the (still operational) school building, the third of their munificent benefactions. The principal duty of the almsmen (who still live in their charming and comparatively unaltered brick and timber cottages round a cloistered quadrangle) is and was to pray for the founders in this south chapel: which thus appropriately contains the tombs both of Alice's father Thomas Chaucer (with its fine brasses and coloured enamel heraldry of his family connections) and of Alice herself – a monument which is Ewelme's most famous and magnificent possession. There the great lady's alabaster effigy lies serenely at prayer, the insignia of the Order of the Garter tied round her left forearm: while angels support her pillow, line the elaborate canopy above and, bearing shields, guard the tomb chest where here body rests. Yet beneath all, visible through a grille at ground level, is a second and infinitely grimmer effigy, depicting her not as an elegant aristocrat but as a shrouded and emaciated corpse: a reminder of the mortality which no amount of charity could avert, but from which she hoped the prayers of its beneficiaries would raise her to life eternal.

EWELME Oxfordshire
OS 175 SU 646914
The small and attractive village of Ewelme is some seventeen miles south-east of Oxford; three miles north-east of historic Wallingford and six miles south-west of junction 6 of the M40 London-Oxford motorway, via the B4009 through Watlington. Church, almshouses and school stand together, the church being usually open and the almshouses' courtyard (though not the almsmen's cottages) often accessible to the traveller. Nine miles to the north is Rycote Chapel.

The fame of Eyam rests on the heroism of its clergy and people during the tragic series of events which began in late August 1665, when the village tailor received a box of disease-infected clothes from London, then in the grip of the Great Plague. Within weeks the deadly sickness was spreading through the community, whose people prepared to seek the only remedy then known – that of flight into the surrounding countryside, carrying the plague with them. But the new vicar William Mompesson, aided by his wife Catherine and by a Puritan minister named Thomas Stanley, persuaded them to stay within the village limits: promising to remain with them and to arrange for supplies to be brought to certain points on the parish boundary (including Mompesson's Well, a mile to the north-west) where money could be left "disinfected" in vinegar or running water. For a full twelve months the plague raged in Eyam, the dead being laid in makeshift graves near their homes: many of which are still marked, like the poignant Riley Graves where Mrs. Hancock single-handedly buried all seven members of her family. Yet the villagers' resolution held firm, and though Mompesson wisely closed the church for fear of infection, he continued to hold open-air services in the natural amphitheatre called Cucklett Delf, using a limestone outcrop as his pulpit.

When at last the pestilence ceased (after a final onslaught which carried off the fearless Catherine Mompesson) some 224 of Eyam's

350 inhabitants were dead: but their self-sacrifice had saved the Peak District from almost certain disaster, and it has rightly never been forgotten. Eyam, indeed, is full of reminders of that dreadful time. In the restored medieval parish church of St Lawrence, for example, Mompesson's chair stands by the altar, and at the west end of the north aisle is a cupboard reputed (somewhat improbably) to have been made from the fatal clothes-box; while in the opposite aisle is the Plague Register recording the names of the dead. The fine and unusual series of Jacobean wall paintings in the nave, however, date from some time before the disaster, and depict the (imaginary) coats of arms of the Twelve Tribes of Israel, with an ominously prophetic figure of Death the Grim Reaper over the tower arch. Far earlier still is the magnificent ninth century Saxon standing cross – probably brought from the surrounding moorlands – in the churchyard, near the flat-topped tomb of Catherine Mompesson and the grave of the Puritan Thomas Stanley.

Just to the west and across the road, a path beginning by the ancient village stocks leads to the Delf, the pretty wooded ravine used as a place of worship during the epidemic. Here, each "Plague Sunday" (the last in August, and the anniversary of the outbreak's beginning) an open-air service is held to commemorate the Eyam men and women who died that the neighbouring communities might live.

EYAM Derbyshire
OS 119 SK 218764
Eyam (pronounced "eem") stands in the dramatic countryside of the Peak District National Park, eleven miles south-west of Sheffield via the A625, the B6521 to Grindleford, and a minor road: it can also be reached from the M1 motorway (some eighteen miles to the east) via junctions 29 or 30, Chesterfield, and the A619/A623; following signs first to Buxton, then to Chapel-en-le-Frith and (west of Stoney Middleton) finally to Eyam. The church is in the middle of the village, and other places connected with the Plague are well signposted: Mompesson's Well (SK 223773) is by a minor road to Grindleford; and the Riley Graves stand (SK 229765) by a footpath turning north off the road to the east of the village; while Cucklett Delf is accessible from the path by the village stocks, via a locked gate whose key can be obtained (except on Sundays) from the house opposite with the white gate and outside staircase.

FAIRFORD Gloucestershire
OS 163 SP 152012

The attractive stone-built town of Fairford is eight miles east of Cirencester on the A417 and some sixteen miles north of junction 15 of the M4, via the A419 Swindon by-pass, the A419 to Lechlade, and then the A419 west. St Mary's church is near the town centre, and in its churchyard are many fine tombs, not forgetting that of "Tiddles" the church cat (1963–80) by the porch. All around are prosperous medieval wool towns with splendid churches, notably Cirencester to the west, Lechlade to the east, and Northleach to the north.

The great wool church of Fairford is outstanding even in a region famous for its fine medieval churches. Built within a very short space of time (c.1490–1500) by the wealthy clothier John Tame and his son Sir Edmund, it is thus a remarkably unified example of the most sumptuous phase of late Gothic Perpendicular architecture. It retains much of its original stone and wood-carving, all of the highest quality; and, most notably of all, it preserves its complete set of twenty-eight original stained glass windows. Sculpture abounds on its exterior: heraldry on the parapets of its noble tower, mingling with clothiers' scissors, merchant's marks and the image of Christ in Pity on the western face; and rows of figures line the battlements lower down, the most lifelike being the boy apparently preparing to jump from the parapet to the right of the porch.

Immensely spacious within, the church is lit by its famous (though now admittedly rather faded) windows, probably the work of Henry VII's Master Glass Painter, the Fleming Barnard Flower: certainly they have a rather Germanic air, particularly the Crucifixion scenes in the east window. To see them as they were meant to be seen, portraying every principal element of the Catholic faith (and a few "holy legends" besides) the traveller should begin on the north side, with the Fall of Man in the fifth window from the left as viewed from the entrance. Continuing east-

wards and clockwise into the Lady Chapel (via the childhood of the Virgin and of Christ) notice the heraldic wall brass of Sir Edmund Tame (d.1534) and his two wives: and then the tomb of the founder himself, between the Lady Chapel and the choir and surmounted by a fine original wooden screen. On it John Tame the merchant is represented in brass as an armoured gentleman; while the inscription beneath his feet, begging the traveller to pray for his soul, underlines his hope that his great church might buy him entry into Paradise.

In the chancel, facing the glass Crucifixion scenes, are a set of early Tudor stalls carved with comic low-life subjects, and in the Corpus Christi chapel the Bible story continues with the Resurrection and Ascension, Christ's feet disappearing into Heaven on the last but one panel to the west. Back now in the nave, rows of glass apostles and saints (while Martyrs defy Persecutors of the Church across the nave roof) lead westwards to the climax of the whole scheme, the overwhelming Last Judgement in the great west window. Here Christ sits on His rainbow with the world as His footstool, surrounded by concentric rings of saints and angels: while below St Michael divides the saved from the damned, one of whom a blue devil wheels in a barrow to the hideous Satan in the window's bottom right-hand-corner.

See **The Great Wool Churches.**

FINCHALE PRIORY Durham
OS 88 NZ 297471

The priory is three miles north-east of the famous and historic city of Durham, with its outstanding Norman cathedral: and is accessible from there via the A691 north-west, the A167 north, and a signposted minor road turning east. It is also easily reached, via Durham or Chester-le-Street, from the nearby A1 trunk road.

Delightfully set against a backdrop of woodland by a great loop in the fast-flowing river Wear, Finchale Priory was a most unusual monastery, and owed its origins to an altogether exceptional saint. His name was Godric, and after starting life as a Norfolk pedlar he took to the sea as a merchant-cum-pirate, voyaging to Spain, Denmark and Flanders and in 1102 helping the King of Jerusalem to escape from pursuit by the Saracens. From the beginning, however, he was addicted to pilgrimages, visiting St Andrews in Scotland, Compostela in Spain, and St Giles in France, and walking barefoot to Rome accompanied by his aged mother. Eventually he abandoned travel for the life of a hermit and, directed by a vision of St Cuthbert to seek out a place called Finchale, settled in a turf hut here in 1115. From then on he strove to expiate his past sins by spectacular penances such as continually wearing a coat of mail over a hair shirt, though he also wrote poetry and kept adders as pets: and before long his sanctity was attracting many visitors, great bishops and abbots among them. Their donations built him a little stone chapel dedicated to St John the Baptist, and within it he died in 1170 at the age of no less than 105, being buried beneath the place where his death-bed had stood.

St Godric's coffin, hewn from a single

block of stone and only about five feet long (he is known to have been a stocky man) is still to be seen amid the foundations of his chapel, surrounded by the chancel of Finchale Priory church. Founded in 1196 as an outpost of the great cathedral priory of Durham, three miles to the south-west, the monastery was at first of normal type, with a sizeable church dating from about 1250 and extensive buildings round the adjacent cloister. This accomodation, however, proved too large for the resident monks (there were never more than fifteen of them): and in 1365 the church was reduced in size by demolishing its redundant nave aisles. At much the same time a new use was found for the beautifully positioned priory, and the place once famous for the penances of its hermit became quite literally a holiday home for Durham monks.

By an arrangement formalised in 1408, it was permanently staffed only by a prior and four monks, while groups of four "players" (as the holidaymakers were known) visited in rotation for three week stays. During these rest periods they took turns in reciting the monastic offices, those off duty being permitted to "walk honestly and religiously" in the surrounding countryside. Meanwhile they were accommodated in the prior's house north-east of the cloister, which was enlarged and altered so that it resembled a contemporary private mansion: at its east end is the prior's chamber, which has a fine traceried window overlooking the river, and is flanked by a chapel and a study with a protruding oriel window. Any woman who sat there, according to a ribald tradition which may reflect the popular view of the "players'" leisure activities, would be cured of sterility and blessed with children.

See **Monasteries and Religious Houses.**

Set against the backdrop of a great mansion, and overlooking splendidly landscaped parkland, St Peter's at Gayhurst is the perfect Georgian country gentleman's church. It was built for George Wright, son of a successful political lawyer, to replace a "very old and uncomely" medieval church which spoilt the view from his house – for the same reason, old Gayhurst village was tidied away to its present site by the road – and remains almost exactly as its unknown architect left it in 1728. Basically a classical building (though the windows in its charmingly cupolad tower nod respectively to the Gothic) its light and cooly dignified interior is original in every detail of its furnishing and decoration, from its box pews and towering marquetry-inlaid pulpit to its richly decorated plaster ceiling. There, in the chancel, fat-cheeked cherubs peer from the clouds above the altar: while below the cornice of the nave ceiling are alternating Bibles and bishop's mitres, which flank the Royal Arms above the chancel arch and thus underline the Georgian alliance of Church and State – as yet unthreatened by Methodism and Revolution – epitomized by this fine church. Perhaps its most memorable feature, however, is the vast and superb monument to George Wright and his father the judge, the son elegantly pointing to his father's insignia as Keeper of the Great Seal. Oddly enough it lacks an inscription, an omission attributed to the parsimony of the church-building squire's descendants.

See **The Prayer Book Church.**

GAYHURST Buckinghamshire
OS 152 SP 846463
Gayhurst village is on the B526, eleven miles south-east of Northampton and only four miles north-west (via Newport Pagnell) of junction 14 of the M1 motorway: the church and house are reached via a signposted drive turning off the B526 at the south (or Newport Pagnall) end of the village. A fearsome array of notices proclaims that the house (Jacobean with Georgian additions) is closed to the public, but the church is accessible via a right of way and is generally unlocked.

The Wright monument at the east end of the south aisle.

GEDNEY Lincolnshire
OS 131 TF 403244

The church stands in dead-flat Fenland ten miles east of Spalding, and is clearly visible from the A17 midway between Holbeach and Long Sutton, which both also have large and fine churches.

One of the grand, isolated, "Marshland" churches which are so striking a feature of eastern England's Fen country, St Mary Magdalen's tiers of huge clear glass windows make it seem from a distance almost transparent. Its west tower, topped by a sadly unfinished spire, was built in the thirteenth century; the lower windows, with their flowing tracery, are in the Decorated style of the fourteenth; while the twelve great Perpendicular windows of the oversailing clerestory date probably from the early Tudor period.

Like so many other East Anglian churches, its interior is spacious, bare and full of light, with a splendid roof. The unusual south door has an inset ivory crucifix and an original fourteenth century lock; the south aisle contains monuments to a thirteenth century knight and a lady of *c.*1400, life sized in brass; and the north aisle east window displays a little medieval glass – a reminder that the vast glazed areas of such churches once glowed with colour.

The south front of the grand church of St Mary Magdalen.

56

Set in the wooded fringes of once-great Epping Forest, the charming little church of St Andrew at Greensted has pretty dormer windows in its nave roof, a Tudor brick chancel, and a miniature Essex tower of white-painted timber boarding, topped by a shingled spire. Its most remarkable and most famous features, however, are its nave walls of vertically split oak-logs, set upright in a horizontal sill: for these make it the sole surviving example of an Anglo-Saxon "log-cabin" church, such as must have been common in the forested areas of England during the centuries before the Norman Conquest. How long they have stood here is uncertain, but they are probably those of the building in which the relics of St Edmund of East Anglia rested in 1013, on their way from London to Bury St Edmunds. Thereafter St Andrew's slipped back into obscurity, and unlike most of its contemporaries was never reconstructed in stone during the middle ages, remaining a unique memorial to a long-vanished building tradition.

See **The Anglo-Saxon Church.**

GREENSTED Essex
OS 167 TL 539030
Greensted is a mile west of Chipping Ongar, and some twenty-five miles north-east of central London, via the M11 (junction 7), the A414 east, and signposted minor roads turning south.

Near the western edge of the Cotswolds and ringed by wooded hills, the hamlet of Hailes was once thronged with pilgrims to no less a relic than a phial of Christ's own blood. The most prized possession of Cistercian Hailes Abbey – founded in 1246 by Richard of Cornwall, son of Henry III and nominal King of the Romans – the phial was presented by Richard's son Edmund, and bore the guarantee of the Patriarch of Jerusalem himself: almost at once it attracted hordes of pious sightseers, continuing to do so right up until the Reformation. "You would wonder to see", wrote a Warwickshire vicar in 1533, "how they come by flocks out of the West Country to many images, but chiefly the Blood of Hailes". A mere five years later, however, Henry VIII's commissioners bore the relic off to London, and having declared it to be "no blood, but honey clarified and coloured with saffron" – though some argued it was the blood of a duck or a drake – consigned it to the flames: and shortly afterwards the abbey itself was suppressed. Comparatively little now remains of its monastic buildings, and scarcely anything of its church – except for the pedestal of the Holy Blood's shrine, in a specially enlarged east end: but the little parish church which stood here before the abbey has also survived it.

Honey-coloured without and cream-plastered within, the church was refurbished and given its fine set of thirteenth century wall-paintings by the monks, doubtless with pilgrims in mind. Of special interest to way-farers, certainly, would have been the giant but now faded St Christopher – the patron saint of travellers, a sight of whose image guaranteed them against sudden death – on the nave wall opposite the door: and the more worldly pilgrims must have enjoyed the spirited hunting scene on the facing wall. The finest paintings, however, are in the chancel, including the repeated heraldic devices of Richard of Cornwall on the side walls and the especially well executed figures of Saints Catherine and Margaret (both with kneeling Cistercians at their feet) in the blocked arches flanking the altar: while a whole unnatural history book of fantastic beasts – a winged elephant and a griffon, a unicorn and a dragon, basilisk, leopard, hare and goat – are locked in combat across the arches of the north and south windows.

Perhaps the greatest contribution to Hailes' special character, nevertheless, is provided by its furnishings – the fifteenth century screen and nave benches; the canopied Jacobean pulpit and box pew; and above all by the seventeenth-century panelled pews in the chancel, which are ranged round three sides of a central free-standing communion table set at right angles to the east wall. Once the pews extended round the fourth side of the table as well, where now the altar stands in the conventional position. But apart from these confusing Victorian alterations, Hailes preserves the old Puritan arrangement of its chancel, whereby communicants sat round a table and took the bread and wine as a genuinely communal meal, not as a sacrament dispensed from the altar.

See **The Prayer Book Church, Shrines and Pilgrimages.**

HAILES Gloucestershire
OS 150 SP 050301
Hailes is just east of the A46, eight miles north-east of Cheltenham and two miles north-east of picturesque Winchcombe with its fine fifteenth century church: it is also easily accessible from junction 9 of the M5 motorway (eight miles west) via the A438 to Toddington and then the A46 south. The abbey ruins (whose excellent museum contains most interesting sculpture and other remains) are open daily from 9.30 a.m. until 4 p.m., but closed on winter Sunday mornings; while the parish church across the road keeps broadly similar hours. Nearby (south-east of Winchcombe) is medieval and later Sudeley Castle.

Pleasantly situated on rising ground above the river Blithe, with the gaunt ruins of a great Tudor mansion behind it, St Michael's at Hamstall Ridware is a long, low, and engagingly simple parish church, mainly of the fourteenth and fifteenth centuries. Among its treasures are a Norman font now used for growing wallflowers outside the door, and the table tombs of the Strongintthearm family by the churchyard path, with their shields punning on the family name. Its most notable possession, however, is the Cotton tomb in the chancel, which not only commemorates John and Joanna Cotton (d.1502) but also (and most unusually) provides painted biographies and small representations of each of their children along three of its sides. The girls are represented by the arms of the men they married, but some of the boys are shown as delightful little painted figures, among them "Christopher, the first Englishman that ever was Friar Observant", Walter the parson, and William "who died here at the age of six".

HAMSTALL RIDWARE Staffordshire
OS 128 SK 106194
One of four delightfully named villages (Hamstall, Mavesyn, Pipe and Hill Ridware) in the pleasant rolling country north of Lichfield (six miles to the south) Hamstall Ridware lies two miles west of the A515 via signposted minor roads: the clearly visible church stands alone in a field, a list of keyholders being attached to a notice by the gate.

Shrines and Pilgrimages

The pilgrimage impulse – the desire to visit places made sacred by God or by holy men and women – is common to all world religions, and may indeed be a basic human need. Throughout the recorded history of Britain, certainly, and most of all during the middle ages, pious wayfarers have journeyed to shrines up and down the land: and to follow in their foot-steps is one of the most revealing and rewarding itineraries for the modern traveller in search of places of worship.

The reasons why medieval pilgrims set out on their travels, often so very much more arduous than those of their present day successors, were many and various. Some hoped, quite simply, that to tread where the saints had trod, and perhaps to come into contact with their earthly remains, would afford them both a unique spiritual joy and an new insight into the sacred truths of their religion. Yet these seekers after pure spiritual uplift were probably a minority: and many more travelled with the purpose of gaining forgiveness of their sins, or at least of shortening the time their souls would spend in the fires of Purgatory before being admitted to Heaven. From the eleventh century onwards, indeed, the amount of posthumous relief they could expect was laid down precisely by the "indulgences" offered at many shrines. Those who visited Canterbury on the occasion of the removal of St Thomas's relics to a new shrine in 1220, for example, were guaranteed no less than 540 days remission from the purgatorial flames: and it was theoretically possible, by totting up sufficient pilgrimages, to escape purgatory altogether. Nor, at least according to late medieval popular belief, was it necessary to gain such indulgences by actually making the pilgrimage in person: and wealthy men frequently willed money to hire professional pilgrims to undertake the journey on their behalf.

The most hardened sinners, however, might be ordered by the civil or ecclesiastical authorities to make one or more pilgrimages as a form of penance: and indeed most pilgrimages had their deliberately penitential aspects. According to Anglo-Saxon and later custom, a true pilgrim should travel weaponless and barefoot – as St Godric of Finchale travelled to Rome with his aged mother: he or she, moreover, should never spend more than a night in one place, should willingly undergo fasting and privations, and should cut neither hair nor nails during the course of their journey. This journey, in itself, was likely to be both difficult and dangerous, especially if a sea crossing – like that from Llandanwg or Mwnt to Bardsey – was involved: or if, like the Welsh pilgrims who travelled from Holywell via Clynnogfawr and Nevern

to St Davids, the way lay through wild and mountainous country. Pilgrims who made the demanding journey to St Davids twice, indeed, were held to gain as much merit thereby as those who undertook a single but much longer trip to Rome.

Not content with suffering the rigours of the road, some pilgrims put themselves through additional ordeals, such as loading themselves with chains and manacles or wearing hair shirts: while on arrival at their goal they might indulge in further displays of spiritual athleticism, crawling round Canterbury Cathedral on their knees or poising themselves above the sheer drops of St Michael's Mount. It is no wonder, then, that such pilgrims were generally regarded with respect (if not awe) by the stay-at-homes along their routes: who could, however, obtain some small share in their merit by helping them along their way with free food and lodgings. More meritorious yet was the endowment of permanent pilgrim hostels, like that still to be seen on the Eastbridge at Canterbury. Here, as in many similar establishments, the rules laid down that healthy visitors might stay only one night, a sensible precaution which demonstrates that pilgrims were not always accepted without reservation as being free from selfish or even sinister motives.

The staff, pouch and broad-brimmed travelling hat which marked out the pilgrim did not, indeed, invariably guarantee unblemished holiness. Some apparently pious travellers were undoubtedly little better than vagrants and spongers, or even wandering thieves. Others, journeying through lands not their own, fell under suspicion of being spies – so that foreign pilgrims to Whithorn were required to travel by a set route, and to authenticate themselves with badges issued by the shrine's authorities. A less serious but probably more justified complaint (levelled in particular during the later middle ages) was that many pilgrims were no more than holidaymakers, who overlaid their desire to go sightseeing with a thin veneer of piety: and this is certainly the impression gained from Chaucer's famous Canterbury Tales, purportedly a collection of (sometimes racy) stories told by a very worldly party of pilgrims on their way to the shrine of St Thomas Becket.

There (as at every other shrine in Britain) they will have encountered many travellers who had a far more pressing reason for journeying – or in some extreme cases being carried – to the holy place: the sick, crippled and infirm, who hoped for a miraculous cure. A shrine's popularity, indeed, was directly proportional to the number of such healing miracles reported from it: and shrine custodians were accordingly anxious to publicise them, both for reasons of prestige and in order to attract more visitors (and therefore more offerings) to their church. The beautiful thirteenth century stained glass windows which still surround the site of St Thomas's shrine in Canterbury Cathedral are in fact a fascinating pictorial catalogue of the cures wrought by the martyr, either there or elsewhere. They advertise, among many other wonders, how prayers to the saint delivered Stephen of Hoyland from persistent nightmares, and Robert of Cricklade from swollen feet; how Adam the Forester was saved from a poacher's arrow, and Little Robin of Rochester was resuscitated after drowning in the Medway; and how Eilward of Westoning, blinded as a punishment for theft, had his eyesight restored. As a salutary warning to the ungrateful, moreover, they also tell the story of Sir Jordan Fitz Eisulf, whose dead son the martyr revived, but who failed to thank St Thomas by honouring his shrine: thereupon another of his children died, and he himself only narrowly avoided the same fate by setting off for Canterbury forthwith.

Whatever the motives for undertaking it, a pilgrimage would very often be the most exciting event in the pilgrim's life: and many not unnaturally wished to bring home some souvenir of their travels, both as a focus for future devotions and to display to their admiring neighbours. The very best souvenirs, of course, were fragments of the holy relic they had venerated, so that early pilgrims to Jerusalem were carefully watched to see that they did not bite off splinters from the True Cross when kissing it: while even the pious bishop St Hugh of Lincoln did not scruple to chew away two embalmed fingers from the supposed hand of Mary Magdalen. Relics therefore had to be closely guarded by their custodians (a "watching chamber" for this purpose still exists at St Albans), who also frequently had to restrain pilgrims form acts of pious vandalism like hacking away lumps of the pillars near a saint's tomb. Visitors were, however, generally permitted to touch their own handkerchiefs or rings (or similar articles belonging to bedridden friends) against the shrine, thereby permanently endowing these keepsakes with some of its virtue. More commonly still, pilgrims carried home phials of wonder-working water from the holy wells and sacred springs which most shrines possessed, and often these leaden phials took the form of badges, depicting either the relevant saint or the symbol of the holy place. The very considerable number of such badges that even now survives shows that they were the most popular of pilgrim souvenirs: proudly worn by the dozen in the hat of an experienced wayfarer, they attested as plainly as campaign medals his wanderings round the shrines of Christendom.

The most highly honoured of all pilgrim badges was the palm, proclaiming that the wearer had journeyed to Jerusalem. "Palmer", indeed, was a synonym for pilgrim, while the verb "to roam" commemorates the British pilgrims who visited the seat of the Popes in Italy, with its innumerable shrines; and others braved the notorious Bay of Biscay crossing to the tomb of St James at Compostela in northern Spain, remarking with feeling –

"He may leave all games
That goeth to St James."

Those who preferred to remain in Britain had plenty of holy places to choose from, and could even venerate a supposed relic of Christ Himself, the phial of the Holy Blood at Hailes in Gloucestershire, with its surviving pilgrim church. The Virgin Mary, too, was believed to have visited Britain, at least in the form of a vision, and thousands flocked annually to see the replica of her Holy House at Walsingham, which also boasted a sample of her milk.

Undoubtedly the most famous of British shrines, however, was that of the martyred archbishop St Thomas Becket at Canterbury – where, in addition to the miracle-working tomb, pilgrims were also shown many other wonderful relics, including the Virgin Mary's bed, a fragment of the infant Christ's manger, and a piece of the clay from which Adam was made. Another famous martyr, one of the first Christian missionaries, was venerated at St Albans: while elsewhere saints who had died less violent deaths were as greatly honoured, as was the Saxon abbess St Etheldreda at Ely and the Romano-British evangelist St Ninian at Whithorn, Scotland's oldest amd most internationally renowned shrine. Some pilgrimage centres, moreover, did not display the bodies of saints at all: wayfarers were attracted to Holywell by a miraculous healing spring, and to St Michael's Mount by tales that the archangel had appeared there to Cornish fisherman.

Pilgrimages were likewise made to the shrines of "saints" who were never officially canonised, one of the most famous being Master John Schorne, an early fourteenth century vicar of North Marston near Aylesbury in Buckinghamshire. He was famous during his lifetime for his miraculous cures of leg and foot aliments like gout, and was thus often depicted (as on the painted screen at Cawston) conjuring the Devil into (or out of) a boot – a trick which is sometimes said to be the origin of the children's toy called "Jack-in-the-box". After his death pilgrims flocked to his tomb at North Marston, bathing in the nearby healing well which he was believed to have summoned from the ground during a drought: and by the later fifteenth century the popularity of his cult attracted the covetous attention of the canons of St. George's Chapel in Windsor Castle, just then being rebuilt in its present magnificent form. Determined to secure the donations of Schorne's devotees for their building works, and anxious to enhance the fame of their chapel with the relics of a renowned (if unofficial) miracle worker, the canons removed his remains to Windsor in 1475, compensating the residents of North Marston with a fine new chancel for their parish church. They thus displayed more scruples than the eleventh century monks of St. Augustine's Abbey at Canterbury, who shanghaied the bones of St. Mildred from their resting place at Minster-in-Thanet by getting the locals drunk at a feast, and then breaking open her tomb with crowbars at the dead of night.

In 1484, moreover, the canons of Windsor secured the body of a second uncanonised "saint", of even great status: namely the Lancastrian King Henry VI, who had been assassinated in the Tower of London thirteen years earlier. Intermittently insane throughout his long and disastrous reign, the pious Henry had achieved a reputation for holiness, but his posthumous popularity may have owed much to a feeling of resentment against the rival Yorkist dynasty which had instigated his murder. It was partly to assuage such resentment – and partly to salve his own conscience, since he had almost certainly been implicated in the assassination – that Richard III had Henry's body transferred from its first humble tomb at Chertsey to a splendid shrine at Windsor. He was wise to do so, for rulers and statesmen murdered or executed for purely political reasons were frequently revered as holy martyrs by their supporters – a tendency which still prevails in the modern world: and if not carefully handled, the cults of such uncanonised "political saints" could easily become the focus for rebellion.

After the execution of Earl Thomas of Lancaster by Edward II in 1322, for example, pilgrimages were soon being made to the site of his death near Pontefract in Yorkshire, and veneration for "St Thomas of Lancaster" – in life a stern and brutal politician – helped to bring about Edward's downfall five years afterwards. When Edward himself was savagely murdered on the orders of his queen and her lover, however, the pendulum of public opinion swung in the opposite direction, and the king's splendid tomb in Glouscester Cathedral temporarily became one of the most popular English shrines. So numerous and so generous were the pilgrims who visited it, indeed, that their offerings substantially financed the rebuilding of the cathedral choir wherein it still stands, perhaps the finest early Perpendicular building in Britain. A less controversial royal martyr (and one who, unlike Edward II, was officially recognised by the

Church) was St. Edmund of East Anglia, an Anglo-Saxon monarch shot to death by pagan Vikings, in 869 – most probably at Hoxne in Suffolk, where the collapse of "St Edmunds Oak" in Victorian times revealed the head of an arrow allegedly fired by his tormenters. Greatly revered all over England, his martyrdom is depicted in many medieval churches, most notably by the vivid wall painting at Pickering. But this famous shrine at Bury St Edmunds, where his body was lain after a brief sojourn at Greensted, was destroyed during the dissolution of the monasteries.

All these shrines were (to a greater or lesser extent) known throughout Britain, but there were many others, particularly in the north and west, which enjoyed only a strictly localised fame. Among these were the burial places of the teeming Celtic saints of Wales and Cornwall, including Clynnogfawr and Partrishow; Kirkwall in Orkney, where the Norsemen's patron St Magnus was venerated; and, in the Saxon west country, the shrines of the shadowy St Urith at Chittlehampton and the better-authenticated St Wite at Whitchurch Canonicorum. This last retains a special atmosphere of sanctity, and continues (in its quiet way) to attract pilgrims: perhaps because – with the single exception of Westminster Abbey, whose famous tomb of St Edward the Confessor was spared because of his royal status – it is the only English shrine which still undoubtedly preserves the remains of its original occupant.

All the rest (along with most Scottish and many Welsh shrines) were swept away in the holocaust of the Protestant Reformation, when the veneration of relics came to be regarded as a useless and idolatrous superstition. The official zeal for their destruction, nevertheless, may well have had something to do with the often fabulously rich treasures lavished on them by generations of pilgrims, which promptly disappeared into the coffers of the impoverished Henry VIII. In the centuries that followed, pilgrimages were frowned upon and sometimes forbidden by law, though they continued more or less surreptitiously at Holywell and elsewhere. Since the Roman Catholic emancipation of the Victorian era, however, they have once again been performed openly, and hundreds of thousands of Christians (including increasing numbers of Anglicans) now journey to pray at shrines like Walsingham. The modern traveller touring Britain's places of worship, moreover, is to some extent obeying the ancient pilgrim impulse, an impulse which has deep roots in human nature.

See **The First Christian Missionaries, Holy Wells and Sacred Springs, The Reformation.**

One of the loneliest places of worship in southern England, yet scarcely thirty miles from the outskirts of London, St Thomas's at Harty overlooks the arm of the sea dividing the Isle of Sheppey from mainland Kent. Worth visiting for its atmospheric salt-marsh setting alone, the wooden-belfried and essentially thirteenth century church (still lit by oil lamps) also contains much of interest, including a medieval rood screen and a miniature hand-cranked organ which played only three tunes. Its chief treasure, however, is a delightful late fourteenth century chest depicting a pair of jousting knights with pages waiting behind them, flanked by two armed onlookers in little towers. Almost certainly of Flemish origin, it is said to have been dredged up from the nearby Swale, but was more probably purchased as a "parish chest" for wills and documents.

Above, thirteenth century St Thomas's church at Harty.

HARTY Kent
OS 178 TR 023662

Marked only on large-scale maps, the handful of houses (and the Ferry Inn) which make up Harty are in the south-east corner of the Isle of Sheppey, some six miles south-east of Minster-in-Sheppey Abbey at the end of a minor road turning south off the B2231 midway between Eastchurch and Leysdown. From junction 5 of the M2 motorway (about twelve miles to the south) Harty may be reached via the A249 onto Sheppey and then the B2231 east.

HOAR CROSS Staffordshire
OS 128 SK 125230

Hoar Cross is situated amid the attractively wooded but little visited countryside of Needwood Forest, just to the west of the A515 and some ten miles north of the cathedral city of Lichfield: the church stands on a ridge to the east of Hoar Cross hamlet, next to Victorian Hoar Cross Hall, which was once the Meynell-Ingram seat but is now "the Home of Medieval Banquets". Hamstall Ridware is three miles to the south-west via minor roads; and three miles to the west is Abbots Bromley, the scene of the famous Horn Dance whose ancient regalia hangs in its church.

The large and lavishly appointed Gothic Revival church of the Holy Angels at Hoar Cross is a unique and remarkable demonstration of a very rich woman's devotion, both to her dead husband's memory and to her extreme "Anglo-Catholic" faith. Emily Charlotte, sister of the Viscount Halifax who strove to reconcile the Church of England to Rome and wife of the foxhunting squire Hugo Meynell-Ingram, lost her husband in 1871 after only seven years of marriage: and almost at once she commissioned in his memory the church which was to obsess her for the remainder of her life. To build a church at all was, in fact, not strictly necessary, since a parish church already existed: but Mrs. Meynell-Ingram succeeded in creating a new parish round her mansion, and by 1876 the Holy Angels was complete. Its patroness, however, was not easily satisfied, soon afterwards rebuilding the west end to improve its proportions and subsequently adding two further chapels. By the time of her death in 1904, indeed, she had spent so much on the church that she ordered her accounts destroyed, so that none should ever know the extent of her vast outlay.

Such virtually limitless resources enabled her architect, G. F. Bodley, to build an exceedingly grand pink sandstone church with a fine central tower, employing through-out a style which closely approximates to his favourite mid fourteenth century Gothic. On entering it, the traveller is at first plunged into the almost impenetrable gloom (or "religious twilight") of the nave, which is dimly lit only by high stained-glass windows depicting Mrs. Meynell-Ingram's selection of saints: this device is quite deliberate, and succeeds admirably in its intention to lead the eye towards the gorgeously decorated and sculpted east end. There, behind an elaborate screen surmounted by a great crucifix, stands the brilliantly lit and richly coloured chancel – markedly larger and loftier than the nave, to emphasise its importance – with its serried ranks of carved and painted saints, high altar, and towering organ case. The "chantry" chapels to the south of the chancel are equally luxuriant, but most sumptuous of all are the two huge Gothic tombs there of the patroness (whose beautifully carved effigy wears the lace collared gown of a great Edwardian lady) and of her husband Hugo Francis. Occupying the place of honour traditionally reserved for saints and founders, the squire lies beneath a curlicued Gothic canopy in his uniform as Colonel of the Staffordshire Yeomanry, with a foxhound at his feet; still a Victorian country gentleman amid all his devoted wife's medieval splendour.

See **The Gothic Revival.**

HOLME-BY-NEWARK
Nottinghamshire
OS 121 SK 802591

The tiny village of Holme stands by the river Trent, three and half miles north of Newark (with its fine church and castle) and thirteen miles south-east of Lincoln. It is easily reached from the nearby A1 by turning west near Newark onto the A46 towards Lincoln: after about a mile turn north onto the A1133 towards Collingham, then turn westwards onto a signposted road just north of Langford (which stands near the turning) and continue on over a level crossing to Holme. The church is usually locked, but there is a list of keyholders (who live nearby) in the porch.

The undeservedly little-known church of St Giles at Holme-by-Newark is a truly remarkable monument to the pride and piety of a late fifteenth century merchant, John Barton. A Lancashire immigrant to the rich sheep-grazing lands of east Nottinghamshire, Barton grew immensely wealthy in the thriving English wool trade with France, and acquired both the manor of Holme and a number of influential relations among the county gentry: but he never forgot the basis of his prosperity, and the windows of his now-vanished mansion were inscribed:

> "I thanke God and ever shall
> It is the sheepe hath paid for all"

Nor did he forget to repay God's interest by reconstructing and doubling the size of Holme's parish church, where he was to be buried in 1491: and like a good businessman, he took care to blazon his trademarks on almost every surface of the new building.

Added by one of Barton's descendants, the church porch prepares the traveller for the amazing display of family and commercial advertisement within: for here are the heraldic arms of Barton's grand connections, side by side with the bucks' heads which the middle-class merchant, lacking genuine ancestral heraldry, borrowed from his better-born wife's family as his own device. Here too, in the central place of honour, are the lion and emblematic sea-waves of the Merchants of the Staple of Calais, the great trading company to which Barton belonged; and his own trademark of a cross and two triangles, once stamped on the woolsacks shown below to proclaim that here was John Barton's merchandise. The all-important sheep – two fine rams – also figure in the frieze, as do the founder's initials and his punning device of a bear and barrel (or "tun"), whence "bear-tun" and so "Barton".

Within the church (which still has its original early Tudor pews) Barton's badges are repeated again and again – on wall-shields, on roof bosses, in the now fragmentary glass of the east windows, and of course on the tomb where the founder himself lies with his aristocratic wife, midway between the chancel and the Barton family chapel. With the curious mixture of piety, blatant display and morbidity so typical of the later middle ages, John had this tomb constructed during his own lifetime: and to be doubly sure that neither he nor succeeding generations ever forgot the end to which even the wealthiest merchant must come, he had carved beneath his effigy the figure of a rotting corpse.

Before leaving Holme's unusually complete early Tudor church, the traveller should climb the tower stair to the priest's room above the porch: this is traditionally known as "Nan Scott's Chamber", after the old lady who took refuge there from a seventeenth century plague epidemic.

See **The Great Wool Churches; Tombs and Monuments.**

St Winefride's is undoubtedly the most famous holy well in Britain, not only because it retains its magnificent medieval buildings intact, but also because it has attracted pilgrims without interruption since at least the Norman Conquest, and even now claims to offer supernatural healing to those who use its water aright. According to legend, the wonder-working spring first appeared in the early seventh century, when a local Welsh princess named Gwenfrewi (anglicised as Winefride) was beheaded here by an enraged suitor whose advances she had resisted. Where her severed head struck the ground, however, a curative stream burst forth: but Winefride's uncle St Beuno of Clynnogfawr, reuniting the virgin's head to her body, restored her to life; while the hapless murderer was swallowed by the earth, never to be seen again. Whatever the truth of this tale – suspiciously similar to those told not only about other saints like Hieritha of Chittlehampton, but also about Celtic pagan gods – the well certainly came to be revered by Welsh, English and Norman alike. Throughout the middle ages pilgrims flocked to the chapel beside it, which was replaced in about 1500 by the present two-storeyed building.

Much the largest and most splendid of all surviving well chapels, this was probably founded by the pious Lady Margaret Beaufort, mother of Henry VII and wife of Thomas Stanley, Earl of Derby, a great landowner hereabouts. Rich in carved bosses of wood and stone, its upper storey consists of an octagonal chancel built on solid ground, its nave and aisle being constructed above the pillared well-chamber beneath, a lofty three-sided crypt opening onto a courtyard. At this chamber's centre is the sacred spring itself, its waters bubbling strongly up into a star-shaped inner basin beneath a vault carved with scenes from the saint's life, and thereafter flowing into an outer basin which has steps leading down into it. Here pilgrims customarily immerse themselves in the water three times, remembering St Beuno's prophecy that Winefride will grant their request, if not at the first time of asking, then at least at the second or third: while sufferers too infirm to bathe unaided are carried through the pool on the backs of friends – a practice dating from the middle ages, and depicted on a stone corbel by the arch of the stairway

to the upper chapel. Bathing is allowed only at set times on weekday mornings, men and women being strictly segregated: but less determined (or perhaps less afflicted) visitors may at any time dip their hands into the courtyard pool, fill their bottles with holy water from the adjacent pump, and light a candle before a Victorian statue of St Winefride. They traditionally complete their devotions by kneeling on a rough stone by the pool steps, said to be the one on which St Beuno sat to instruct the well's patroness.

Those who do so have illustrious forebears, including Henry V, who journeyed here to give thanks for his victory at Agincourt, and Henry VIII's unhappy first wife Catherine of Aragon, whose arms are carved on the well-chamber roof and who doubtless prayed here for a son – for the virgin saint's well, curiously enough, was commonly believed to promote fertility. Nor did the shrine lose its appeal after the Protestant Reformation, despite periodic government attempts to suppress pilgrimages to it: indeed, it became a focus for clandestine Roman Catholicism, visited by the Gunpowder Plotters and later by the Catholic James II, also hoping for a male heir. Protestant travellers like Celia Fiennes – who in 1698 thought the pilgrims "deluded by ignorant blind zeal, and ought to be pitied by us" – were less impressed, or (like Dr. Johnson) shocked at the custom of "indecently bathing in full view of all the company". Yet throughout the eighteenth and nineteenth centuries Catholic devotees came from far and near, many of them (including one T. M. Carew of Westmeath in Ireland, whose name is prominently carved by the bathing basin) proclaiming the miraculous cures the well had wrought for them.

Now that the shrine is officially in Roman Catholic care they come in still greater numbers, even though the waters that now flow here are no longer those of the underground stream which fed the original well – and which was accidentally cut through by mining operations in 1917, so that another watercourse has been diverted to supply the loss. Details like this, however, are perhaps irrelevant in a place with so long a history of prayer and pilgrimage, and which continues to give comfort to so many.
See **Clynnogfawr, Holy Wells and Sacred Springs, Shrines and Pilgrimages.**

HOLYWELL Clwyd
OS 116 SJ 183763
Holywell town is some seventeen miles north-west of Chester, on the main A55 trunk road to the North Wales coast and Anglesey. St Winefride's Well, on its western outskirt, is signposted from the town centre, and is open throughout the year: it is in the care of the Roman Catholic Church, and services take place there daily at 11.30 a.m. from Whit Sunday until late September; the key to the upper chapel (in state custody) is obtainable from the shrine guardian. The adjacent parish church is largely a Georgian rebuild. There is much else to draw the traveller to this historic and much fought-over part of Wales, including the ruins of Basingwerk Abbey immediately to the north-east of Holywell, off the A548; Flint Castle, four miles south-east on the same road; and Rhuddlan Castle and St Asaph Cathedral, both just over ten miles to the west.

Reputedly the oldest English Nonconformist chapel still in regular use, the delightful Old Meeting House at Horningsham is said to have been founded during the 1560s by Scots Presbyterian masons working on the nearby mansion of Longleat: but this tradition cannot be confirmed, and the present building probably dates from around 1700. Modest and unobtrusive, the thatched stone chapel looks at first sight more like a substantial cottage or a small barn: once entered,

however, its atmosphere is almost palpable; and it is immediately clear that here is a place of worship in the simple and dignified Nonconformist manner, with no frills or nonsense about it. Nor could anyone ever mistake it for an Anglican or a Catholic church, for in the place of honour there reserved for an altar stands a towering pulpit, flanked by brass candlesticks and lit by a pair of double windows: where, beneath the inscription "God is Love", worthy ministers preached no

HORNINGSHAM Wiltshire
OS 183 ST 813412
The scattered village of Horningsham stands outside the park gates of Elizabethan Longleat House, one of England's most famous and popular stately homes, and is some six miles south-west of Warminster via the A362 and signposted by-roads through Longleat park. The unobtrusive chapel (built on a slope so that it is below road level) is not far

63

from the Bath Arms Inn, from which
it is signposted. Bradford-on-Avon is
twelve miles to the north, and to the
east is the wide sweep of Salisbury
Plain.

doubt excellent sermons, timing themselves
by the clock on the facing gallery – which only
they and the deacons seated round the table
below could see without obtrusively turning
their heads. That they preached (and indeed
still preach on occasion) to numerous congregations is proved by the fact that the
chapel was provided from the first with galleries round three of its sides. These were
once assigned to the younger and less staid
worshippers, the men sitting on the south
side beneath a row of wooden hat-pegs and
the girls (who kept their bonnets on and, it
is to be hoped, their eyes decently cast down)

in the gallery opposite: while the choir, and
perhaps the chapel band, occupied the gallery facing the preacher.

No verbal description, however, can do
proper justice to this lovingly-kept and altogether laudable Congregationalist chapel:
which is all the more impressive because its
constant use and little unobtrusive
modernisations have preserved it from mere
quaintness. It is worth journeying many miles
to see and appreciate, and is especially
recommended as an antidote for the traveller
sated with the aristocratic splendours and
Safari Parks of nearby Longleat.

THE HURLERS Cornwall
OS 201 SX 258714

*The circles are approximately five
miles north of Liskeard, via the
B3254, a minor road turning west at
Upton Cross to Minions, and a short
walk along a signposted track (which
continues past the Hurlers to Rillaton
Barrow and the Cheesewring). There
is much else of interest in the
immediate area, including King
Doniert's Stone (two miles south-west,
at SX 236688) commemorating a
ninth century king of Cornwall: and
the spectacular Stone Age burial
chamber of Trethevy Quoit (two miles
south, at SX 259688). The village of
St Cleers (three miles south) has a
fine medieval church, with a chapel-
covered holy well just north of its
churchyard: while the church of
St Neot (six miles south-west)
contains the best medieval stained
glass in Cornwall.*

*A fallen stone against the backdrop of
Stowe's Hill and the Cheesewring.*

Set in the windswept, awe-inspiring landscape of Bodmin Moor, and surrounded by
abandoned mine-workings, the three prehistoric stone circles called the Hurlers are
among the most starkly impressive in
southern England. Like so many other
circles, they were once believed to be men
petrified for profaning the Sabbath (in this
case by playing the Cornish game of "hurling
the ball") while the musicians who encouraged them were transformed into a pair of
outlying stones called the Pipers. Another
tradition relates that the stones cannot be
counted, but in fact there seem originally to
have been some ninety of them – of which
only thirty-nine now survive – very carefully
spaced in three almost perfect circles aligned
on a north-north-east to south-south-west
axis. The largest and best-preserved is the
midmost circle, with a diameter of about 135
feet: near its centre is a fallen stone, and
excavations have revealed that the whole
circle was once floored with quartz crystals,
either for some ritual or decorative purpose
or as a result of hammering the circle stones
into regular shapes. Both this and the smaller
north-western circle were partially restored in
the 1930s, when markers were erected to
show the positions of missing stones, but the

south-western circle has been ruinous for
centuries.

Exactly why the circles were raised here,
probably in the early Bronze Age, remains a
mystery. They stand, however, by an ancient
route across the high moorland, and it is clear
that the surrounding area was of considerable
religious significance to prehistoric man,
perhaps because of its proximity to the
Cheesewring, a fantastic natural granite feature crowning nearby Stowe's Hill. To the
east and west are groups of burial mounds,
and the circles' alignment points directly up
the slope towards Rillaton Barrow, a quarter
of a mile to the north-north-east. There, in
a stone chamber which can still be entered
(with difficulty) by the more intrepid traveller,
one of the richest Bronze Age grave deposits
ever found in Britain was discovered in 1837.
Its chief treasure, indicating that the person
buried with it was someone of great wealth
and importance, was an exquisite cup of
beaten plate gold: after being lost for some
time, this came to light in George V's dressing
room (doing duty as a receptacle for collar
studs) and is now on display at the British
Museum.
See **Prehistoric Religion.**

Inchcolm – alias "St Colm's Inch" or St Columba's Isle – is the most beautiful of the rocky islands in the Firth of Forth. Here, according to tradition, St Columba once dwelt during his mission to the eastern Picts, and (as at Iona off the west coast) his sanctifying presence subsequently made the place a favoured burial ground. Another unsubstantiated tale, indeed, relates that the Vikings defeated by Macbeth at nearby Kinghorn purchased the right to lay their dead here, a legend perhaps substantiated by the Danish-style "hog-back" tombstone on the knoll immediately west of the abbey. When King Alexander I's ship was storm-driven onto the island in 1123, however, it was occupied only by a solitary hermit, who for three days shared his diet of milk and shellfish with the monarch and his followers: and in gratitude Alexander founded here an abbey for Augustian "black canons", which today remains one of the most complete in Scotland.

The earliest building in the monastery is said to be the simple cell of the original hermit, much repaired in the later middle ages. The canons' first church was likewise comparatively plain, but as the abbey prospered it was progressively extended eastwards (being given its fine rectangular tower in the thirteenth century) until at last a new church was built east of the older structure, and linked to it by a courtyard. This later church is now ruinous, but the old still retains

its roof: it was converted into an abbot's house in the fifteenth century, and here it was that Abbot Bower of Inchcolm wrote his well-known chronicle of Scotland. Remarkably well preserved, too, are the adjacent monastic buildings, including the octagonal chapter house with its pointed roof, one of only three of this type in Scotland: still more unusually, it is of two storeys, the upper being the "warming house", one of the few places in the abbey where a fire was allowed. In the middle of its floor is an aperture through which a lamp could be lowered into the vaulted chapter house proper beneath, and round its walls were inscribed improving sentiments, such as "It is foolish to fear what cannot be avoided."

That Inchcolm's canons stood in need both of spiritual and physical comfort is plain from the cloister itself, whose walk (again unusually) passes beneath the surrounding buildings rather than outside them. Austere, small-windowed, and fortress-like, they underline the fact that the isolated little community had to cope not only with the gales roaring up the Firth but also with frequent attacks by sea-raiders: burnt in 1384, in 1421 the abbey was temporarily deserted "for fear of the English", and during the 1540s its existence was effectively ended by successive English and French occupations.
See **Iona, Monasteries and Religious Houses.**

INCHCOLM Fife
OS 66 NT 189828
Inchcolm island lies in the Firth of Forth, approximately a mile and a half south of Aberdour, from which it is accessible by boat during the summer months, when the abbey is open to the public. Aberdour is some fifteen miles north of Edinburgh by road, via the A90, the Forth Road Bridge, and the A92.

The beautiful island of Iona is a place of tremendous significance in the history of Britain's conversion to Christianity. Here, in 563, came St Columba, also known as Colum Cille, "the dove of the church": despite his pacific name, this Irish abbot of royal descent had previously led a turbulent life, vigorously supporting his O'Neill relations in the feuds with their Ulster rivals which culminated in the bloody battle of Cooldremney. Fearing that such divisions might destroy the Irish church, his fellow abbots thereafter ordered him into exile, laying on him the task of converting more souls to Christ than he had caused lives to be lost in warfare. With twelve companions, he therefore set off across the Irish Sea in an open hide boat, and made landfall on the isle of Hi or Iova, the "place of yew trees" whose present name, ironically, is the product of a medieval mistranscription. There, having beached his coracle in St Columba's Bay to the south of the island, he is said to have mounted the clifftop and looked back south-westwards to ensure that his native land was out of sight, lest a distant view of it should draw him home.

In coming to the west of Scotland, Columba was not entirely separating himself from his people, who had already colonised these shores and established there the kingdom of Dalriada. But these Irish "Scots" (of whom the saint became the spiritual leader)

were at least nominally Christian, and Columba's principal mission was to the Picts of the north and east, still largely pagan despite the efforts of St Ninian of Whithorn. He made many journeys through their lands, tirelessly preaching and founding new monasteries (traditionaly including Inchcolm). Among his miracles there is said to have been the vanquishing of a water monster in Loch Ness, and by this and other wonders he converted the powerful Pictish king Brudei, thus ensuring the ultimate success of his mission. Iona, nevertheless, always remained his home and his great love, and it was there that he died in 597, a few months before St Augustine arrived in Canterbury.

Columba's monastery on the island, moreover, remained the supreme spiritual powerhouse of northern Britain for two centuries after his death, despatching monks to Lindisfarne to convert the Northumbrian English and serving as the hallowed burial place first of the monarchs of Dalriada and later of the kings of the united Picts and Scots, including the famous Kenneth mac Alpin. But during the early ninth century the scourge of the Vikings descended on it, and after repeated raids (and the slaughter of sixty-eight monks in "Martyrs' Bay") the community appears to have fled to Ireland, bearing with them their founder's body; some say it was later returned, and lodged in the shrine

IONA Strathclyde
OS 48 NM 287245
The island of Iona lies off the west coast of Scotland, near the south-western tip of Mull. It is reached from Oban (123 miles north-west of Edinburgh) first by taking the car ferry to Mull (a forty-five minute passage) and then driving across that island to Fionnphort, whence a five minute crossing takes the traveller to Iona. Between April and September Iona ferries sail between 9.00 a.m. (10.00 a.m. on Sundays) and 12.30 p.m., and between 1.30 p.m. and 5.00 p.m.: in winter the service is much more restricted. No cars are allowed on Iona, but most of the sites are within easy walking distance of the pier, and are well signposted.

of St Columba by the cathedral. Yet Iona was too renowned a holy place to remain desolate for long. St. Margaret, Malcolm Canmore's queen, may have re-established some kind of monastery on the island in about 1080, and in the first years of the twelfth century the local chieftain Reginald mac Somerled certainly founded here both a Benedictine abbey and an Augustinian nunnery, the former's church becoming the cathedral of the Western Isles in 1507.

The remains of these later monasteries now dominate the island, including the nun's church by the ferry landing place, dating from the thirteenth century but (like so many of Iona's buildings) appearing older because of its archaic Irish style of architecture. Of Columba's original community few traces remain, though part of its enclosing earthwork is visible by the road from the pier, while on the hill called Tor Abb (west of the cathedral) are the excavated remains of what may have been the saint's cell, floored with pebbles and equipped with a stone-cut bed. Between this and the cathedral, moreover, is a well probably used by the Celtic monks, and here too stand three tall Celtic crosses, all that remain of the hundreds which once graced the island. These date from the ninth or tenth centuries, and the finest is the fourteen foot high St Martin's Cross, carved with the Virgin and Child at its centre and with Biblical scenes on its shaft.

From this area the bodies of the great and the pious were carried, via the partly surviving red marble roadway called "the Street of the Dead", for burial in the cemetery of Reilig Odhrain, about a hundred yards to the southwest. Here, it is said, rest more than sixty Scots, Norse and Irish kings, together with the Highland chiefs who continued to be buried in the sacred ground long after the last of the kings – probably Duncan, murdered by Macbeth in 1040 – had been lain there. Most of the oldest gravestones have now been transferred to the museum, but the restored chapel of St Oran still remains, dedicated to one of Columba's followers and believed to stand on the site of the oratory. Traditionally the oldest complete building on Iona, this chapel – which contains the fine late medieval tomb of the chieftain Lachlan Mackinnon – is said to have been built either by Kenneth Mac Alpin in the ninth century or by Queen Margaret in the eleventh: but was in fact probably raised in about 1200 by the newly-introduced Benedictine monks.

To them also belonged the largest of Iona's places of worship, the cathedral or abbey church. A sturdy cruciform building with a low central tower, the present building dates mainly from the early sixteenth century, but was much restored in about 1900. Many of its monastic buildings (including the old Infirmary, now a museum housing the stone called St Columba's Pillow) have moreover been rebuilt by the Iona Community, an inter-denominational Christian group set up here in 1938. They are now once again used for prayer and meditation and as a place of religious retreat, partly fulfilling a prophecy attributed to the island's patron saint.

> In Iona of my heart, Iona of my love
> Instead of monks' voices shall be the
>   lowing of cows
> But ere the world shall end
> Iona shall be as it was

KEMPLEY Gloucestershire
OS 149 SO 670313
St Mary's church, long redundant but now happily in the care of English Heritage, is a mile north of Kempley village – whose "new church" of St Edward the Confessor (SO 671297) is a fine example of the Edwardian Arts and Crafts style. Kempley is five miles north-east of Ross-on-Wye, and thirteen miles north-west of Gloucester, via the A40, the B4215 through Newent and Dymock, the B4024 turning west a mile north of Dymock towards Much Marcle, and finally via a farm road: St Mary's is well signposted by name both from the B4215 and the B4024. Much Marcle church, just over a mile north-west of St Mary's, has a fine collection of medieval monuments, and the Forest of Dean lies not far to the south-west.

The great majority of medieval churches now have scraped or white-plastered interiors, and it is easy to forget that most of them once glowed with the dramatic colours of wall paintings. In the small and remote Norman church of Kempley, however, the removal of a coat of whitewash in 1871 revealed the most complete surviving series of twelfth century wall paintings in Britain, painted in "fresco" while the original plaster was still wet. Almost entirely covering the roof and walls of the tiny round-vaulted chancel, their effect is still overwhelming, and for the medieval parishioners of Kempley they must have been a powerful reminder that an all-seeing God was waiting to judge them at Doomsday. For their imagery is taken from the Book of Revelations, which foretells the End of the World, and at the centre of the roof vault Christ in Majesty looks down from His rainbow, with one hand raised in blessing while the other holds an open book. Clustering round him are the symbols of the Four Evangelists – an eagle, a lion, an ox and a man, all winged – with the sun, moon and stars: the seven golden candlesticks of Revelations; and the Virgin and St Peter: while at the four corners of the roof multiwinged Seraphim stand guard. On the side walls of the chancel the Twelve Apostles – six on each side, under arched canopies – gaze up in adoration: and the remainder of the chancel's surfaces are crowded with angels, bishops, fortresses and pilgrims with staff and hat. The style of the figures is decidedly Byzantine, and indeed the visitor to Kempley's chancel almost has the impression of being transported from rural Gloucestershire to some Orthodox church in Greece or Southern Italy.

Kempley's nave, moreover, also has its share of wall paintings, though these are neither as accomplished, as well-preserved, or as ancient as those in the chancel. Dating mainly from the thirteenth and fourteenth centuries, they include a Wheel of Life on the north wall, St Michael weighing souls on a nearby window splay, and the surcoats of knights murdering St Thomas Becket on the wall opposite. Above the exterior of the chancel arch is a fragmentary Doom.
See **The Norman Church.**

Christian church within pagan henge at Knowlton.

The tiny Dorset hamlet of Knowlton posseses one of the most graphic illustrations in England of the relationship between paganism and Christianity. At some time probably between 3000 and 2500 B.C., for reasons that we can only guess at, New Stone Age people dug there three great "henges", internally-ditched earthwork rings almost certainly used for religious ceremonies. They are carefully laid out in a line running from south-west to north-east, decreasing in size as they go: the best preserved and most accessible being the 350 foot diameter central ring, which may well have contained a circle of timber uprights, the counterpart of the stone circles erected in henges elsewhere. Between it and the southern henge, moreover, is a great tree-covered burial mound, probably a Bronze Age round-barrow and thus dating from a period perhaps a thousand years after the henges were constructed; while several other less obvious round-barrows also cluster around the three rings.

For many generations of prehistoric worshippers, then, Knowlton was clearly a place of special religious significance: but during the succeeding centuries (and particularly after the coming of Christianity) its atmosphere of holiness seems to have been transmuted into one of fear, its gods remembered only as pagan demons. A need to exorcise these terrors must surely be the explanation for Knowlton's most striking feature, the church built in the middle of the central henge. Long since ruined, it apparently dates from the Norman period (though it has the remains of a fourteenth century tower) and presents a most interesting comparison with the earlier church at Avebury. There, however, the Saxons built their place of worship *outside* a great prehistoric temple, as if they feared that the new religion might not yet be able to tackle the ancient gods on their own ground: whereas the Norman builders at Knowlton had no such qualms. Does their boldness indicate that paganism hereabouts had declined into mere rustic superstition, to be scorned rather than feared? Or were the atmosphere and associations of the henge still so strong that only a head-on attack would serve to dispel them? *See* **Avebury, Prehistoric Religion.**

KNOWLTON Dorset
OS 195 SU 024103
Knowlton is nine miles north of Wimborne Minster and three miles south-west of Cranborne, near the junction of the B3078 and a signposted minor road to Gussage All Saints: in the care of English Heritage, it is always open. Seven miles to the south-west (off the B3082 from Wimborne Minster to Blandford Forum) is the great Iron Age hillfort of Badbury Rings.

The Medieval Parish Church

It is difficult to overestimate the importance of the part played by the parish church in the life of medieval man. The modern traveller may attend service at a place of worship as he or she pleases, and then forget its existence: but for the medieval parishioner it was not so simple, for the Church influenced every aspect of the society in which he lived. It was from the parish priest, for example, that he received the vital seven sacraments of the Church – including baptism, marriage, and unction at the point of death – as well as probably the only education he possessed. Wall paintings such as the magnificent series at Pickering; windows like the graphic examples at All Saints' in York or the Doom at Fairford; and fonts like those depicting the seven sacraments at Cley-next-the-Sea were all dramatic visual aids for a priest preaching to a largely illiterate congregation.

The parish priest, therefore, was one of the most powerful and respected figures in the community, if not always the best loved – for he had the duty of supervising his flock's moral welfare, and the power to arraign them from the pulpit for misdemeanours. In return for administering the "cure of souls", he could likewise claim "boon" or "love work" – supposedly voluntary labour – from his parishioners at certain times of the year, in order to work the "glebe" land belonging to the church: and above all he had the right to collect tithes, which is to say one-tenth of all his parishioners' produce, be it corn, honey, or cloth. The collection of these tithes was not always an easy matter, for parishioners were adept at evasion, and on occasion whole parishes mounted "tithe strikes", refusing to pay up at all until some grievance was remedied. But in the end the clergy always had the upper hand, for in the last resort they could excommunicate defaulters, thus excluding them not only from the services of the church but also from the company of their neighbours and, most important of all, from any chance of entering heaven if they died excommunicate.

The frequency of such disputes must have depended greatly on the character of the parish priest. Some priests (especially in the period following the Black Death of 1348–9, when the horrifying mortality rate among parish clergy led to the ordination of unsuitable candidates as replacements) were undoubtedly both ignorant and negligent. Yet the high mortality in itself demonstrates how faithfully many priests had performed their duty in plague time, and both then and later many made strenuous efforts to care for the spiritual and material welfare of their flock. Neither can their position have been made easier by the fact that, in many cases, they were themselves merely deputies for some greater absentee cleric: a situation which arose from the peculiar nature of the English parochial system.

The word "parish" was originally applied to an area roughly equivalent to a modern bishopric: but by the later Anglo-Saxon period (when England was divided into the administrative units which, albeit much modified, still survive today) it had come to be applied to subdivisions of a bishopric, each served by a resident priest. The patron of such a parish – usually a nobleman or other landowner – owned the "advowson", or right to appoint a "rector"; and he in turn frequently appointed a substitute (or "vicar") to perform the services and other duties, receiving the lesser part of the parish tithes as payment. The rector, meanwhile, was expected (from the "greater tithes") to maintain the church fabric, in particular that of the chancel where Mass was celebrated. That some rectors took this duty seriously is demonstrated by such features as the finely carved sedilia, piscina and Easter Sepulchre in the chancel at Patrington: but elsewhere they woefully neglected their obligations – as at Westonzoyland, where the chancel appears absurdly small and mean when compared to the great Perpendicular nave and tower erected at the expense of the parishioners.

The division between rector and parishioners was, from the thirteenth century onwards, still further emphasised by the erection of richly decorated choir screens like those of Cullompton and Partrishow: which separated the chancel from the nave where the congregation stood or knelt to hear Mass – only in the later middle ages were they provided with pews or benches, like the satirically carved examples at Brent Knoll. To care for their section of the church, and collect money for its maintenance, the parishioners appointed "churchwardens", an office which still flourishes today. It became increasingly common, moreover, for parishioners to join together in a fraternity or "guild", which cared for widows and orphans, financed funerals and memorial Masses, and – imitating on a smaller scale the rich merchants who raised the great wool churches – sometimes beautified or added to their parish church. Features like the "Plough Gallery" at Cawston serve as a reminder of their activities: and though the Reformation was to sweep away much of the embellishment which late medieval congregations delighted to lavish on their places of worship, enough remains to prove the paramount importance of the parish church in the everyday life of the medieval community.

See **The Great Wool Churches, The Reformation, The Prayer Book Church.**

One of the most atmospheric places of worship in northern England, the tiny "chapel of the Blessed Mary at Lead" stands alone in a field near the haunted site of the battle of Towton, where the Yorkists routed the Lancastrians during a Palm Sunday snowstorm in 1461, with such great slaughter that the nearby Cock Beck is said to have run red with blood. At that time the chapel was already old – the present building apparently dates from the early fourteenth century, though parts of it may be earlier – and also somewhat larger, for it then had a chancel whose outline is marked in the grass outside the eastern wall. Nor did it then stand alone, for it originally served the now-vanished mansion of the knightly Tyas family, four of whose members lie beneath a row of heraldic tombstones set into the chapel floor.

With the abandonment of the mansion St Mary's fell on hard times, and by 1596 it was "in utter ruin and decay". Yet someone clearly still loved it, and it was probably during the seventeenth century that it was provided with the rustic furnishings – simple rough-hewn bench pews and a minute three-decker pulpit – which lend it so much of its charm: while an eighteenth century refurbishment contributed the edifying advice "Prepare to meet thy God", "Give almes of thy good and turn not thy face from anye poor man" painted on the wooden plaques round its walls. Decaying once more by the 1930s, it was saved and overhauled (though not heavy-handedly "restored") by the voluntary efforts of public-spirited ramblers from Leeds and Bradford: only to be again threatened with closure in the 1970s, and again reprieved, this time by the Redundant Churches Fund. A fence has now been built to protect it from the cattle which browse round its walls: and this unspoilt rural chapel lives on as a memorial to the devotion of many generations and a delight for the passing traveller.

LEAD CHAPEL Near Saxton, North Yorkshire
OS 105 SE 464369
The chapel is four miles south-west of Tadcaster, in a field by the B1217 Aberford-Towton road, opposite the Crooked Billet Inn. It can be reached from York (twelve miles to the north-east) via the A64, the A162 and the B1217 turning south-westwards at the south end of Towton: or from the nearby A1 (two miles to the west) by taking the Aberford exit and turning eastwards onto the B1217. The chapel is never locked, but ingenuity is required to operate the latch. The surrounding area is full of interest half a mile to the west (by the B1217) is the great tree-grown dyke called the Rein, of unknown but probably Anglo-Saxon date, and Lotherton Hall, with its fine collection of paintings and costume.

LEIGHTON BROMSWOLD Cambridgeshire
OS 142 TL 115753
The small and peaceful village of Leighton Bromswold is eight miles west-north-west of Huntingdon and six miles west of the A1, via the A604 Huntingdon-Kettering road and signposted minor road turning north, about a mile west of Spaldwick. The building across the field east of the church is the gatehouse of Leighton Bromswold Castle, a projected Jacobean mansion which was never completed. Little Gidding is some four miles to the north, via minor roads.

Matching pulpit and reader's desk flank the chancel arch.

From a distance the church appears medieval, but as the traveller walks past an ancient Saxon moot-stone and into the churchyard, the realisation grows that here is something very special and unusual: and when the church itself is entered that realisation is confirmed. For the great cream-coloured tower was built in 1634, and the light and nobly dignified interior, with its complete set of furnishings of much the same date, transports the visitor straight back to the decade before the Civil War. What we see here is, in fact, a perfect seventeenth century church within a largely medieval shell, the work of the famous poet George Herbert and his friends the Ferrars of Little Gidding. When Herbert took over the parish in 1626, he found "the fair church of Layton fallen down a long time, and lay in the dust", so that the parishioners were forced to use a nearby manor house for services: so, "sparing not his own purse", Herbert set about raising the large sum needed for total restoration, and soon after 1632 "a fine neat church was erected, not only to the parishioners' own much comfort and joy, but to the admiration of all men".

St Mary's is, indeed, surely almost the ideal Anglican village church, furnished and decorated by John Ferrar not in a gaudy, half-classical style (like the near-contemporary St Katherine Cree in London) but with a marvellously unified scheme in locally carved and turned woodwork. Matching pulpit and reader's desk flank the chancel arch, and the honest unstained oak furnishings – pews, lectern, desks, tower screen, the little vestry in the south transept, the cover of the font and the low children's seats behind it – have the same restrained lathe-turned decoration throughout. The fine roof, too, is largely seventeenth century, and the plain glass windows (together with the fact that the transept pews face inwards towards the preacher, and those in the chancel inwards towards an intended communion table, not eastwards towards the altar) emphasise that this is truly a Protestant place of worship, not an imitation Catholic church. Herbert died at a tragically early age in 1633, and thus can never have seen his church completed: but the spirit behind this labour of love is summed up in a poem (now a well-known hymn) he bequeathed to the Ferrars.

"Teach me, my God and King
In all things thee to see
And what I do in anything
To do it as for thee

This is the famous stone
That turneth all to gold
For that which God doth touch and own
Cannot for less be told".

See **Little Gidding, London – St Katherine's Cree, The Prayer Book Church.**

Prisoners' stalls within Lincoln Castle's place of worship.

LINCOLN Lincolnshire
OS 121 SK 975719

The fascinating city of Lincoln is 131 miles north of London, via the A1 and the A46. The chapel is within the great medieval castle (open seven days a week from April until November, and closed only on winter Sundays) which stands across the square from the famous Early English Gothic cathedral, sometimes held to be the finest in Britain. Within a short distance is much else of interest, notably the Norman "Jew's Houses" on the steep and picturesque cobbled hill leading down into the city centre, with its medieval guildhalls and Saxon church of St Peter-at-Gowts.

A few hundred years from Lincoln's noble medieval cathedral, in the disused Victorian prison within its ancient castle walls, is a "place of worship" of a very different kind: a chapel Christian in name, but in fact a chilling demonstration of man's inhumanity to man. Under the "separate system" which prevailed when it was built in 1842, prisoners were confined in solitary cells and never allowed to meet, even during the compulsory services held once daily and twice on Sundays: and the prison chapel's designers, with truly devilish ingenuity, ensured that this principle should be observed with maximum efficiency. One by one, the "congregation" were herded into their individual stalls, the door of each being shut before the next was

occupied and all the doors of a row being simultaneously locked by an underfloor device when that row was full. Each "upright coffin" – as the half-roofed stalls were graphically nicknamed – is moreover built so that the occupant could see neither above, below, nor behind him, nor to either side, lest he catch a glimpse of his companions in misfortune: but only straight ahead, to the pulpit where the prison chaplain preached his improving sermons. Neither could he take refuge from pious exhortations by dozing, or even sit comfortably; for the seats in the stalls slope sharply forward, banishing all ease, and vigilant warders could of course see into all seventy-eight of them.

The walls of this horrifying chapel are stark

white, its windows barred, and its stalls a dreary unrelieved brown: as is even the screened-off gallery to the right of the pulpit for the governor's family; and the box below it where those imprisoned merely for debt were graciously allowed to sit together on pews, albeit behind spiked railings. A place less conducive to worship, indeed, can scarcely be imagined.

The "Holy Island" of Lindisfarne, off the Northumbrian coast, was the great powerhouse of early Christianity in northern England. Its beginnings date from 634, when the Christian King Oswald Of Northumbria, after a seemingly miraculous victory over pagan invaders, sought for missionaries to complete the conversions of his kingdom. Having himself been baptised in exile by Scots Celtic monks, he naturally looked to Iona for aid: and thence came a party of monks led by St Aidan, who at his own request was granted Lindisfarne as his headquarters. Doubtless it reminded him of the island monastery he had left, but it also had other advantages: for it was within sight of Oswald's coastal fortress-capital at Bamburgh and (being cut off by the tide twice a day) was easily defensible against pagan attack from the land, while its little harbour allowed ready access to ships from Scotland. Here, then, a Celtic monastery was established, and from here the Gaelic-speaking Aidan (with the king himself acting as his interpreter) undertook many missionary journeys throughout Northumbria. It was subsequently provided with an oaken church "thatched with reeds after the Scots manner", and its influence continued to grow first under Celtic abbot-bishops and then (after a dispute over doctrine) under Englishmen following the traditions of the Roman Church, the greatest and most famous of whom was St Cuthbert.

Beginning life as a shepherd boy on the border hills, this truly extraordinary man became a monk and an untiring missionary, penetrating even the wildest and most dangerous parts of Northumbria. He then retired as a hermit to the remote Farne Islands seven miles south-east of Lindisfarne, where he dwelt within an earthwork so high that he could see neither sea nor land, but only the heaven he so much desired. Yet his reputation as a saint and miracle-worker – enhanced by his remarkable power over the seals and eider-ducks which were his only companions – pursued him even there, and in 685 he reluctantly agreed to return to Lindisfarne as abbot. After his death two years later his enshrined body at once became the goal of pilgrimages from all over northern England: and in the decades that followed, the abbey reached the zenith of its fame both as a place of worship and a centre of learning and culture, producing among other treasures the beautiful Lindisfarne Gospels now displayed in the British Museum.

With the growth of the Viking menace, however, its once advantageous island situation rendered it particularly vulnerable, and in 793 it fell victim to one of the first recorded Danish raids on Britain – an event apparently depicted on a tombstone in the site museum. Eventually, in 875, the whole "community of St Cuthbert" abandoned the island, bearing with them their patron's hallowed bones: which after a hundred and twenty years of wanderings – once as far afield as Whithorn – found their present resting place at Durham. For more than two centuries thereafter Lindisfarne remained desolate, so that scarcely any trace of the Celtic and Saxon monasteries survives there today. Yet St Cuthbert's congregation at Durham never forgot their origins, and in 1083 Bishop William of St Calais decided to re-establish a monastery on the "Holy Island" (as it then became known) as an outpost of his Durham Cathedral Priory.

The splendid red sandstone ruins of this monastery's Norman church still stand today, albeit weathered and engraved with tortuous patterns by their long exposure to the North Sea gales. Built between about 1090 and 1140, and thus almost exactly contemporary with the present Durham Cathedral, it not surprisingly shares some of the architectural characteristics of its mother church, including the boldly incised decoration of its sturdy nave pillars: which, since Lindisfarne priory is so much smaller than the great cathedral, appear even more massive here than they do at Durham. Perhaps the priory's most impressive remaining feature is the west front, with its richly carved projecting Norman doorway flanked to the south by a fortress-like turret, part of the monastery's defences against the unceasing threat of French and Scottish raiders. More memorable yet, however, is the graceful "rainbow arch" springing across the centre of the cruciform church, a chance survivor of the ribs that once supported the vault beneath its vanished tower.

Lindisfarne Priory was dissolved at the Reformation, being thereafter plundered for stone to build the Tudor fort (restored as an individualistic Edwardian mansion) which stands so impressively on a crag in the distance. Yet this well-named Holy Island is not bereft of places of worship. For the largely thirteenth century church of St Mary (immediately west of the ruins) continues in parish use: and also forms the focus of a Christian community which – as at Iona – strives to recreate the spirit of the island monastery's founders.

See **The Anglo-Saxon Church,**
The First Christian Missionaries, Iona.

LINDISFARNE
Northumberland
OS 75 NU 126418
Lindisfarne (or Holy Island) is sixteen miles south Berwick-on-Tweed, and is reached by turning east off the main A1 five miles north of Belford onto a signposted minor road. Prominently displayed tide-tables indicate the (variable) times when it is possible to drive across the causeway: and these must also be checked to avoid the possibility of being temporarily marooned on the island until the next low tide. Should this occur, however, there is much to see (including Lindisfarne fort or "castle", open April – October) and several hospitable hotels and cafes.

The narrow nave of the community's church at Little Gidding.

LITTLE GIDDING
Cambridgeshire
OS 142 TL 127816

The handful of houses which make up Little Gidding lie some nine miles north-west of Huntingdon and three miles west of the A1, at the end of a signposted lane between Great and Steeple Gidding. It may be reached from the A1 via the B660 westward through Glatton and then a minor road turning south-east in Great Gidding: or (with careful navigation) from Leighton Bromswold, four miles south, via minor roads through Homerton, following signs first to "the Giddings" and then to Little Gidding.

Minute, distinctly odd-looking from outside, and set in a copse by a remote farmhouse, Little Gidding is nevertheless one of the most famous churches in England. Its fame derives from the religious community established here in 1625 by Nicholas Ferrar, a scholar, businessman and M.P. who declined high office and retired to what was even then a deserted village: moving into its (now vanished) manor house, he and his family surrounded themselves with like-minded people and devoted themselves to prayer, meditation and charitable works, including the refurbishment of a derelict church previously used as a haystore-cum-piggery. Yet they were too close to the Great North Road to escape either visitors or comment, some admiring but more of it disapproving – the latter especially from the Puritans who unjustly suspected Ferrar of Catholic sympathies, and his community of being a "secret nunnery". Eventually, after giving hospitality to a defeated and fugitive Charles I, the community's church was ransacked by Parliamentarian troopers, and in 1657 the "holy experiment" came to an end – or rather a temporary halt, for the church is now once again used by a Christian community centred on Little Gidding.

How much of its present fabric survives from Ferrar's time is uncertain: though its west end (and curious pinnacled bell-cote facade) undoubtedly dates from a reconstruction of 1714, and its east window (the only jarring note) from a restoration in 1853. But much of the furnishing of its delightful interior – a kind of panelled wooden tunnel, flanked by single rows of seats – may well come from the original community's church: and the brass tablets of prayers and Commandments, the unusual brass pillar-font, and the curly hour-glass stand near the chancel arch – the sand-glass it held was used to time sermons – are all certainly theirs. So too is the great brass eagle lectern, a medieval piece presented to the church by Nicholas Ferrar, who himself lies buried beneath the movingly simple table tomb outside the church door.

What strikes most visitors to the church, however, is neither its architecture nor its furnishings, but its atmosphere of almost palpable peace and tranquility. It is easy to see what the great Anglo-American poet T. S. Eliot meant, when he wrote of Little Gidding in his "Four Quartets":

> "You are not here to verify
> Instruct yourself, or inform curiosity
> Or to carry report. You are here to kneel
> Where prayer has been valid".

See **Leighton Bromswold,
The Prayer Book Church.**

LITTLE SNORING Norfolk
OS 132 TF 953326
*Little Snoring is three miles north-east
of Fakenham, via the A148 and a
signposted minor road turning north.
Walsingham is three miles further
north, Binham Priory six miles north-
east; and Cley-next-the-Sea some ten
miles away in the same direction.*

*The church at Little Snoring was a
place of worship for the servicemen
who were based at the nearby airfield
during World War II.*

Little Snoring (nothing to do with sleep, but
the settlement of the Saxon followers of a
certain "Snear", "the swift one") has a church
as charming and unusual as its name. For
though its flint and probably Saxon round
tower is of a type not uncommon in parts of
East Anglia – especially where lack of building
stone for corners made conventional towers
expensive to erect – in only one other place
is the round tower detached from the church:
and no other round tower has such a delightful conical roof, giving it an aspect almost
more French than English. St Andrew's
tower, as is clear from the arch on its east face,
was once attached to a Norman church,
which for some now inexplicable reason was
demolished and replaced – also during the
Norman period – by the present building a
few feet to the north. This in turn was altered
during the thirteenth century, when the wide
chancel with its three narrow lancet windows
was built in the Early English style of Gothic:
and at the same time the second of Little
Snoring's unusual features, its extraordinary
triple south doorway, was constructed by
rearranging carved Norman masonry into a
sharply pointed arch, encircled by a wider
horseshoe and itself enclosing an innermost
round arch.

Llandaff is one of the lesser-known British
cathedrals, and fate has dealt hardly with it
over the centuries: yet it has risen triumphantly above its misfortunes, and today is
well worth visiting for its blend of the old and
new in church architecture. The original
"church on the river Taff" was traditionally
founded by the missionary St Teilo during
the sixth century, but nothing now remains
of this "little minster" (which was only twenty-
eight feet long) except a battered Celtic standing cross in the south choir aisle. The much
larger cathedral which replaced it was begun
in about 1120 by Urban, the first Norman-
appointed bishop: and of this considerable
portions of the east end survive, notably the
splendid Norman arch behind the high altar.
Building then continued westward with the
nave, which is in the new Early English style
of Gothic: as is the charming west front of
about 1220, flanked by the asymmetrical
towers that give the cathedral its distinctive
appearance. The northern, named after
Henry VII's uncle Jasper Tudor, dates from
the late fifteenth century; while the southern
tower, with its soaring spire, is entirely
Victorian.

The last major part of the medieval
cathedral to be completed was the fine Lady
Chapel at the eastern end, raised in the later
thirteenth century by Bishop William de
Braose, whose tomb still remains there. There

LLANDAFF South Glamorgan
OS 171 ST 156781
*The cathedral lies in a hollow below
the village city of Llandaff, now
virtually a suburb of Cardiff: it is some
two miles north-west of Cardiff city
centre, via Cathedral Road (the
A4119) and four miles south of
junction 32 of the M4 motorway.
Cardiff, the capital of Wales, has many
attractions, including the restored
Norman castle in the city centre: while
four miles to the west is the
outstandingly interesting Welsh Folk
Museum at St Fagans, with
farmhouses, chapels and other
characteristic buildings from all over
Wales reconstructed about its
extensive grounds.*

73

too stood the silver shrine of St Teilo, a magnet for pilgrims until its destruction at the Reformation, whereafter the cathedral went into an accelerating decline. Used after the Civil War as an alehouse-cum-post office, its nave roof and south-west tower collapsed during the early eighteenth century, when ivy colonised the desolate ruins. Georgian "restoration" as an "Italian Temple" scarcely improved matters: and a more sympathetic Victorian reconstruction (including the south tower and spire and the distinctive "pepperpot" chapter house roof) was brought to nought when, on the second of January 1941, a German landmine fell immediately south of the cathedral, virtually destroying its interior and severely shaking the whole fabric.

The disaster, however, was turned to opportunity by the cathedral authorities, who strove not merely to copy what was lost but rather to create something new. Instead of dividing the east and west ends of the interior by a conventional screen, therefore, they commissioned a daring and outstandingly effective alternative, the great concrete parabolic arch which springs across the centre of the cathedral and leaves the vista from end to end uninterrupted at ground level. This graceful bow-like arch supports (at a height of twenty-five feet) a towering cylindrical organ case, adorned with sixty-four gilded figures from the wrecked Victorian choir stalls. On its western face, His hands outstretched towards the congregation in the nave, is a tremendously elongated statue of Christ in Majesty, designed by the famous sculptor Sir Jacob Epstein and cast in unpolished aluminium. Other new work includes the David Chapel jutting from the north side to the cathedral, a fine piece of modern architecture constructed in round river-washed stones and beautifully lit within: but it will be the great arch and its still more effective Christus that the traveller chiefly remembers from Llandaff.

See **The Reformation.**

LLANDANWG Gwynedd
OS 124 SH 569284

The church stands on the seashore some two miles south of Harlech, with its famous and outstandingly impressive medieval castle: and is reached by turning south-west off the A496 at Llanfair onto a minor road signposted for Llandanwg Beach. To the north and south stretch the great sandy tracts of Morfa Harlech and Morfa Dyffryn, and to the east are the Rhinnog Mountains, with Cader Idris beyond: the beaches and dunes hereabouts are noted for their unusual plants and plentiful seashells.

Once the mother church of the large parish which included Harlech Castle, the little beachside chapel of St Tanwg is now partly engulfed by encroaching dunes for much of the year, and the sand thrown by winter gales against its door must be laboriously dug away to allow occasional summer services to be held there. Comparatively little is known about the origins of this ancient place of worship, and its patron saint is equally obscure: but sixth century memorial stones preserved within suggests that (like St Piran's Oratory) it may have been founded by a Celtic evangelist who landed here from Ireland. Subsequently (like Mwnt chapel) it is said to have become a chapel of rest for seagoing pilgrims travelling to the holy isle of Bardsey, thirty miles to the west, and for the corpses they carried with them for burial there. Apart from a pretty fifteenth century east window, however, the simple single-chambered church now retains few furnishings, though the tombstones which lean all about its sandy churchyard demonstrate that it was still in full use until quite recently: and in fact the dunes only began to threaten it during the present century.

See **Shrines and Pilgrimages, St Piran's, Oratory, Mwnt.**

LLANIDLOES Powys
OS 136 SN 954847

The attractive market town of Llanidloes, with the church at its centre, is set amid the beautiful but comparatively little-visited countryside of mid-Wales, on the A470 twelve miles west of Newtown and some twenty-five miles east of Aberystwyth and the coast.

Though it was by no means unusual for monastic churches to be taken over for parish use after the dissolution of religious houses by Henry VIII, it was altogether more uncommon for large sections of them to be transported bodily to a new location. This, however, is precisely what befell sizeable portions of the church of Abbey Cwmhir, a now almost entirely vanished Cistercian monastery amid the Radnorshire hills of mid-Wales: for in about 1542 over a third of its notably long and splendid nave arcade was dismantled, loaded into carts, and hauled more than twelve miles northwards to the market town of Llanidloes. There it was re-erected (somewhat out of order) to form the greater part of St Idloes's parish church, where it remains to surprise and impress the traveller.

The nave arches (five of the original fourteen sets at Abbey Cwmhir) date from about 1200, and are notable examples of the Early English Gothic style, their pillars ringed with clustered shafts and topped by capitals sensitively carved with foliage. Soaring above them is an equally magnificent wooden roof – indeed, one of the finest in all Wales – whose arched and traceried braces are supported on projecting "hammer beams", each guarded by a rather dissolute-looking angel. One of these carries a shield with the date 1542, but whether the roof was constructed then to complement the newly-acquired arches, or whether it too was shanghaied from Cwmhir by the proverbially thrifty Llanidloes men remains a matter for conjecture.

Many of the London places of worship described here (in the approximate chronological order of their building) are very close to each other. Since parking in central London is difficult and expensive, these are best visited via public transport and on foot (with the aid of an easily available "A–Z Guide").

Walks through the City of London are invariably full of interest in themselves, and one from the Tower westwards to the Temple Church could easily take in St Mary Abchurch, the Temple of Mithras, St Paul's Cathedral and St Bride's Fleet Street en route.

London was founded by the Romans soon after their invasion of Britain in A.D. 43, and by the second century had become both the capital and much the largest city in Roman Britain. Many of the multifarious gods of the Empire must therefore have had places of worship there, yet no physical trace of such was known until 1954, when work on a new building in Queen Victoria Street brought to light a remarkably complete "Mithraeum", or temple of Mithras. Over 80,000 people flocked to view the sensational discovery, but it proved impossible to preserve on its original semi-subterranean site, and it was accordingly dismantled and re-assembled above ground some sixty yards away, on the forecourt of Bucklersbury House. Replicas of the fascinating sculptures found within it are displayed in the entrance hall of Bucklersbury House: the originals – together with other carvings probably from the temple, found in Victorian times – being on view in the Museum of London.

These, taken in conjunction with the temple ruins, reveal much about the worship of Mithras the Bull Slayer, an originally Persian deity whose cult swept the Roman Empire towards the end of the second century, when this London temple was founded. His statue – whose head, wearing the characteristic "Phrygian" cap, was found in 1954 – doubtless stood at the semi-circular western end of the shrine, overlooking a sunken central space (built too high in the reconstruction) where his mysteries were enacted, watched by worshippers from the raised flanking aisles. Performed in strict secrecy and by night, the rites of Mithras were open only to initiates, who were required to undergo a series of terrifying ordeals before being "baptised" in the blood of a cock or a bull. This, they believed, would guarantee them a happy after-life: but the London Mithraists seemingly hedged their bets by also honouring several other gods connected with the underworld, including the Egyptian Serapis (whose beautifully carved image was found in the temple) and Bacchus, the orgiastic Greco-Roman god of wine. Particularly disliked by Christians, in the early fourth century they were apparently forced to hide their images from adherents of the new religion by burying them beneath the temple floor: but the building continued in use for at least another fifty years, and its threshold is worn by the feet of countless devotees of Mithras, "the lord of light and life".

See **Carrawburgh, The Gods of Rome.**

LONDON The Temple of Mithras, Queen Victoria Street, E.C.4.
OS176 TQ 325813
The reconstructed temple stands on a raised platform outside Bucklersbury House, on the south side of the north-eastern end of Queen Victoria Street and some two hundred yards south of Bank Underground station (Northern and Central lines). The original sculptures from it are in the new and outstandingly interesting Museum of London in the Barbican Centre (Barbican Underground station, Metropolitan and Circle lines). St Mary Abchurch is within a few hundred yards of the temple site.

No complete place of worship survives from the post-Roman or Anglo-Saxon periods of London's history, but the capital possesses one of the earliest and least altered Norman chapels in England, and perhaps the noblest of them all – the chapel of St John the Baptist in the Tower of London. Built in the 1080s as an integral part of the great keep called the White Tower – the original "Tower of London", from which the whole of the vast royal fortress-palace takes its name – its rounded or "apsidal" east end accounts for the semi-circular projection rising from floor to roof at the south-east corner of the otherwise rectangular stronghold. Within, on the keep's two lowest floors, are the chapel's lower and upper crypts: while the chapel itself soars clear from the second floor to roof height, its lower level ringed on three sides by a vaulted and round-arched passage.

Massively built and strikingly austere, its only decoration the severely restrained carving on the capitals of its squat pillars, the chapel's almost overwhelmingly powerful atmosphere reduces the noisiest visitors to immediate silence. "Here", in the words of Professor Allen Brown, "one can get closer to the Conqueror and the Conquest than anywhere else in England": for this was indeed the private chapel of the stern and unbending Norman kings, whose quarters lay just outside its door and who most often have worshipped here. Here too Henry VI's body lay in state in 1471, after his murder in the Wakefield Tower: and here the "knights of the bath" (the favoured young men who, having undergone ritual purification by bathing, were knighted at medieval coronations) kept their night-long vigils before the altar.

The huge Tower complex was, of course, a great armoury and a notorious prison as well as a royal palace, and it is appropriate that its "parish church" (technically one of the Chapels Royal) should be dedicated to St Peter-ad-Vincula, or "St Peter in chains". Ominously positioned near the site of an execution block on Tower Green, the present building dates from about 1520 and has a light and pleasant interior with several fine monuments, notably that of John Holland, Duke of Exeter. Beneath its floor, however, are buried some 2,000 bodies, including the decapitated remains of two of Henry VIII's unfortunate queens, Anne Boleyn and Catherine Howard.

See **The Norman Church.**

LONDON The Chapels of St John and St Peter-ad-Vincula, Tower of London, S.E.1.
OS 176 TQ 337805
The Tower of London, famous also for its Crown Jewels, its ravens and "Beefeaters", and its unrivalled collection of arms and armour, is open daily and on Sunday afternoons from March until October, and from Monday to Saturday in winter: St John's chapel is freely accessible, but the interior of St Peter-ad-Vincula can normally be viewed only in the course of the racy and informative guided tours led by Beefeaters. The Tower is best reached via Tower Hill Underground station (District and Circle lines) or, as an attractive alternative in summer, by river boat from the pier near Westminster Abbey. St Katharine Cree is within easy walking distance of the Tower.

LONDON St Bartholomew-the-Great, Smithfield, E.C.1.
OS 171 TQ 320818
St Bartholomew's is most easily reached from Barbican Underground station (Metropolitan and Circle lines) by turning right outside the station into Long Lane, and shortly afterwards left into West Smithfield Square, continuing along the east side of the square to the half-timbered gatehouse: the church is generally open daily from 10.30 a.m. until 5 p.m. A short distance to the south-west, past St Bartholomew's Hospital with its wall plaques the the Smithfield martyrs, is
St Sepulchre's-without-Newgate.

An aura of legend surrounds the origins of London's largest Norman church, which lies behind a half-timbered gateway off West Smithfield, a square once notorious for martyr-burnings and now associated with the capital's principal meat market. In 1119, the story runs, the courtier Rahere's carefree existence was shattered by the shipwreck which drowned his dearest friends, whereupon Rahere went on a repentant pilgrimage to Rome – only to contract malaria there, from which he himself almost died. Vowing in his sickness to found a hospital for the London poor, he was ordered by a vision of St Bartholomew to build an Augustinian priory as well, and to site both establishments nowhere but at "Smoothfield": this area (as the saint and perhaps the courtier knew well) was then a valueless swamp, and Rahere had little difficulty in obtaining land there, beginning his twin foundations in about 1123.

Both still continue, the modern St Bartholomew's Hospital being one of the best in Britain and the priory church of St Bartholomew the Great ranking among London's most atmospheric places of worship, notwithstanding the hard times it fell on after the Reformation. The originally cross-shaped church then lost its nave and transepts, while its Lady Chapel was used in succession as a house, a printing shop where Benjamin Franklin once worked, and a fringe

factory: but its splendid choir survived as a parish church, being given a brick tower in 1628, and despite heavy Victorian restoration its cavernous interior is quite magnificent. Two tiers of great Norman arches (the lower resting on mighty pillars and the upper filled with slender columns) are topped by a third storey of Gothic windows, and march eastwards to the semi-circular apse, a Victorian rebuild designed to reproduce the plan of Rahere's original church. Rahere himself lies by the altar, in a canopied tomb remodelled during the later middle ages: his effigy wears the black robes of an Augustinian prior, and is flanked by two miniature canons reading from Bibles, one of them open at the founder's favourite text, "For the Lord shall comfort Zion; he will comfort all her waste places . . ." Opposite, set high up in the Norman gallery, is a delightful Tudor oriel window, that of a chapel built by Prior Bolton and carved with a pun on his name, a crossbow "bolt" piercing a barrel or "tun": while all round the walls are Elizabethan and later monuments, including one in the north aisle to John and Margaret Whiting, whose inscription ends:

"She first deceased. He for a little tried
To live without her, liked it not, and died."

See **Monasteries and Religious Houses.**

LONDON The Temple Church, Middle Temple, E.C.4.
OS 176 TQ 313813
The church is tucked away off the west end of Fleet Street, behind a labelled archway (a paper stall on weekdays) almost exactly opposite the junction of Fleet Street and Chancery Lane. It can be reached via Temple Underground station (District and Circle lines) by walking up Arundel Street, turning right into the Strand (past St Clement Danes and the Law Courts) and continuing eastwards to the archway: or, from St Paul's Cathedral, by a longer walk westward down Ludgate Hill and along Fleet Street, taking in St Bride's Fleet Street en route. The Temple Church is generally open on weekdays from 10 a.m. to 4 p.m., but is sometimes closed on winter Mondays and Tuesdays: opposite the archway, across Fleet Street, is the octagonal Gothic Revival church of St Dunstan-in-the-West, with a display of Rumanian Orthodox icons.

The remarkable church of St Mary in the Temple stands in an area which is now the hub of legal London, but which was once the English headquarters of the crusading order of Knights Templars. Sworn to defend the holy places of Jerusalem, and in particular the famous round church of the Holy Sepulchre there, these "monks of war" reminded themselves and others of their mission by building all their major churches with round naves, such as survives here despite drastic restoration in 1841 and disastrous bomb damage a century later. One of only a handful of round churches still standing, the London Temple's nave is all the more notable for having been built (probably between 1160 and 1185) at a time when the Norman style of architecture was beginning to give way to the new Gothic style, and thus displays an instructive juxtaposition of the two forms. Its outer door, for example, has a pointed Gothic arch, but the inner portal is round-headed and Norman, as are the windows in both the lower and the uppermost of the nave's three circular storey's. Within, how-

ever, the arches separating the round central space from the encircling "ambulatory" or processional aisle are pointed Gothic again, as is the decorative arcading round the walls of the ambulatory and the triforium storey above: while the clustering arch pillars and arcade columns are of dark Purbeck marble, a material much beloved by builders in the new style.

Purbeck marble, indeed, also appears prominently in the church's fine vaulted rectangular choir, which was built between 1220 and 1240 in a style now unreservedly Gothic, and which is a fine example of the first or Early English phase of the new architectural form. The same attractive stone is used for the famous series of thirteenth century effigies of Knights Templar in the nave, many of them renewed after the bombing: they include that of the renowned William the Marshall, who began as a penniless knight errant and died in 1219 as Earl of Pembroke and Regent of England.

See **Monasteries and Religious Houses.**

LONDON St Helen's, Bishopsgate, E.C.3
OS 176 TQ 333184
Set back behind office buildings at the southern end of Bishopsgate (just before it divides into Threadneedle and Gracechurch Streets) St Helen's

Though dwarfed by the towering skyscrapers which surround it, St Helen's is one of the largest of the City's medieval churches, remarkable alike for having escaped both the Fire of 1666 and the bombing of 1941, for its unrivalled collection of pre-Fire monuments, and for its unusual "double church"

plan. It did indeed begin as two churches, each with its own nave and chancel: the northern belonged to a nunnery which was established alongside the (southern) parish church in the early thirteenth century, a reversal of the order of events at Minster-in-Sheppey. Originally separated by a tall screen (over which the nuns were accused in 1385 of waving to the parish congregation) the two churches are now divided only by a central row of late medieval arches, and both (along with the fourteenth century chapels to the south east of the parish section) are packed with monuments. Perhaps the finest of all is that of Sir John Crosby (d.1475) in the parish chancel, which shows the great London merchant in armour with a Yorkist livery collar of suns and roses: but certainly the most curious are those of Sir Julius Caesar Adelmare (d.1636) in the nun's chancel (a black slab with a marble "deed" recording that this lawyer had "paid the debt of nature") and of Captain Martin Bond (d.1643) on the north wall, which depicts the soldier sitting in a tent guarded by sentries. Just east of the last is an unusual Easter Sepulchre of 1525, where the consecrated host was symbolically "buried" from Good Friday until Easter Sunday: this incorporates an angled "squint", so that nuns in a chamber outside could keep watch on the altar.

Finally, spare a glance for the bearded seventeenth century beggar supporting the poor box by the west door.

St Katharine Cree (or "Creechurch", after the nearby priory of Christ Church) is a most unusual church, dating from an unusual period for church-building, the late 1620s. It was raised as part of Bishop Laud's campaign to revive within the Church of England what he called "beauty in holiness", but his Puritan opponents regarded as blatant Popery and superstition: one of the accusations made against him at his trial, indeed, was that during his "pompous" consecration of St Katharine's in 1631 he had "thrown dust into the air" and "uttered divers curses". The church he blessed remains substantially unchanged, though its side aisles, ironically, are now shut off and used as offices. Painted blue and white, its interior is a curious blend of the old Gothic and the coming Classical styles, with ornate 'Grecian' pillars and round arches supporting rows of late Perpendicular Gothic windows rising to a Gothic plaster-vaulted roof: while the eastern "rose" (or "Katharine Wheel") window also recalls the medieval past, but is set in a totally un-Gothic square frame and filled with carefully non-representational glass of the 1630s.

A valuable architectural link between London's pre- and post-Fire churches, (St Katharine's is also notable for a touching memorial to Sir Nicholas Throckmorton (d.1571); a fine "Father Smith" organ played by Purcell and Handel; and its "Lion Sermon", endowed in 1648 by Sir John Gayer, donor of the font. Still preached annually on October the sixteenth (generally by some leading churchman), this commemorates Sir John's escape from a prowling desert lion, which he warded off by the power of prayer.

LONDON St Katharine Cree, Leadenhall Street, E.C.3. OS 176 TQ 334812
Standing at the corner of Leadenhall Street and Creechurch Lane, St Katharine's is a short distance west of Aldgate Underground station (Metropolitan and Circle lines) via Aldgate High Street and Aldgate: it is always open from 9 a.m. until 5 p.m. Monday to Friday, when visitors are most welcome, but is closed at weekends. St Helen's Bishopsgate is a few hundred yards to the west.

On Sunday the second of September 1666 the Great Fire of London began at a baker's shop in Pudding Lane, and when the conflagration finally burnt itself out five days later – at Pie Corner, near St Bartholomew the Great – virtually the entire capital lay in ruins, with eighty-seven of its 108 churches destroyed or irreparably damaged. Within the next two decades fifty-one of them were to be rebuilt by the famous architect Sir Christopher Wren: who, far from producing anything like a standardised building, displayed true genius in the extraordinary variety of his designs both for the churches themselves (which range from square through cross-shaped to ten-sided) and for their amazing belfries – which ring the changes from simple towers to breathtaking combinations of domes, columns, pinnacles and spires. A fine selection of these renowned belfries can still be seen by walking, say from St Paul's Cathedral to the Tower: but comparatively few Wren interiors have escaped the onslaught of Victorian restorers and the far more devastating bomb damage of the Second World War; and of these probably the least altered is that of St Mary Abchurch.

Externally a simple brick rectangle with a modest but delicate cupola-spire, St Mary Abchurch reserves its treasures for the traveller who steps inside, and whose eye is immediately swept upward into the wonderful dome which roofs the whole building. Gloriously and ingeniously painted in 1708–9 by William Snow, this seems to open into a cloudy Heaven where the Hebrew name of God is adored by angelic choirs, surrounded by an outer ring of symbolic Christian virtues; and like the rest of the church it is lit by clear glass windows, as all Wren churches were intended to be. Equally notable, once the surprise of the dome has passed, it is the sumptuous and largely original woodwork, dark-stained throughout – the raised pews round three sides; the west gallery above the mighty vestry doorcase; and the amazing "wine-glass" pulpit with its spiral-columned stair and great spreading canopy, ornately (and perhaps even excessively) embellished with carved cherubim, eagles, grapes and foliage. More restrained, yet dominating all, is the tremendous columned altarpiece, the finest example in London and the only authenticated work by the master-carver Grinling Gibbons in a City church. What remains most impressive about St Mary Abchurch, however, is its completeness as an original "post-Fire" church, and a rare example of the great Sir Christopher's work as he meant it to be seen.

See **London – St Bartholomew's, Smithfield, The Prayer Book Church.**

LONDON St Mary Abchurch, off Cannon Street, E.C.4. OS 176 TQ 328810
The church is hidden in tiny Abchurch Lane, a narrow passage opposite 100 Cannon Street (the Banco de Bilbao) and almost equidistant from Monument (to the east) and Cannon Street (to the west) Underground stations, both on the District and Circle lines: at present it is reliably open only between noon and 2 p.m. on Wednesdays and Thursdays, and always closed at weekends. Nearby, just to the west of Cannon Street station in College Street, is the restored Wren church of St Michael Paternoster Royal.

LONDON St Sepulchre's-without-Newgate, Holborn Viaduct, E.C.1.
OS 176 TQ 318815
Easily seen in conjunction with a visit to nearby St Bartholomew-the-Great, St Sepulchre's stands near Holborn Circus, about a quarter of a mile eastwards along Holborn from Chancery Lane Underground station (Central line). It is open from Monday to Friday (9 a.m.–4 p.m.) but closed at weekends.

Properly the Church of the Holy Sepulchre, this largest of the City's parish churches has a medieval shell and porch and a fine (if much altered) Classical interior, perhaps the work of Sir Christopher Wren. Yet it is generally visited for its associations, the best-known of which is as melancholy as its name: standing opposite the Central Criminal Court of the Old Bailey and near the site of notorious Newgate gaol, its great bell once tolled prisoners to their execution, and its handbell (preserved by a pillar near the south pulpit) disturbed their last night on earth. Paid by a charity endowed in 1605, the parish bellman rang this outside their cell at midnight, reciting a rhyme which began.

"All you that in the condemned hole do lie Prepare you, for tomorrow you shall die"

and ended;

"And when St Sepulchre's Bell in the
morning tolls
The Lord above have mercy on your souls".

Here too is buried – and commemorated by a window in the south aisle – the flamboyant Captain John Smith, the Jacobean Governor of Virginia whose life (at least according to his own account) was saved by the Indian princess Pocahontas.

LONDON Christ Church Spitalfields, Commercial Street, E.1
OS 176 TQ 337817
Set among bustling fruit and vegetable markets, Christ Church is best reached from Liverpool Street Underground station (Metropolitan, Circle and Central lines) by turning north up Bishopsgate and then east down Brushfield Street, which frames its unforgettable tower. The interior is currently under restoration, but a key can usually be obtained by enquiring at the church's crypt which commendably serves as a rehabilitation centre for homeless alcoholics. Opposite the church is a pub named "Jack the Ripper" after a notorious Spitalfields denizen: and St Helen's Bishopsgate and St Katharine Cree are within walking distance to the south-west.

Surely one of the very grandest and without doubt one of the most distinctive of London churches, Christ Church, Spitalfields was a product of the Fifty New Churches Act of 1711, which strove to provide places of worship for the population of the capital's ever-expanding suburbs. It was designed by Nicholas Hawksmoor, once Wren's personal assistant and also associated with the colossal country palaces of Blenheim and Castle Howard: and at Spitalfields too he worked on a massive scale. Dominating the surrounding vegetable markets, his tremendous spire-capped Portland stone tower (fronted by the equally tremendous columned portico he apparently added as an afterthought) seems almost as broad as it is high, and has no parallel in Britain for rampant individualism: and his interior, though more conventionally Baroque, is equally magnificent in conception. Wonderfully lofty, its dominant features are the exceptionally tall Classical columns (raised still higher by mighty pedestals) which flank the central space and support the richly decorated multiple vaults of the aisles: while at the east end a gargantuan cross beam, topped by the Royal Arms, divides off the sanctuary with its great altarpiece.

Begun in 1715, this "stately Fabrick" – as it is called on the monument to Edward Peck, a sullen-looking Georgian gentleman surrounded by weeping cherubs – was completed in 1729, but drastically altered in 1866 by Victorian "improvers". Now it is being restored to its original Hawksmoorian glory, and is thus temporarily stripped of its fittings: but its current bareness only serves to emphasise both its grandeur and the vast outlay required for building fifty new churches on this scale – which in the end "so far exceeded the Calculations formerly made" that only a dozen new places of worship were actually constructed.

LONDON All Saints, Margaret Street, W.1
OS 176 TQ 289814
All Saints is at the east end of Margaret Street, which runs to the north of and parallel with busy Oxford street in London's West End. From Oxford Circus Underground station (Victoria, Central and Bakerloo lines) walk northwards up Regent Street, and Margaret Street is the second on the right. The church is frequently open, but if not the key is obtainable from the adjacent parish office.

All Saints, Margaret Street is a church which the traveller is likely either to love or to hate. The pioneer and still a revered shrine of the Gothic Revival in London, it was built in 1850–59 as the "model church" of the Tractarian movement within the Church of England. Rejecting Classical architecture as essentially pagan, and the light-filled, pulpit-focused churches of the Georgian era as barren of "holy mystery", the Tractarians chose instead to build in the "pure and Christian" medieval Gothic style and to focus their places of worship on a high altar in a richly decorated chancel, clearly visible to all as a symbol that the sacraments, not the preacher, were the true basis of Christian life. William Butterfield, the architect they selected, fulfilled these aims in a manner which was controversial at the time and is still startling. For he deliberately built in brick, and because brick cannot be effectively carved he achieved his decorative effects by the use of many-coloured materials, with results that are striking enough on the multi-striped exterior of the church and its attendant buildings, and absolutely overwhelming within.

There, amid the Anglo-Catholic gloom, colour glimmers from glazed and patterned brick, from tile-painted Bible stories and from gilded walls and pillars of polychromatic granite and marble, alabaster and serpentine: and dominating all is the kaleidoscopic chancel, with its towering altar backed by a golden reredos of tiered and serried saints. All this richness of shade and texture, combined with Butterfield's use of architectural devices such as particularly high and wide arches, conceals the fact that the church is in fact a small one, built on a cramped site: church and tower (whose spire is one of the highest in central London), choir school and vicarage are all ingeniously fitted into a space some hundred feet square. That All Saints achieves to admiration an atmosphere of "holy mystery" is also undeniable: but whether the visitor actually likes it or not must remain a matter of personal taste.
See **The Gothic Revival.**

A church of the High Gothic Revival and certainly among the finest of its period in England, St Augustine's was built in 1871–80 for a group of Anglo-Catholics who had broken away from their parish church after a doctrinal wrangle, and who accordingly needed a building suited to their ritualistic manner of worship. Its architect, John Loughborough Pearson, favoured a style of Gothic based on French thirteenth century models: and he designed an ambitious church with a particularly successful west end (with a great rose window between two pyramid-roofed turrets) and a splendid tower with a soaring 250 foot spire. Within, the large and almost cathedral-like church is more impressive yet, indeed breathtakingly so. Constructed largely in red brick but vaulted with stone throughout, its most memorable features are the aisles (doubled in the nave) which run uninterrupted all round the church, so that they can be used for processions. Above them, supported on a continuous series of low arches and roofed by a much loftier arcade, is an upper processional gallery which cuts through the buttresses and bridges the transepts to follow the same path. Besides affording unrivalled opportunities for complex ritual, this remarkable two-storey processional way has the effect of creating an almost endlessly changing panorama of vistas, varying at every viewpoint: an affect further enhanced by the complex nature of the building, which has chapels in both transepts.

LONDON St Augustine's, Kilburn Park Road, N.W.6
OS 176 TQ 247831
St Augustine's stands in the north-western suburbs of London, near the junction of Kilburn Park Road and Maida Vale: it is easily reached from Kilburn Park Underground station (Bakerloo line) by walking some two hundred yards south-east down Cambridge Gardens and Rudolph Road. If it is locked, the key can usually be obtained at the modern vicarage immediately north of the church.

Probably the best known of the many City of London churches "bombed out" during the Second World War was Wren's St Bride's, Fleet Street, famous for its "wedding-cake steeple" of four diminishing octagons, pierced by tiers of arches and topped by a delicate spirelet. This steeple and a gutted shell were all that remained of the church after the great fire-bomb raid of December the twenty-ninth 1940, but by 1958 St Bride's had been rebuilt as a virtual replica of the original, though with a completely different seating plan and an entirely redesigned set of modern fittings. What is perhaps most remarkable about the reborn St Bride's, however, is the evidence of no less than six earlier churches on the same site, revealed by post-War excavations and now imaginatively displayed in the crypts beneath it – which also contain (though they do not display) the bones of some 7,000 skeletons, neatly piled in a medieval charnel-house. The first St Bride's was apparently a simple Saxon building of the sixth century, later given a semi-circular apse at its east end and subsequently replaced by a series of progressively larger and more complex churches, culminating in the late-medieval St Bride's destroyed by the Fire of 1666. Services are now held daily in a chapel within the Saxon foundations, and there is no better place than St Bride's crypt to study and reflect on the history of places of worship in London.

LONDON St Bride's, Fleet Street, E.C.4
OS 176 TQ 306813
Instantly identifiable by its famous steeple, St Bride's is just off the east end of Fleet Street, opposite the Daily Express building: a short walk westwards from St Paul's Cathedral, and about a hundred yards north of Blackfriars Underground station (District and Circle lines) the church is open daily from 9 a.m. until 5 p.m. The Temple Church is within easy reach at the far end of Fleet Street, as are St Bartholomew-the-Great and St Sepulchre's-without-Newgate, both to the north-east via Ludgate Hill and Old Bailey.

One of the largest and most splendid even of the great late medieval parish churches of East Anglia, the church of the Holy Trinity presents an unforgettable sight across the wide village green of Long Melford, with brick Elizabethan almshouses to its front and the domed turrets of Melford Hall away to the east. As the many proud inscriptions round its exterior walls proclaim, it was built between c.1460 and 1496 by the wealthy cloth merchants of this then prosperous region, foremost among them the Clopton family: and like so many such great wool churches, it was clearly built to impress. In this it succeeds admirably, its immense length being still further increased by the low and triple-gabled Lady Chapel attached to its east end, and its height emphasised by the verticals of its serried Perpendicular windows and of its elaborate "flushwork" wall decoration in flint and stone. This last does not, significantly, extend to the north side, which faces away from the village and would thus be rarely seen.

Within, the first impression is of greater plainness, largely due to the loss of medieval fittings: yet the north windows of the spacious and lofty nave display a splendid collection of stained glass knights and ladies in heraldic tabards and mantles, the patrons and family connections of the Cloptons; while the Cloptons themselves kneel with their patron saints in the east window. At the east end of the nave aisles are some fine brasses and effigies, and in the chancel the exceedingly large and pompous Elizabethan monument of Sir William Cordell (d.1580), builder of nearby Melford Hall.

The two most delightful and interesting parts of Holy Trinity's interior, however, are not immediately apparent, though all the better for their unexpectedness. The first (entered through a tiny priest's room at the east end of the north aisle) is the Clopton chantry chapel, with its wide east window containing an exquisite stained-glass "Lily Crucifix"; its founder's tomb of John Clopton; and its painted roof encircled by a long medieval English poem inscribed on a series of scrolls. This is unusual, but more unusual and striking still is the much larger Lady Chapel, which is reached via a vestry behind the high altar and is in effect a totally separate building. Also raised by the Cloptons, it consists of a central sanctuary for the altar, surrounded on all four sides by an ambulatory or indoor walkway for processions in honour of the Virgin.

See **The Great Wool Churches.**

LONG MELFORD Suffolk
OS 155 TL 865468
The large and attractive village of Long Melford stands on the A134, twelve miles south of Bury St Edmunds and three miles north of Sudbury: the church stands by the green at the north end of the village, and opposite is Melford Hall, while just to the north is Kentwell Hall, both these large Elizabethan mansions being open to the public. This is an area of pretty countryside and fine churches, notably those of outstandingly picturesque Lavenham (four miles north-east) and of Kersey (nine miles east).

The Great Wool Churches

"Wool churches" is the name frequently given to a group of splendid late medieval places of worship, many of which were indeed built with the profits of the immensely lucrative trade in wool and cloth, the mainstay of England's wealth in the fourteenh and fifteenth centuries. Not surprisingly, they occur principally in the main sheep-raising areas of medieval England; which is to say in East Anglia, Lincolnshire and Nottinghamshire, and in the counties from Wiltshire and Gloucestershire westward to Devon. In East Anglia, particularly, they may well tower over tiny villages like Salle, thus illustrating the point that their often vast proportions were not necessarily commensurate with the size of the population they served. Their grandeur, rather, was at least nominally an offering to the greater Glory of God, for whom only the highest of towers, the grandest of angel roofs, and the finest stained glass that money could buy would do. So contemporaries were swift to point out, and when John Clopton added his beautiful Lady Chapel to the already magnificent church of Long Melford, he had inscribed round its walls, "Let Christ be my witness that I have not exhibited these things in order to win praise for myself, but in order that the Spirit may be remembered".

This pious declaration loses some of its force, however, when a close observation of Long Melford church reveals that its external decoration is concentrated on the side facing towards the village, and is decidedly scanty on that which would rarely be seen. It is tempting, therefore, to view this and other great wool churches as manifestations of the late medieval principal known as "largitas", which may be translated either as "conspicuous consumption", or more bluntly as showing off. Their builders, the wealthy businessmen of their day, certainly had no scruples about reminding all and sundry of their generosity, and both at Long Melford and Cullompton prominently placed inscriptions record the names of those who contributed to the work. At Holme-by-Newark and elsewhere, moreover, both the inside and the outside of the church are most liberally decorated with the trademarks and (not entirely genuine) heraldic arms of the founder: as well as with the sheep which (like the sailing ships carved on John Lane's aisle at Cullompton) were the source of his wealth.

That rich men should wish to display their riches is only natural. In earlier times they had done so by founding monasteries and religious houses, and in later periods they would build vast and showy mansions, or endow international scientific institutes bearing their names. When the wool trade reached its zenith in the fifteenth and sixteenth centuries, how-

ever, the emphasis was on the parish church, and it was here that they lavished their generosity. Yet personal or familial aggrandisement was not by any means their only motive: for they were also moved by the equally human desire to outdo their neighbours by building bigger parish churches than those of the surrounding villages. John Lane's aisle at Cullompton, for example, was raised as a direct response to similar additions to the churches of two rival clothtowns: while the groups of wealthy parishioners who built the intervisible churches of Cawston and Salle must surely have kept half an eye on their neighbours' doings. The magnificent and cathedral-like church of St Mary Redcliffe at Bristol, moreover, is an expression of civic pride second to none, designed to demonstrate that the great seaport was the equal of any town or city in England.

Civic pride, combined with a determination to score off their monkish rivals, likewise prompted the townsmen of Wymondham to raise a loftier and more elaborate bell tower at the west end of their church than the monks had already built over the centre of the same shared place of worship. Many of the ancient towns and cities of England, indeed, possess late medieval churches which testify graphically to the wealth and self-confidence of their inhabitants. Norwich, one of the richest communities in fifteenth century England and the focus of the East Anglian wool trade, has many such churches, much the most notable being stately St. Peter Mancroft, appropriately positioned by the city's principal market: while several of the ports from which East Anglian wool was shipped to Europe, including King's Lynn, Ipswich and Cley-next-the-Sea, also boast fine churches. Moving further north, the prosperity of the Lincolnshire wool trade is proclaimed by the great churhes at Gedney, Louth, Grantham, Spilsby and Boston, to name but a few: and Tattersal church in the same county remains as a memorial to that wily politician Ralph Lord Cromwell, Lord Treasurer of England. The neighbouring county of Nottinghamshire likewise displays great wool churches, notably at Newark, Holme-by-Newark, and Nottingham: while Holy Trinity at Hull, the largest of all medieval English parish churches, demonstrates the success of that port as an outlet for Yorkshire wool, cloth and lead.

The other principal wool producing regions of England lay to the west and south, and included the relatively small area in the middle Welsh borderlands which bred the fleeces called "Leominster ore", the costliest and most sought after grade of English wool: hereabouts stand the great parish churches of Ludlow in south Shropshire and Ledbury in Herefordshire.

Perhaps the most impressive collection of wool churches, however, is centred on the wide sheep grazing lands of the Cotswolds, largely in Gloucestershire but touching also the fringes of Oxfordshire, Worcestershire and Warwickshire. Among the outstanding late medieval parish churches of the first county are those of Chipping Campden, Cirencester, Fairford, Northleach and Winchcombe: while Oxfordshire wool churches include Burford and Witney, and that of Broadway is one of the finest in Worcestershire. Further south, the chalk downs of Wiltshire and Dorset were likewise good sheep country, whose prosperity is commemorated by the Wiltshire churches of Cricklade and Steeple Ashton and by the fine parish church of St. Thomas in cloth-trading Salisbury: as well as by the spacious places of worship at Beaminster, Cerne Abbas and Yetminster in Dorset.

Somerset, too, was a leading fleece producer, with a fine collection of wool churches, some (like Chewton Mendip) in the hilly north of the shire – but most in the area of marshland grazing between Glastonbury and Taunton: these include the parish church of St. John in Glastonbury itself; High Ham; Huish Episcopi; Ilminster; Ilse Abbotts; and Westonzoyland. Devon likewise boasts a number of large and splendid late medieval parish churches, either "built on wool" or with the proceeds of the equally lucrative tin trade: among them are Crediton; Cullompton; Ottery St. Mary; Tavistock and Tiverton. Cornwall, though essentially a region of small churches, also has a few of the larger type, notably at Bodmin, Launceston and Liskeard.

Wherever they stand, such lavishly built places of worship are to a very considerable extent the product of a desire to show off wealth, and to exalt the status both of the builder himself and of his community. To attribute them entirely to such worldly motives, nevertheless, would be both over-cynical and mistaken. For many of their builders were undoubtedly men of genuine piety – St Mary Redcliffe's William Canynges, indeed, ended his life as a priest – and all of them were unquestionably concerned with the fate of their souls after death, especially when they remembered how proverbially difficult it is for a rich man to enter heaven. According to late medieval popular belief, however, it was possible in effect to "purchase paradise", or at least to shorten the period which all but the very best or worst of mortals must expect to spend in the fires of Purgatory before being admitted to bliss. This could be achieved by deeds of charity during life, such as the foundation of almshouses like the fine example at Ewelme: but the surest way was to have as many Masses as possible said for one's soul after death. All who could afford to do so therefore willed cash or property to pay for such Masses, and the less well-off joined guilds whose collective funds employed a priest to mention all subscribers in his prayers.

The wealthy, however, endowed "chantry priests" of their own, or better still arranged for a succession of such priests to sing Masses for their souls in perpetuity: and in the case of the very rich they would do so in chantry chapels specially built for the purpose, and generally containing the founder's tomb. Often (as at Cullompton) these chapels would be attached to an already existing parish church or (if the deceased was influential enough) built within a cathedral, while occasionally they took the form of separate buildings near the founder's mansion, like Rycote Chapel. Nearly all the great wool churches likewise contain them, generally in the position of honour flanking the chapel and its high altar: and their presence surely reveals the principal reason why these magnificent places of worship were built. When the plutocratic wool merchant John Tame raised the huge and splendid parish church of Fairford, for example, he took care to emblazon it with his merchant's marks and other symbols of his worldly prestige, and he was equally anxious to provide his home town with a church to rival or outdo those of its wool producing Cotswold neighbours.

His primary concern, nevertheless, was that he should be fittingly commemorated after his death, and above all that he should be insured against the unknown both by the Masses of his chantry priests and the prayers of ordinary worshippers, requested on his tomb in the following words

"For Jesus's love pray for me
I may not pray now, pray ye
That my pains released may be."

The Masses of John Tame's priests ceased at the Reformation, when chantries were abolished as "popish": but the modern traveller who visits this and the other great wool churches may care to spare at least a thought for the men who raised them. Whatever their motives, they have bequeathed some of the finest places of worship in Britain.
See **The Medieval Parish Church, The Reformation.**

MARSTON MORETAINE
Bedfordshire
OS 153 SP 996413

Marston Moretaine (sometimes spelt "Moreteyne") is within easy reach of the M1 motorway, being three miles north-east of junction 13 and six miles south-west of Bedford (and John Bunyan's Elstow) on the A421. The church is set back from the road, at the end of a signposted lane at the south end of the village: it is kept locked, but the key can be readily obtained from the Post Office (in the middle of the village, on the A421) which is open every weekday morning and most afternoons.

The lower stages of the tower predate the church of St Mary of which it is now a part.

Much the most striking feature of St Mary's church at Marston Moretaine is its massive detached belltower: such towers are unusual in England (though there is another at nearby Elstow) and the reason why Marston's was built in this manner is far from clear. Folklore insists that the Devil stole it away, but found it too heavy to carry and so dropped it in its present position: while others suggest that it was raised there either as a refuge from the flooding frequent in this marshy region or else to take advantage of firmer ground. None of these explanations, however, are entirely convincing: and it is more likely that (though its topmost storey is plainly contemporary with the existing chancel) the tower's thick-walled lower stages stood here before the present church, as a safe stronghold against raiders: a conclusion reinforced by the opening high up in its southern face, probably an original entrance accessible only by ladder.

The main body of the church proclaims its origin far more clearly, with an east end con-structed of yellow-brown ironstone in about 1340 and a higher nave of lighter stone, built in the Perpendicular style about a century later: and its interior, though sadly in need of refurbishment, contains much of interest. The lofty nave has a largely original roof flanked by ten crowned angels, and a faded but still dramatic "Doom" painting (*c*.1505) over the chancel arch, full of naked souls rising from their graves for the Last Judgement: while in its north aisle is part of a sixteenth century painted screen with four prophets. There is also a fine series of monuments to successive lords of the manor, starting by the altar with the plate-armoured brass of Thomas Reynes (who began the nave, and died in 1451) and continuing into the south nave aisle, where a pair of Tudor helmets – part of the accoutrements carried at funerals – hang near the Elizabethan "bedstead" monument of Thomas Snagge, Speaker of the House of Commons in Armada year. *See* **Elstow.**

The great Tweed-side monastery of Melrose is not only the finest of the famous Border abbeys, but also one of the most beautiful monastic ruins in Britain. It was founded in 1136 by that enthusiastic patron of the church King David I of Scotland, who brought here from Rievaulx in Yorkshire the "white monks" of the new Cistercian order. So called from their mother house of Cîteaux in France, these Cistercians followed an austere rule which emphasised the value of manual labour: and in the rich valley lands around Melrose they prospered exceedingly as sheep and cattle farmers, exporting wool to Flanders through the port of Berwick-on-Tweed, where they owned much property. Estates all over southern Scotland, indeed, were bestowed on them by King David, his royal successors, and their subjects great and small: so that in the first 150 years of its existence Melrose was among the wealthiest and most successful in the northern realm.

To these palmy days belong the extensive monastic buildings which, probably because of better drainage there, were laid out on the north side of the church. Like the Cistercian order itself, they were divided into two separate sections, those to the west (including a 355 foot long dormitory and refectory range) being for the "conversi" or lay brothers, who did most of the abbey's manual work, and of whom there were nearly two hundred during Melrose's heyday. These also had their own cloister and their own part of the church, at the west end of the nave. The white monks proper, called "choir monks" because they were literate and sang the monastic offices, had their quarters round the great cloister, to the east and nearer the church: and there too was the chapter house where the business of the monastery was done, and where its greatest abbots (including St Waltheof, famous for his learning) were buried.

During the bitter Anglo-Scottish wars of the fourteenth century, however, the abbey fell on hard times. For the nearby main road from Edinburgh to the border, which in the days of peace had increased its prosperity, now brought only invading armies, and Melrose was several times attacked, most seriously in 1322. The damage was to some extent repaired by generous grants from King Robert Bruce, who loved Melrose and whose heart (after being carried on crusade by Sir James Douglas) was eventually buried here, probably near the high altar – though it may have been laid by the shrine of St Waltheof in the chapter house, where a mummified heart was discovered and replaced in 1921. With a fresh outbreak of conflict in 1385 a still greater disaster occurred, when the abbey church was burnt to the ground by a raiding force under Richard II of England: yet within four years a new church had begun to rise in its stead, and this is now the greatest glory of Melrose.

Building began at the east end, one of the contributors being a presumably repentant King Richard: and it may be that English masons (probably from Yorkshire) designed the huge and splendid east window, its delicate grid-like tracery surmounted by a row of image niches in the gable. Further west, however, a different style comes into play, most noticeably in the great south transept window with its complex flowing curves, perhaps the work of the French-born "John Morow" (Jean Moreau?), who left his architectural testament inscribed on a panel within the transept. All round this window are examples of Melrose's famous figure sculpture, and the little images of monks, angels and fantastic beasts continue westward again along the south side of the building, where an array of windows mark the positions of the eight separate chapels which lined this flank of the immensely long nave. Part of it (formerly the monks' choir at the eastern end) is roofed over and dourly barrel-vaulted, having served as the Presbyterian parish kirk between the seventeenth and nineteenth centuries: while at the extreme western end remain traces of the original pre-fire church, demonstrating that the new building never attained its intended length. For before it could be completed the wars returned, and from the successive English attacks of 1544 and 1545 there was this time to be no recovery.
See **Abbey Dore, Dundrennan, Monasteries and Religious Houses.**

MELROSE Borders
OS 73 NT 550343
Set against the backdrop of the triple-peaked Eildon Hills, Melrose is some forty miles south-east of Edinburgh, on the A6091 which links the A7 and the A68, both picturesque routes through the border country. The lovely ruins of Dryburgh Abbey are three miles to the south-east, off the A68, and further south on the same road are the well-preserved remains of a third border monastery at Jedburgh. The attractive burgh of Selkirk, to the south-west, is also worth a visit, and beyond it is the beautiful valley of the Yarrow Water.

In England only by a few yards, the delightful church of St Peter at Melverley stands on the bank of the frontier river Vyrnwy, with the outliers of the Welsh mountains rearing up to the west. It is a rare example of an entirely "timber-framed" church, constructed as a cage of closely-set oaken beams, infilled with interwoven and plastered-over wattles: and was probably built in the fifteenth century or early sixteenth century to replace an earlier building destroyed in the Anglo-Welsh border wars. The font from this earlier church, indeed, is almost the only stone object in the church, even the doorstep being a huge baulk of wood, with the marks of the adzes that hewed it into shape still clearly visible. From the outside, therefore, only its little bell-turret distinguishes St Peter's from a timbered house or barn, an effect underlined by its rectangular, domestic-looking windows, largely Victorian replacements: and within the church is even more barn-like, a simple rectangle divided into three by great horizontal tie-beams.

Above its westernmost section (a screened-off entrance foyer) is an Elizabethan gallery reached by an alarmingly twisting stair, and itself crazily buckled and canted by the warping of its imperfectly seasoned timbers. From here the traveller looks into the main body

MELVERLEY Shropshire
OS 126 SJ 333166
The hamlet of Melverley is fifteen miles west of Shrewsbury, via the B4393 and a signposted road turning north at Crew Green, near the Fir Tree Inn: the church stands in meadows by the river, and is signposted from the Tontine Inn in the hamlet.

of the little church, which is bisected into nave and chancel by a simple tie-beamed floor to ceiling partition; walled and roofed with a chequerboard of timbering; and full of splendidly rustic furnishings – all, of course, in wood. Rows of pews with odd circular ends face towards a fine Jacobean pulpit, a candle-flanked lectern, and a little harmonium, with an Elizabethan altar-table beyond: and though the memorial to Richard and Margaret Downes (d.1730) on the nave wall is cleverly painted to resemble marble, even that is actually timber.

MEREWORTH Kent
OS 188 TQ 660537

Mereworth ("merryworth") is seven miles west of Maidstone and four miles south of junction 4 of the M20 motorway, via the A228: the church stands in the village, and about a mile to the east is Mereworth Castle, Lord Westmorland's Georgian classical mansion. Within five miles to the west are two fine medieval manor houses, Old Soar Manor at Plaxtol and beautiful Ightham Mote.

Its distinctive spire visible for many miles around, the grandiose neo-Classical church of St Lawrence at Mereworth is an odd and rather incongruous sight amid the woods and hop-gardens of rural mid-Kent. The product (like Gayhurst) of Georgian "landscape management", it was built in 1746 for the Earl of Westmorland, to replace the medieval parish church he demolished because it stood too near his new mansion: and, with an almost missionary zeal, imported into the countryside all the latest and most extreme architectural fashions. The exterior – a wide-eaved "Tuscan barn", dominated by the over-sized spire and fronted by a great semi-circular columned portico – borrows quite shamelessly from the design of various well-known London churches, but the interior is altogether more memorable and individual.

Entered via a circular vestibule – which is flanked by chapels containing a fine collec-tion of monuments from the old church – it is a mathematically exact copy of a Roman basilica, built according to the principles laid down by the classical architect Vitruvius. At the east end of the wide, columned, hall is a huge half-moon shaped window glowing with heraldic glass: while the columns and barrel-roofed ceiling are painted all over to resemble marble, plasterwork and panelling, even the "organ pipes" above the west gallery being merely a piece of theatrical scene-painting. This most uncompromisingly classi-cal of country churches, indeed, more nearly resembles a lavish stage set than a place of Christian worship: and here it is easy to see why the earnest church builders of the next century rejected classicism as frivolous or downright pagan, turning instead to the "Christian purity" of the Gothic Revival.
See **The Gothic Revival, The Prayer Book Church.**

Far left, the elaborate west end of the church. Above, the south aisle, and below, the west door.

Tombs and Monuments

From its earliest beginnings, religion has been much concerned with questions of death and the hereafter: and in nearly every period of their history the tombs and monuments of the dead have been closely associated with places of worship. It is likely, indeed, that tombs and places of worship were originally one and the same thing, and that some of the oldest surviving prehistoric places of worship were communal tombs like West Kennet long barrow near Avebury, where rituals seem to have been performed to placate the dead and perhaps to assist their spirits to escape from their bodies. At a later period such ceremonies appear to have been transferred to the great stone circles, and it is surely no coincidence that these circles are more often than not surrounded by burial mounds, which at important sacred sites like Stonehenge and Avebury may be numbered in hundreds or even thousands. The positioning of such tombs testifies to the apparently universal human desire to be laid to rest as close as possible to a holy place. This motif is repeated throughout history, for example in the assemblage of Scots royal tombs on sacred Iona; the clustering monuments of lords and bishops round the shrines of saints at Canterbury, Ely and St Albans; and the still continuing tradition of honouring great personages by burying them in Westminster Abbey.

The Romans, admittedly, deviated from this norm, for their hygene laws prohibited burial in a temple or inhabited place, and the bones or ashes of their dead were generally deposited in cemeteries outside the city walls. There they were frequently commemorated by tombstones, and it is to the Romans that we owe Britain's first memorials proper, in the sense of inscribed stones recording the name, age, and often the profession and birthplace of the departed, sometimes accompanied by a stylised representational effigy. Such tombstones thus provide invaluable information about the population of Roman Britain, and many fascinating examples are displayed in museums all over the country. With the coming of Christianity, the tradition of burial in places of worship reasserted itself (pagan Romans contemptuously referred to early Christian churches as "bone houses") and a number of Christian memorial stones of the late or immediately post-Roman periods survive at Nevern, Whithorn and elsewhere. These are for the most part very simple, consisting merely of the name of the person commemorated and perhaps a cross roughly scratched on a stone: but by the seventh and eighth centuries monuments were becoming increasingly elaborate and carefully executed, as demonstrated both by later examples at Nevern and Whithorn and by such Anglo-Saxon tomb markers as the beautifully sculptured slabs, carved with crosses and interlaced patterns, at St Gregory's Minster in Yorkshire.

Elaborately carved standing crosses or patterned recumbent slabs appear to have been the usual monuments of the better-off dead – the grave markers of the poor, presumably made of wood, have not generally survived – until after the Norman Conquest, when a new type of monument began to make its appearance. This was the effigy, a Roman tradition which continued in Europe but which had apparently been abandoned in Europe until it was reintroduced under Norman influence. The earliest of such representations of the dead, including the monuments of Bishop Losinga (d.1096) in Norwich Cathedral and of Bishop Nigel (d.1133) at Ely were sculptured in low relief on stone or marble slabs. By the early thirteenth century, however, more lifelike effigies carved in the round were becoming widespread, and were to remain the dominant type of monument to wealthy and important personages until the Tudor period and beyond.

These effigies therefore survive in thousands, and are to be found alike in tiny parish churches and in great cathedrals, which often possess dozens of them. Faithfully and accurately depicting the costume, armour, or priestly vestments of those commemorated, they provide the traveller with an unrivalled display of the changing fashions of the centuries: only very rarely, however, do they attempt to portray personal appearance, setting out rather to represent the ideal knight, lady or bishop. Much the most common type of effigy, particularly in the earlier period, is that of the knight or esquire in armour: and from such the development of armour can be traced in great detail from the complete chain mail of Angevin times, via the mixture of mail and plate armour of the mid fourteenth century, to the elaborate suits of plate armour of the later middle ages. Some of the finest "military" effigies belong to the later thirteenth and fourteenth centuries, and many of these (like the pair at Abbey Dore) show the knight, not in a posture of repose, but as if in the act of rising from the tomb, with hand on sword hilt and legs crossed as though about to spring upright. This last, purely stylistic, feature is often but quite wrongly believed to indicate that the knight had fought in the Holy Land: in fact, the Crusades had long since passed into history by the time such "cross-legged" effigies were carved.

Effigies of ecclesiastics – bishops, abbots, and ordinary priests in their Mass vestments – are also relatively numerous: but representations of men in civilian clothes do not become common until the rise of a wealthy and powerful merchant class in the later middle ages. Great ladies, however, are frequently depicted in effigy, being sometimes shown beside their husbands – occasionally hand in hand – and sometimes alone: sometimes clad in widow's mourning, but more frequently dressed in the height of fashion. Here and there, too, the dead are shown in the dress of their profession, for instance in the robes of a judge or with the bow and hunting horn of a forester: while during the turbulent fifteenth century their effigies may bear the badge of a political faction, such as the Yorkist collar of suns and roses or the Lancastrian collar with the repeated letter "S".

Earlier medieval effigies were generally carved from local stone or (like the fine collection in London's Temple Church) from decorative Purbeck marble: from the mid fourteenth century onwards, however, some of the finest examples were sculpted in the translucent and easily worked limestone material called alabaster. The most lavish and costly of all medieval effigies, nevertheless, were the small number made in cast bronze or gilt copper, usually for royal patrons: among these being the figures of Queen Eleanor of Castille, Edward III and Richard II in Westminster Abbey, and of the Black Prince in Canterbury Cathedral.

Metal – this time the hard alloy of copper and zinc technically known as "latten" – was also used for a much cheaper and more widespread type of memorial, the monumental "brass". Here the effigy was not carved in the round, but incised on a flat plate, which was then cut to the outline of the figure and inlaid into a stone slab: slab and brass were then either set into the church floor, fixed atop a tomb chest or, from the fifteenth century onwards, sometimes attached upright to a church wall. Introduced in the late thirteenth century and persisting well into the Stuart period, brasses are most frequently found in the eastern parts of England, where stone suitable for carved effigies is less common. At first almost life sized and favoured by the higher ranks of society, they declined in size and grandeur as their popularity spread down the social scale: some of the smallest later examples, commemorating minor merchants or middling yeomen, are scarcely a foot long.

Among the most extraordinary brasses (found, for instance, at Cley-next-the-Sea and Salle) are those which depict the departed, not as in life, but as a "cadaver" or emaciated corpse: a macabre late medieval fashion also represented by the stone monuments of John Barton (d.1491) at Holme-by-Newark and Alice Chaucer (d.1475) at Ewelme. The latter, one of the finest in Britain, displays the medieval monument at its most sumptuous and highly developed, with sculptured tomb chest, noble alabaster effigy, splendid canopy, brilliant heraldry, and ranks of carved attendant angels. Its completeness is also unusual, for many such monuments were to suffer during the upheavals of the Reformation, when their religious imagery was destroyed or mutilated as "idolatrous", and damage was often inflicted on the effigies themselves.

Elizabethan and Stuart church memorials (of which there are fine collections at Tawstock and in London's St Helen's Bishopsgate) nevertheless continue to include effigies, though the medieval saints and angels were replaced by rows of kneeling children, and the deceased is increasingly likely to be depicted leaning on one elbow or commemorated (as at Brent Knoll) by a painted head-and-shoulders bust.

Full length "Classical" standing figures, however, were favoured for the grandest Georgian monuments, like those at Edenhan and Gayhurst: while the wealthier Victorians, under the influence of the Gothic Revival, sometimes reverted to the medieval tradition, most magnificently at Hoar Cross. The churchyard tombstones of the eighteenth and nineteenth centuries, with their various regional styles and touching or revealing epitaphs, are likewise well worth investigation. Whatever their period, indeed, tombs and monuments provide a fascinating field of study: a mirror of the ages that produced them, and a uniquely personal link with the men and women they commemorate, they will add greatly to the traveller's enjoyment of places of worship.

MINSTER-IN-SHEPPEY Kent
OS 178 TQ 956730

Set on a hill overlooking the Thames Estuary, the abbey church is on the north coast of the Isle of Sheppey, by the B2008 two and a half miles south-east of Sheerness: if it is locked, the key is usually available at the large house north of the churchyard. Some ten miles north of junction 5 of the M2 motorway, it is accessible from there via the A249/250 northwards, turning eastwards onto the B2008 at Halfway Houses. Six miles south-east is Harty church, also well worth visiting.

As both its name and its appearance indicate, the remarkable and undeservedly little-known church of St Mary and St Sexburga is in fact two churches standing side by side, with a grand but never completed tower topped by a pyramidal wooden belfry. The northern church was that of the original "Minster-in-Sheppey", the "monastery in the sheep island" founded in *c*.670 by St Sexburga, widow of a Saxon king of Kent and sister of the formidable St Etheldreda of Ely: and though substantially rebuilt in medieval times it still displays much Saxon work, including a pair of windows (partly built in still older Roman bricks) above the interior arches dividing the northern and southern churches. The former belonged to the Minster nuns: and so that they should not be disturbed at their prayers by the Sheppey farmers and fishermen they employed, the southern or parish church of St Mary was grafted onto it in the thirteenth century, producing the present curious arrangement.

The double church's cavernous interior contains a fine collection of medieval monuments, including two unusually large and early brasses in the south chancel, commemorating a knight and lady (*c*.1330) and probably of French workmanship. In the north chancel are two fifteenth century effigies, one holding a little figure representing his soul: and under the dividing arches is Sir Thomas Cheyne (d.1559) – an assiduous side-changer who acquired the abbey lands in 1539 and held onto them through all the upheavals of the Reformation – in the robes of a Garter knight. The earliest and strangest effigy, however, is that of Sir Robert de Shurland (*c*.1310), set under a later canopy in the south chancel. Wearing a quilted surcoat over his chain mail, he lies in an awkward cross-legged posture, a miniature page at his feet and a horse's head oddly rising from the waves behind him: what this last symbolises is uncertain, some associating it with a famous occasion when Sir Robert's charger saved him from drowning, and others with his feudal right to claim any wreck he could touch by riding into the sea.

That wrecks and the sea have always played a dominant part in Minster's history is plain from the many fascinating tombstones in the churchyard. Near its eastern entrance, for instance, is one to a captain in the Czar's fleet and another to a naval gunner: and at its west end is the sturdy medieval gatehouse which helped protect the abbey against sea-raiders.
See **The Anglo-Saxon Church, London – St Helen's Bishopsgate, Monasteries and Religious Houses.**

MOUNT GRACE PRIORY
North Yorkshire
OS 99 SE 453982

The priory is beautifully sited at the foot of wooded hills, seven miles north-east of Northallerton and immediately east of the A19 trunk road, from which it is rather abruptly signposted: it is open all the year round. The original chapel of Our Lady of Mount Grace (SE 454982) now rebuilt and staffed by Franciscan friars, is accessible from the priory via a stiff uphill climb through the woods, but clear directions should be obtained from the priory custodian before setting out: commanding splendid views, it is more conveniently reached by a signposted footpath from Osmotherley village. Immediately east of the priory are the Cleveland Hills and the dramatic North York Moors, with Whitby beyond them on the coast: and within comparatively easy reach to the south-east are Rievaulx Abbey and St Gregory's Minster.

A community of hermits would appear to be a contradiction in terms, yet this is what in effect existed at Mount Grace Priory during the later middle ages. It is much the best preserved of the nine English monasteries of the Carthusian order, which differed very considerably from other medieval groupings of monks or nuns: for while these stressed a religious life lived in common, the Carthusians – named after their original house at La Grande Chartreuse in the Alps – lived vowed to silence in individual cells, assembling in church only for a minority of services and eating together only on major festivals. Unlike most other medieval orders, too, the Carthusians rigidly maintained their austere standards until the very eve of the Reformation – thus continuing to command the respect of influential laymen long after enthusiasm for their laxer brethren had waned, and to establish new monasteries long after those of their sister orders had slipped into decline.

It was not until 1398, indeed, that Thomas Holland, Duke of Surrey and half-brother of Richard II, founded a priory on a remote site in the Cleveland Hills, naming it after an already ancient chapel of "Our Lady of Mount Grace" in the nearby uplands: now refurbished, this chapel is still a centre of Roman Catholic pilgrimage. As the extensive ruins immediately demonstrate, the new monastery was a very large building – yet it was designed to accommodate less than twenty monks, and its centrally-placed church is small and anything but magnificent: originally it was smaller and meaner still, for its side-chapels are later additions.

These apparent paradoxes are explained by the particular needs of the Carthusian brethren, whose religious life was focused not on the church, but rather upon the individual cells surrounding the immense cloister to the north of it: each of the cells being in fact a two-storied hermit's cottage with its own walled garden. One of them has been reconstructed, and within are four rooms on the ground floor – a lobby, a living-room with a fire-place, a bedroom-cum-oratory where the monk prayed, and a study – with a large room above, apparently used as a workshop: behind the cell is the garden, with the hermit-monk's private lavatory at the end of it, overhanging a drain flushed by water from the hillside.

If these arrangements give the impression of cosy privacy and modest comfort, that impression is quickly dispelled by the extract from the Carthusian rule displayed in the reconstructed cell. Its occupant was admittedly allowed such necessities of life as a washing-up bowl, scissors, writing materials and a wood-chopper: but he was permitted none of its luxuries, wearing a hair shirt at all times and sleeping beneath a single rough sheet and a coarse sheepskin coverlet. Three days a week he fasted on bread and water, and on others his diet was largely vegetarian, neither meat nor game being even admitted

within the priory gates. Perhaps the most graphic reminder of the silent austerity of the Carthusian hermit-monk's life, however, is the stone hatch through which his sparse meals were passed: this has a dog-leg bend in it, so that the monk within might never be tempted to see or speak to the server in the courtyard outside.
See **Monasteries and Religious Houses, The Reformation.**

Set against the steep conical "mount" which both provides its name and shelters it from the worst of the Atlantic gales, the little whitewashed chapel of the Holy Cross at Mwnt is an unforgettable sight. On this mount, according to tradition, the local Welsh won a notable victory over a force of sea-raiders, celebrating by playing football with the pirates' severed heads: and its summit affords sweeping views over Cardigan Bay, the haunt of seals and porpoises. The chapel, indeed, has always been intimately connected with the sea, for here pilgrims are said to have halted to pray before embarking in the cove below for Bardsey, the holy "island of the saints" fifty miles northward across the tempestuous Bay: and here too the bodies of the pious rested before being shipped there for burial. The carved figure of a pilgrim, part of a late medieval rood screen, still remains in the chapel to commemorate these intrepid travellers. Its plain roof is likewise late medieval, but otherwise there is little to date the fabric of this low, battened-down place of worship, with its tiny bellcote: it may well have stood on its windswept headland for over a thousand years.
See **Llandanwg, Shrines and Pilgrimages.**

MWNT Dyfed
OS 145 SN 185520
Mwnt ("munt") chapel stands on a headland, some four miles west of the pretty coastal resort of Aberporth and about the same distance north of Cardigan. It can be reached either by minor roads from Aberporth or by turning off the A487 at Penparc (some two and a half miles east of Cardigan) and following minor roads to the coast. Immediately to the west of the chapel, accessible via a steep pathway, is a delightful little beach.

Nestling in a thickly wooded churchyard which descends down to Mylor Creek, this is perhaps the most delightfully positioned of all Cornish places of worship. It is dedicated to St Mylor or Melorus, one of the teeming Celtic holy men of the far west, and clearly the site has been hallowed since the earliest days of Cornish Christianity, for beside the church stands a Celtic pillar cross some seventeen feet high, the tallest of the 300 or so in the Duchy. The present sturdy building, however, is part Norman, part late medieval – as evidenced by the especially fine and delicately carved entrance doorway – and part Victorian restoration: while the pretty weatherboarded belfry dates from the seventeenth century. Within are an Elizabethan pulpit and an unusually well-preserved rood screen carved with foliage, which retains both its original colouring and its inscription to "Jesw Chrest" in the now-vanished Cornish language. Appropriately placed near the waterside in the churchyard, moreover, is the wooden tombmarker of an unfortunate ship-builder named Joseph Grapp, which records;

"His foot did slip and he did fall
Help help he cried, and that was all"

MYLOR Cornwall
OS 204 SW 820353
The church stands in the hamlet of Mylor Churchtown, which is just over a mile south-east of Mylor Bridge village and about four miles north-east of Falmouth via the A39 and minor roads through Mylor Bridge. There are many other places of interest in this outstandingly beautiful area, including the Tudor coastal fortress of Pendennis Castle (a mile south-east of Falmouth) and, across the inlet of Carrick Roads, St Mawes Castle and St Just-in-Roseland, which also has an attractive creekside church.

Here, and on the previous page, are aspects of the churchyard at Mylor – it is well worth exploring.

NEVERN Dyfed
OS 145 SN 083401

Nevern is some eight miles south-west of Cardigan and a mile and a half north-east of Newport, on the B4582 which turns north off the A487 between Newport and Eglwyswrw. It is set in beautiful but comparatively little-visited countryside, and to the south are the wild Preseli Mountains with their many prehistoric remains, most notably the spectacular burial chamber of Pentre Ifan (three miles south-east of Nevern on a minor road to Brynberian, at SN 099370). Twelve miles to the north-east, on the coast near Aberporth, is Mwnt chapel.

Tucked away in the wooded valley of the river Nyfer, the pretty village of Nevern was once a place of great importance, the principal seat of the Welsh and subsequently the Norman lords of the region between the Preseli Mountains and the sea. It was the latter who built both the ruined castle north-west of the village and the sturdy Norman tower of St Brynach's church, which is otherwise of late medieval date. Yet the origins of the church stretch much further back in time, for on its site stood what was probably one of the earliest Christian places of worship in west Wales, founded during the fifth century by St Brynach the Irishman, a forceful evangelist who is said to have talked with angels on the summit of Myndd Carningli, visible on the skyline away to the south-west. From this ancient building came Nevern's famous collection of Celtic memorial stones, including that to Maglocunus or Maelgwyn, probably the son of the prince who gave Brynach the land for his church. Now forming a window sill in the south transept, this is inscribed both in Latin and in 'Ogham' script, the primitive Irish alphabet based on nicks cut in a straight line.

Undoubtedly the most impressive of the stones, however, is the thirteen foot high "Great Cross" in the churchyard, probably the finest and best preserved of its kind in all Wales: carved all over with wonderful Celtic interlace patterns, its east and west faces also bear panels inscribed with letters which may translate "Hallelulia to the Lord". This dates from the tenth or eleventh century, by which time Nevern was apparently an important stopping place for pilgrims on their way from distant Holywell to the shrine of Wales's patron Saint David, in his cathedral twenty-five miles to the south-west. About a hundred yards west of the church (beyond a stile on the lane to Frongoch) a wayside pilgrim cross is cut into the rock, above a niche here travellers knelt to pray for a safe journey.

See **Shrines and Pilgrimages.**

90

Magnificently and unforgettably dominating the serried stalls of the city's bustling market place, St Peter Mancroft is the foremost, the biggest, and much the most splendid of Norwich's thirty-two medieval parish churches. It was raised between 1430 and 1455, as a demonstration of the civic pride of a town which was then probably the third largest in England, outstripped only by London and Bristol: and whose prosperity is reflected in its great length, the high quality stone of which it is built, and above all in its mighty and sumptuously decorated tower, 146 feet high to the tip of its delicate lead-covered spire. Broadside-on to the market square, and filling one entire side of it, St Peter's noble but essentially simple exterior displays in the Perpendicular manner almost "more glass than wall", with the eight great windows of the main body of the church topped by a continuous row of seventeen lesser windows in the oversailing clerestory above. Within, too, the uncluttered design produces a church breathtakingly open, lofty, and full of light, with no division between nave and chancel to detract from the eastward sweep of the eight towering arches. Above them, lit by the clerestory windows, is a most splendid roof also running the whole length of the church, its angel-ended hammer beams concealed by fan-vaulted coving: while at its eastern and western ends the height of the building is again emphasised by the great window above the altar – full of notable fifteenth century stained glass – and the soaring arch of the tower.

St Peter's interior furnishings likewise manifest its pride in its city and itself. First into view after the traveller has passed through the two-storeyed porch is the font with its astonishing canopy, a domed octagonal superstructure raised on four ornately carved legs: partly fifteenth century and partly Victorian reconstruction, only two more such canopies survive in England. Nearby are the illuminated manuscript rules of the Norwich bell-ringers' society, recalling the fame of St Peter's bells and their claim to have sounded "the first whole Peal that ever was Rung by any Ringers whatsoever": while among the glittering display of church plate in the north transept is a great earthenware jug, capable of holding thirty-five pints of beer for the refreshment of the ringers. All round the walls, moreover, are memorials to famous parishioners, principally merchants and Lord Mayors of Norwich; and against the aisle pillars are decorative rests for the ceremonial swords and maces borne before Lord Mayors when they attended church in state. Yet despite all this, St Peter Mancroft is not merely a museum or a place for municipal pomp: for here services are held daily, and this magnificent church continues to minister to the city centre it has watched over for more than five centuries.

One of the most interesting of all English cities, especially for lovers of things medieval, Norwich is 114 miles north-east of London via the M11 and A11: and St Peter Mancroft stands prominently at its centre, a few hundred yards from the large and splendid Norman castle. Further to the west is the magnificent cathedral, also essentially Norman: and all around (sometimes two to a street) are Norwich's thirty-two medieval parish churches, mainly dating from the fourteenth and fifteenth centuries. Many of these, however, are now redundant and generally kept locked, though some of their treasures are displayed in the fascinating St Peter Hungate Museum of Church Art on picturesque Elm Hill (open weekdays 10 a.m.–5 p.m.). St Peter Mancroft is invariably accessible during daylight hours.

Perhaps the most delightful parish church in Devon, if not in all the West Country, St Petrock's at Parracombe owes its survival to the national outcry which greeted a proposal to demolish it in 1879: a new church was instead built further down the hill, and St Petrock's remains untouched and unspoilt, a village church preserved exactly as it was in the late Georgian period. The fabric of the building – which is sited at the head of the steep "combe" that gives the village its name – is far older than that, its chancel and fortress-like tower probably dating from the thirteenth century and its simple nave and aisle from the later fifteenth. Its plain whitewashed interior, however, is fitted out for Anglican worship as it was in the centuries between the Restoration of Charles II in 1660 and the combined impact of Victorian "Anglo-Catholicism" and the Gothic Revival: which is to say for services strictly according to the Book of Common Prayer, and for preaching rather than Holy Communion. The bare chancel where the rare communion services were held – perhaps twice or three times a year – is indeed almost hidden away, not only by a medieval screen but still more effectively by a great boarded "tympanum", painted with the Commandments, the Creed, and the Lord's Prayer, all overtopped by the Royal Arms: for the Georgian Church of England never forgot that it was "the church by law established", an integral part of the state.

This forthright display of Anglican priorities shares its dominance of the main body of the church with the three-decker pulpit, whose "sounding-board" canopy bears the equally direct (and perhaps necessary) statement, "We preach not ourselves but Christ Jesus". From here the vicar delivered his weekly sermons to the congregation in the packed pews and benches below, descending to the lower deck to read the lessons and during the hymns – which were doubtless conducted by the parish clerk from the lowest of the pulpit's stages. The singing was accompanied, not by a sober organ, but by the far more varied strains of the church band or "playing quire" in the raised tiers of pews at the back of the nave, one of them cut away to make room for the bow of the bass viol.

There are plenty more such small but eloquent details in the church: the hat-pegs along the south wall; the monuments by the door, touchingly painted to look like marble; the raised pew by the chancel screen, the privileged preserve of a squire or wealthy farmer; and the dramatically simple tower interior, its single bell reached by ladders and staging. All of them contribute to the unique atmosphere of St Petrock's, a place of worship frozen in time.

See **The Prayer Book Church.**

Parracombe is on the northern edge of Exmoor, some ten miles north-east of Barnstaple and four miles south-west of the dramatically situated coastal resort of Lynton, via the A39. St Petrock's stands by the A39, or can be reached through the pretty hillside village, passing the "new church" and following signs to Churchtown: if it is locked, a list of keyholders is in the porch.

The great boarded tympanum which separates nave from chancel in St Petrock's, Parracombe.

PARTRISHOW Powys
OS 161 SO 279224

Partrishow (also spelt Patricio) is set high up in the Black Mountains some six miles north of Abergavenny, and is accessible only by narrow mountain roads which may be impassable during winter snow or in very wet weather. The simplest way to reach it is from the A465 Abergavenny–Hereford road, turning west about four miles north of Abergavenny at

92 *Llanfihangel Crucorney onto the road*

Hidden away in a hollow of the Black Mountains, the little church of St Issui at Partrishow is one of the most interesting and visually delightful places of worship in all Wales. As so often in the Celtic lands, the earliest sacred site here was a holy well, which still exists in the "dingle" of the Nant Mair stream just below the church, the way to it marked by a "pilgrim stone" incised with a cross. Nearby, according to tradition, a pious hermit named St Issui or Ishow had his lonely cell at some unknown date before the Norman Conquest:

and his martyrdom at the hands of an ungrateful traveller lent additional power and sanctity to the spring, which soon afterwards cured a wealthy pilgrim of leprosy. In thanksgiving, the pilgrim gave a hatful of gold to build a church on the adjacent hill: and there seems little doubt that parts of the present building, including its massive stone font – whose inscription, in English: "Menhir made me in the time of [Prince] Genillin", dates it to about 1050 – survive from this earliest church. The hermit himself, moreover, almost certainly lies buried beneath the ancient stone altar in the tiny chapel attached to the western end of the church: for this altar stands off-centre, demonstrating that it was too sacred to be moved when the "chapel of the grave" was altered in later medieval times.

Above the chapel altar is a grilled aperture, designed to enable a priest saying Mass in the chapel to concert his movements with colleagues conducting services in the main body of the church: which, despite its small size, has three altars of its own. Two of these stand in front of Partrishow's most famous possession, the splendid and almost perfectly preserved rood-screen and rood-loft spanning the chancel arch, which dates from about 1500 and is a masterpiece of the woodcarver's art. Once surmounted by the Rood itself – a figure of Christ crucified, flanked by the Virgin and St John – the balcony-like loft housed the lights and candles which illuminated those images on holy days. The panels of its western face are pierced with a delicate filigree, and above and below them run horizontal bands of intricately carved running ornament, the widest depicting a twisting vine attacked at either end by winged dragons – a favourite motif on Welsh border screens, of which this is the finest surviving example.

The screen divides the basically Norman nave, with its fifteenth century barrel roof, from the Elizabethan chancel: both of which have treasures of their own. On the nave west wall, for instance, is a painted figure of Death with scythe, spade and hourglass, more comic than frightening; and near the eleventh century font is an ancient "dug-out" parish chest with three locks – one each for the vicar and the two churchwardens. While in the chancel are many attractive Georgian memorial tablets, carved and tinted with bright vegetable dyes by the Brute family of masons from nearby Llanbedr.

Partrishow's fascination, moreover, overflows into its churchyard: where a medieval stone bench along the church's south wall faces a partly restored preaching cross, from which in 1188 Archbishop Baldwin of Canterbury is said to have urged support for the Third Crusade. By the churchyard gate stands a building once used to stable the parson's horse and dry his travelling clothes – a frequent necessity in the wet mountain vastnesses served by this most notable little church.

See **Holy Wells and Sacred Springs.**

towards Llanthony Priory (also well worth a visit): and then west again at Stanton, driving through Forest Coal Pit and towards Llanbedr. The signposted road to Patricio turns north just over a mile west of Forest Coal Pit.

Top, remote and beautifully situated, the church of St Issui. Above, the nave seen beyond the rood screen. Left, intricately carved winged dragons decorate the ancient screen.

The Reformation

The Reformation, the great upheaval which transformed Britain from a Catholic into a Protestant land, is a vast and complex subject, about which whole libraries of volumes have been written: here, however, the traveller must be content with a summary. When Henry VIII's reign began in 1509, there were few signs of the changes to come, and throughout the middle ages both England and Scotland had indeed been famed for the adherence to orthodox Catholic beliefs. For centuries, of course, the manifest temporal failings of the Church – its worldly clergy, its excessive wealth and power, and the increasing financial burdens it laid on worshippers – had attracted criticism (and often bitter criticism) from all classes of society. Yet whether these complaints were voiced in tavern mutterings or in the weighty Latin pronouncements of theologians, the call was always for reform, not revolution; for the Church to keep its own rules, not for the rules to change. During the early years of the fifteenth century, admittedly, the English radical movement known as the Lollards had actually dared to question Catholic dogma and to offer an alternative system of Christian belief: but after a hopelessly abortive rising they had been reduced to a hunted remnant. Nor did the more recent anti-Catholic doctrines of Martin Luther (which began filtering into Britain from Germany during the early 1520s) at first make much impression outside the universities: and King Henry VIII himself publicly condemned them in the book which won him both the Pope's approval and the title "Defender of the Faith".

At first, then, there was little spontaneous desire for sweeping religious change in Britain. The first moves in the English Reformation, rather, were imposed from above by this very Defender of the Faith, and sprang from his overwhelming need for a male heir to carry on the Tudor line. His first wife Catharine of Aragon, though she had borne him the future Queen Mary, appeared unable to produce such an heir: so Henry, voicing pious doubts about the validity of the marriage, resolved to divorce her. To do so, however, he required papal consent, which might have been obtainable had the Pope of the day not been entirely dominated by the Emperor Charles V, Catharine of Aragon's nephew. He dared not, therefore, grant the annulment, despite increasing pressure both from the king and the English clergy, whom Henry (with the aid of parliament) had assiduously bullied into complying with his demands. Thus "the King's Great Matter" dragged on until, in 1533, Henry lost patience with the negotiations and married Anne Boleyn, who soon afterwards bore him, not a boy, but the future Queen Elizabeth. Yet hopes for a son remained high, and in the following year the Act of Supremacy declared Henry VIII "Supreme Head of the Church of England", thus severing the link with Rome.

As head of the Church, Henry lost no time in remedying another of his pressing problems, his desperate lack of funds: and between 1536 and 1539 he not only plundered the major shrines of his realm, but also systematically confiscated the vast estates of all English monasteries and religious houses. This "Dissolution of the Monasteries" was resisted by a northern rising known as "the Pilgrimage of Grace", but elsewhere it proceeded smoothly enough, for monasticism had long been in decline, and in places like Wymondham the monks had been troublesome neighbours. Both there and elsewhere, indeed, monastic churches were swiftly turned over to parochial use, while the emptied monastic quarters became useful sources of building stone – unless, as at Egglestone Abbey, they were converted into mansions for the lords and gentlemen who had eagerly purchased the confiscated estates from the king. This wholesale redistribution of church lands among the laity, moreover, was to prove a vital factor in the Reformation, making the changes it had wrought virtually irreversible. For half the ruling families in England henceforth had a propertied stake in the new order, and thus a vested interest in opposing any return to Roman Catholicism.

In other ways, too, the English Reformation was beginning to pick up its own momentum by the end of Henry VIII's reign. Henry himself was no religious revolutionary. Having gained his immediate ends (and a son, Edward, by his third wife Jane Seymour) he was content that the Church should remain doctrinally much as it had been before the break with Rome: in effect a Catholic Church under new management, ruled by a king instead of a pope. Increasingly, however, his subjects were developing more radical opinions, as genuinely Protestant doctrines became more widespread among them.

One of the most important of these new ideas concerned the Mass or Eucharist, the service which re-enacts Christ's Last Supper before His Crucifixion. The Catholic Church believed (and still believes) that Christ was really present at each celebration of the Mass: that the bread and wine on the altar, though remaining much as it had been before the break with Rome: in effect a Catholic Church under new became not figuratively but actually the Body and Blood of Christ. This miracle, known as "transubstantiation", occurred at the priest's words of consecration, "This is my body", "This is my blood"; but exactly how it happened was held to be a holy mystery, not susceptible to comprehension by human reason or logic. What was certain, nevertheless, was that attendance at Mass and regular reception of the consecrated bread (the wine being reserved for clerics) were absolutely necessary to salvation. Since it was equally sure that only an ordained priest could perform the vital miracle, this doctrine of the Real Presence raised the clergy to a very special and exalted position in society: and it gave the Church absolute control not only over entry into Heaven, but also, by extension, over every aspect of man's earthly life.

By questioning and ultimately rejecting this doctrine, then, the Protestants struck at the very roots of the Church's power. That Christ had indeed instituted the Holy Communion service (as they preferred to call it) they did not doubt, and some held that He was spiritually present during its performance, though the more thoroughgoing reformers taught that it was simply a commemoration of His sufferings. But the idea that a priest could make the physical body of Christ by saying certain words (like a conjurer producing a rabbit from a hat) seemed either a downright blasphemy or a fraud to fool the weak-minded, offensive to God-given reason and (worst of all) not confirmed by the teaching of the Bible.

The importance of the Bible in forming Protestant beliefs, indeed, can scarcely be overestimated. Throughout the middle ages, the Bible had been largely inaccessible to ordinary people, for no official English translation existed, and the unofficial translation compiled by the Lollards was a proscribed work. Only those who could understand Latin – the clergy and the clerically educated – could, the Church believed, be trusted to interpret the scriptures in a correct manner: and to allow a version in everyday language into the hands of lesser folk would only harm both them and the Church itself. The English translations of the Bible which appeared during Henry VIII's reign therefore had a literally explosive effect, for they demonstrated to all that many of the Church's teachings and practices had no basis in either the Old or the New Testament. No mention was made therein, for example, of confession, or Purgatory, of papal authority, or of the many Catholic seasonal rituals, while the worship of "graven images" – as many now interpreted the statues and representations of the saints which filled medieval British churches – was frequently and specifically forbidden. All the long-resented abuses which disfigured the Church, in short, could be seen as unwarrantable (if not pagan and superstitious) accretions on the purity of early Christian biblical religion, and it was the clear duty of all good people to sweep them ruthlessly away.

While the conservative Henry lived – and burnt radical Protestants for heresy – these reforming impulses were held in check. His sickly, bookish son Edward VI, however, was a convinced Protestant, as were the

Protectors who ruled England in the boy-king's name: and under them the English Reformation moved into top gear. First, in 1547, chantry chapels and memorial Masses were prohibited by law, and three years later all images, crucifixes, and "Popish books" were ordered to be burnt or "otherways defaced and destroyed", while "idolatrous" altars were ripped out and replaced by movable communion tables. The old Latin services, moreover, were "clearly and utterly abolished, extinguished and forbidden", and instead Archbishop Cranmer produced his incomparable Book of Common Prayer, from versions of which Church of England services have been taken ever since. Many medieval English churches still bear the marks of this wave of Protestant zeal – empty image niches, wall paintings defaced or whitewashed over (at Binham Priory somewhat inefficiently), and rood screens mutilated or bereft of their crucifixes – and there was even talk of demolishing the chancels where the hated Mass had been celebrated. This was not done, but Edward's premature death in 1553 left the Church of England thoroughly Protestant in both doctrine and practice.

There were, of course, those who resented (and in the traditionalist West Country, rebelled against) these changes, and who were glad to welcome Edward's sister Mary to the throne. The daughter of the rejected Catharine of Aragon, Mary had held firmly to her Roman Catholicism through all the viscissitudes of her father's and brother's reigns, and now she was determined to restore the old faith in her realm at any price. The Reformation, therefore, was stopped dead in its tracks, and from extremist Protestantism government policy swung to bigoted Catholic reaction, reinforced by Mary's unpopular marriage to King Philip of Catholic Spain and by a formal reunion with Rome in 1554. Not content with this, the Queen determined to root out all trace of heresy from the land. In 1555 she began the notorious persecutions which sent nearly 300 Protestants (including Archbishop Cranmer) to the fire for their beliefs, and which earned her the still current epithet of "Bloody Mary". Far from achieving her ends, moreover, Mary's draconian policy damaged her cause irreparably: for henceforth Catholicism would be associated in most English minds with the fire and the torturer's rack, and with the domination of hated Spain.

When Mary's death in 1558 brought her sister Elizabeth to the throne, then, England sent up a collective sigh of relief: especially when it became clear that the new Queen would pursue neither a Catholic nor an extremist Protestant line, preferring a moderate middle way "conducive to decency and good order in worship and to peace in the state". A long-practised pragmatist, Elizabeth never revealed the exact nature of her personal religious beliefs, but her public policy was one of compromise between the traditionalist bishops and the vocal "Puritans", many of whom had gone into exile under Mary. Thus the "images" briefly set up during the previous reign were once again removed, but chancel screens were to be retained, though in place of a crucifix they were now surmounted by "some comely ornament", generally a board decoratively setting out the Lord's Prayer, the Commandments and the Creed and often including a fine representation of the royal arms. Mary's fixed Catholic altars were likewise abolished, but the moveable communion tables which replaced them were to be set altarwise at the east end of the church, placed upon a carpet, and covered with "a fair linen cloth, in as beautiful a manner as possible". What Elizabeth sought, was to adapt traditional church interiors to the Protestant worship of the book of Common Prayer, thus creating the Prayer Book Church.

The Elizabethan settlement likewise perpetuated, albeit in much modified form, some aspects of the organisation and ritual of the pre-Reformation Church. The system of church government by archbishops and bishops, for example, was continued virtually unaltered, despite the protests of those who regarded it as unscriptural. Unlike Catholic priests, however, Anglican ministers were permitted "to marry at their own discretion, as they shall judge the same to serve better to godliness". The Catholic doctrine of purgatory, along with prayers for the dead and the veneration of saints' images and holy relics, was rejected as "a fond thing vainly invented": but the ceremonies of baptism, confirmation, marriage, the ordination of ministers and the last rites for the dying were continued. So too, shorn of their "Popish superstition", were such picturesque practices as "beating the bounds" of the parish. This had originally been intended to bless and drive evil spirits from the crops, but now became an annual procession of vicar and people round the parish borderline, designed to ensure that boudary markers were maintained and remembered.

Perhaps most important of all, however, was the Elizabethan clarification of the Anglican doctrine concerning Holy Communion, which firmly stated that the bread and wine distributed during the service represented the Body and Blood of Christ only 'after an heavenly and spiritual manner": the Catholic dogma of transubstantiation being dismissed as "repugnant to the plain words of Scripture". This essentially Protestant belief, along with the other tenents of the Elizabethan Church, was codified in the famous "Thirty-nine Articles", to this day the official basis of the Anglican faith. Still worth reading for their fine language, these Articles reveal a church which blended the old with the new, rejecting both Catholicism and Puritanism in favour of a moderate Protestantism that remains – despite the assaults of Victorian Anglo-Catholics and their modern suc-

cessors – the hallmark and glory of the Church of England.

The Elizabethan compromise suited most Englishmen admirably, and the tensions within it were submerged throughout her long reign by their personal loyalty to the Queen and the national unity engendered by the threat from Catholic Spain. After her death in 1603, however, the disagreements between moderate and radical Protestants – between bishops and Puritans – became more and more acute, culminating in the Civil Wars of 1642–51, the temporary Puritan triumph which followed, and the restoration of the Anglican Church in 1662. That England would adhere to Protestantism of some kind, however, was never really in doubt after Mary's reign. James II's attempt to reintroduce Catholicism, indeed, swiftly brought about his deposition in 1688: and two years later the Presbyterian kirk was confirmed as the established national church of Scotland, thus likewise bringing the Scottish reformation to a triumphant close.

The Reformation in the independent kingdom of Scotland, however, had followed a quite different and rather more violent course. Far from being initiated by the crown, as in England, it had begun as a groundswell of popular protest against a government-backed Catholic church: and had soon become involved in international politics, with Protestant England supporting the reformers and Catholic France aiding the regent who ruled in the name of the young Mary Queen of Scots. An English army, indeed, guaranteed the temporary victory of the Scots Protestants in 1560: but the faith these adhered to was far removed from the English model of Protestantism. It was, rather, based on the more uncompromisingly radical doctrines of Calvin, as canvassed by the fiery preacher John Knox, and would have no truck with bishops or other remnants of the old order. Instead, its organisation was based on a system of "presbyteries", individual congregations electing their own ministers, elders and deacons: these were co-ordinated by a General Assembly of the Kirk, which (in the absence of a Protestant monarch) increasingly came to see itself as the true government of Scotland.

The Presbyterians likewise found little use for the "Popish" medieval churches of Scotland, many of which (like Elgin Cathedral) were severely damaged during the long drawn out religious upheavals of the 1560s and 70s. After a lull under James VI, moreover, religious strife broke out again when Charles I unsuccessfully attempted to replace Presbyterianism with a Protestant Church along English lines, and yet again when Charles II and James II made the same attempt. Yet the Presbyterian kirk was too firmly rooted among the people of Scotland ever to be defeated by kings, and in 1690 its ascendancy was finally recognised.
See **The Prayer Book Church, The Gothic Revival.**

The huge and stately church of St Patrick well deserves its title of "the Queen of Holderness": for not only does its towering 190 foot spire – rising from a delicate coronet of pinnacles – dominate the level Holderness countryside for miles around, but it is also one of the most beautiful of all English parish churches. Largely the product of the earlier fourteenth century – and therefore essentially Decorated in style – the great cruciform church has a strikingly spacious and light-filled interior, perhaps best appreciated from a viewpoint beneath the central tower, midway between the two transepts which are the earliest parts of the building. Both these transepts have east and west aisles (a feature more characteristic of cathedrals than of parish churches) and each once housed three side-chapels. From the vault of the south transept's restored Lady Chapel depends a hollow boss (perhaps originally a receptacle for holy relics) which is delightfully carved with figures of the Virgin and other saints: while a glance upwards to the transept's main arch reveals by contrast a splendidly hairy devil, who supports the pre-cipitous stairway to the bellringing chamber.

Patrington, indeed, is justly famous for the sculpture lavished everywhere on its column capitals, roof bosses and corbel stops, particularly attractive being the heads of humans, animals and fantastic creatures (nearly two hundred in all) in the nave. Ornately carved, too, are the sedilia (or priests' seats) and piscina (the sink where sacred vessels are washed) on the south side of the chancel, which is entered through a restored fifteenth century screen. The rather gaudy modern reredos, behind the high altar and below the great Perpendicular east window, may not however be to everyone's taste: and for many the highlight of the chancel is the early fourteenth century "Easter Sepulchre" on the north wall. Here, before the Reformation, the consecrated communion wafer was "entombed" from Good Friday until Easter Sunday, to symbolise Christ's death and resurrection: and the Sepulchre therefore depicts Christ rising from His coffin, while beneath slumber three tomb-guarding Roman soldiers in the guise of medieval knights.

See **The Reformation.**

PATRINGTON Humberside
OS 113 TA 315225
The small town of Patrington is about fourteen miles south-east of Hull (which itself has the largest of all medieval parish churches, Holy Trinity) via the A1033: the Hull-Patrington road passes through Hedon, which also has a fine medieval church with a splendid tower. Eight miles east of Patrington is Spurn Point nature reserve, jutting into the Humber Estuary.

PICKERING North Yorkshire
OS 100 SE 799840
The small market town of Pickering stands on the southern edge of the picturesque North York Moors, some thirty miles north-east of York via the A169, and about twenty miles south of Whitby. The church is clearly visible in the town centre, and there is much else to see in Pickering; including the medieval castle, the Beck Isle museum of Yorkshire life, and a popular steam railway which offers trips across the moors. To the west, off the A170 towards Helmsley, is St Gregory's Minster, with Helmsley Castle and Rievaulx Abbey further on.

A medieval representation of St George slaying the dragon, and on the following page, the martyrdom of St Edmund.

Set in a churchyard entirely surrounded by old houses, and accessible only by steps and alleyways, Pickering's parish church of St Peter and St Paul is famous for its stunning medieval wall paintings – perhaps the most complete and certainly the clearest series in Britain, though their clarity admittedly owes much to heavy restoration after their discovery under whitewash in 1851. Ranged along both sides of the nave, and all

97

painted in about 1490 (rather than *c.*1450 as is usually stated) this vivid medieval picture-book begins at the west end of the north side with a fine St George and the Dragon, continuing eastwards with a giant St Christopher – placed (as at Hailes) opposite the door, where travellers could easily see him and thus supposedly guarantee themselves against sudden death. On his left (and also of interest to wayfarers) is a miniature hermit shining a lantern to guide the saint across the snake-infested stream: and to his right is a strip-cartoon style representation of St John the Baptist denouncing Salome at Herod's feast, and his subsequent beheading at her behest; with the Coronation of a rather horse-faced Virgin Mary in the panel above. Next, above the easternmost northern arch, comes Pickering's most memorable painting, the martyrdom of St Edmund of East Anglia, who is shown bound to a tree and shot full of arrows by life-sized archers wearing a variety of curious headgear. Above, four knights in elaborate armour prepare to murder St Thomas of Canterbury as he kneels at an altar.

Crossing now to the south side of the nave, the paintings resume at the east end with eleven incidents from the legendary life of St Catherine – another "strip-cartoon", which among other things shows her shattering the "Catherine Wheels" intended to crush her: and continue westward with the Seven Christian Works of Mercy, from the giving of food and drink to staff-bearing travellers to the burial of the dead – scenes worth comparing with those at All Saints, North Street, York. These merciful acts (no doubt by deliberate design) merge directly into seven scenes from the Passion and Crucifixion of Christ: above which are panels of the death and the burial of the Virgin; while below, between the arches, Christ descends into a terrifying hell-mouth to free the souls there – who are naked but for "decency plates". Finally, by the westernmost south arch, Christ rises from His tomb, thus triumphantly completing a series which affords the traveller a uniquely immediate insight into the workings of late medieval popular religion.

See **Hailes, York.**

The jagged granite outcrop of Roche Rock rises like a broken tooth amid a weird lunar landscape, with the dead-white cones of china clay dumps all around: and it is scarcely surprising that many legends cluster about the ruined chapel that clings precariously to its summit. Some say, for instance, that here once dwelt a leper priest, shunned by all save his faithful daughter – probably a version of a tale about St Roche, the patron of plague-sufferers: while others tell how the tortured spirit of wicked Jan Tregeagle sought refuge here in vain from the hell-hounds that pursued him, and which can still be heard baying for his soul on stormy nights. Such traditions may well indicate that the Rock was originally a place of pagan worship, later taken over by a Cornish hermit-saint: and certainly its chapel is dedicated to St Michael the Arch-

Below left, the extraordinary spectacle of the chapel on Roche Rock.

angel, who is the leader of the Heavenly Host against the powers of darkness as well as the guardian of high places. Built in 1409, the chapel is an amazing feat of engineering: seeming almost to grow out of the Rock, it is constructed from great granite blocks laboriously hauled up the sheer face of the outcrop and mortared directly onto its surface, so that the Rock itself forms the fourth wall of the lower storey. This was the living quarters of the chapel's resident hermit priest, while the much-ruined storey above was the chapel proper, once the goal of many pilgrimages.

Roche village's parish church of St Gonardus (perhaps the name of the Rock's original hermit) is also worth a visit. For though the main body of the building dates from the nineteenth century, its tall granite tower is medieval, and it contains a splendid Norman chalice-font of typically Cornish type, fantastically carved with moustachioed angels and writhing serpents. In its churchyard is a still more ancient Celtic "wheelhead" cross, which perhaps marked the first place of worship on the site.

ROCHE Cornwall
OS 200 SW 991596
Roche village is five miles north-west of St Austell, and six miles south-west of Bodmin via the A30 and the B3274. St Gonardus's parish church (SW 988598) stands in the village, and opposite is a minor road leading to Bugle: the Rock and chapel are immediately south of this road. Four miles to the north-west of Roche (via the B3274, a minor road towards St Columb Major, and a footpath) is the impressive Iron Age hillfort of Castle-an-Dinas (SW 945624).

ROSLIN Lothian
OS 66 NT 275631
Roslin is six miles south of Edinburgh, via the A701 and the B7006: the chapel (still used for episcopalian worship) is reached via a minor road turning off the B7006 in the village, and like the adjacent medieval and sixteenth century castle (sometimes open to the public) enjoys fine views over the valley of the North Esk.

The outside of the chapel is almost as ornate as its interior.

St Matthew's Chapel at Roslin is by far the most richly decorated medieval place of worship in Scotland, a country whose pre-Reformation churches were generally distinguished by their plainness: and by any standards the lavishness of the carving which

encrusts it both within and without is amazing – so much so, indeed, that Spanish or other foreign influence has been suggested, but is both unproven and unlikely. Founded in about 1450 by William Sinclair, Earl of Orkney and owner of the adjacent castle, it was intended to be the eastern arm of a much larger cruciform church. In the event no more was built, and what is now to be seen is a high clerestoried choir, with lower aisles on either side and an ambulatory (or processional way) passing round the east end and opening into three little chapels there.

The exterior pinnacles and windows are all sumptuously sculptured enough: but within the decoration borders on excess, covering almost every available surface; even the pillars are fluted, while the main arches are surmounted not merely by one but by three intricately carved bands of ornament. The aisles, moreover, are downright fantastic, with multiple-vaulted roofs resting on lintels thickly coated with small-scale sculpture, those in the south aisle being particularly notable. There the easternmost lintel expresses (in Latin) the opinion that "Wine is strong; kings are stronger; women are stronger yet; but truth conquers all": while the next to the west depicts in minute detail the Seven Deadly Sins and the Seven Acts of Mercy. At the eastern end of this aisle stands the most famous and elaborate of all Roslin's decorative features, the so-called "Prentice Pillar". This virtuoso tour-de-force of stonecarving, wreathed with entwining tendrils of foliage, derives its name from the oft-repeated but completely unfounded tale that it was sculpted by a brilliant apprentice in the absence of his master, who returned and killed the boy in a fit of jealous rage. Like the ornament of the rest of the chapel, however, it is better seen as an almost freakish expression of what could be achieved by imaginative medieval masons, working for a master who was perhaps a little too determined to impress.

Complex vaulting encrusted with decoration.

RUDSTON Humberside
OS 101 TA 097677
Rudston is six miles west of Bridlington and some thirty miles east of York, via the A166 and the B1251; the latter being a picturesque route over the high Wolds, passing through the attractive estate village of Sledmere with its Georgian and Edwardian stately home. Rudston's All Saints church has a fine Norman font, and in its churchyard is also the grave of the novelist Winifred Holtby. There is much to see in the surrounding area, including the impressive prehistoric burial mound called Willy Howe (three and a half miles to the north-west, between Burton Fleming and Wold Newton at TA 063724): while a few miles to the north-east are the dramatic chalk cliffs at Flamborough and Bempton, a sanctuary for nesting seabirds.

High on the windswept chalk Wolds of East Yorkshire, Rudston takes its name from the "rood-stone" or "stone with a cross on it" – the great monolith in its hilltop churchyard. The largest standing stone in Britain, this grit-stone pillar is over twenty-five feet high and six feet wide: and many stories are still told about it, some saying that it was an arrow shot by the Devil at the church and others calling it "the worshipping stone" or "the grandmother of the church". Such tales reveal something of the truth, for the monolith is indeed far older than the church, a much restored Norman and medieval building whose predecessor was deliberately placed here in order to counteract the power of the pagan stone: which had perhaps already been Christianized by the addition of a (now vanished) crucifix, whence its title.

Like most such standing stones, the monolith is virtually impossible to date pre-

cisely. Yet it is clear from the very large number of burial mounds and other prehistoric remains hereabouts that Rudston was a place of considerable religious significance in both the New Stone Age and the Bronze Age: while the great Arkam Dyke (clearly visible as a belt of trees stretching away to the north-east of the village) is thought to date from the later Iron Age. The stone was probably erected during the first or second of these periods, and there must have been some special reason for dragging it at least eleven miles from the nearest outcrop of similar grit-stone material. Perhaps, indeed, the monolith was the focus of the whole prehistoric sacred complex: and the determined efforts made to neutralise it surely prove that it remained powerful and potentially dangerous well into the Christian era.
See **Knowlton, Prehistoric Religion.**

RUTHWELL Dumfries and Galloway
OS 85 NY 101683
Ruthwell is nine miles south-east of Dumfries and some fifteen miles west of the point where the A74 crosses the Anglo-Scottish border at Gretna Green. The village is just south of the
B724 back road from Dumfries to

"It is the custom of the Saxon race, that on many estates of nobles and good men they are wont to have, not a church, but the standard of the Holy Cross dedicated to our Lord and reverenced with great honour, lifted up on high". Thus wrote the eighth century St Willibald, referring to the sculptured "high crosses" which are unique to Britain, and of

which the Ruthwell Cross is the earliest and perhaps the finest example. Rescued from neglect as a garden ornament and now re-erected within a typical Scots Presbyterian kirk, the fifteen foot high red sandstone pillar cross was probably first set up in about 680, at a time when the Anglo-Saxon kingdom of Northumbria controlled this part of southern

Scotland. Originally it doubtless stood alone in the open air, a sculptured gallery of Christian truths as well as a focus for daily prayer and the preaching of visiting missionaries: and the carved scenes on its two widest faces are indeed of quite astoundingly high quality, contrasting with the rather crude nineteenth century work on the "restored" cross-arms.

Eight of the ten shaft panels are devoted to the life of Christ, the largest panels on each broad face showing Christ Himself in Glory: on the southern side His feet are being washed by an ungainly and rather Epsteinish Mary Magdalen, who holds a lock of her hair in a massive hand; while on the opposite face the principal panel of the whole cross shows Him trampling two bears, thus perhaps symbolizing His triumph over chaos and evil. Here, significantly, Christ is not depicted with the conventional beard, but with the drooping moustache which was the hallmark of the Saxon warrior-hero. The reasons why such a hero should tamely submit to shameful execution cannot have been easy to explain to the warlike inhabitants of seventh-century Northumbria, and perhaps for this reason the Crucifixion scene is relegated to the lowest panel on the south face: while an inscription in Anglo-Saxon runes drives home the voluntary and heroic aspects of Christ's death with an extract from the contemporary poem called "the Dream of the Rood".

"The young hero (that was God almighty) strong and resolute, mounted the high cross, Brave in the sight of many, when He would redeem Mankind".

See **Aberlemno, The Anglo-Saxon Church.**

Annan via Clarencefield, and the church wherein the cross stands is well signposted; if it is locked, the key can be obtained at a nearby (labelled) cottage. A mile north-west of Ruthwell via Clarencefield, is Comlongon Castle: and five miles west (via the B725) is the magnificent red sandstone castle of Caerlaverock.

The south face of the Saxon cross within the body of the church, which is shown below.

Standing astride Roman Watling Street, a day's ride north-west of London, St Albans has always been a popular stopping-place for travellers: and from at least the eighth century onwards it also attracted pilgrims to the famous shrine of St Alban, the earliest known British Christian martyr. A citizen of the nearby Roman town of Verulamium,

St Alban gave shelter to a Christian priest fleeing from persecution, and having been converted by him was martyred in his stead, probably in A.D. 209. Many wonders are said to have accompanied his death on a low hill outside Verulamium, and the church built there (itself renowned for miraculous cures) developed by the Norman Conquest into a

ST ALBANS Hertfordshire
OS 166 TL 145071
The small and attractive city of St Albans is some twenty miles north-west of central London, via either the A1 and A6 or the M1 motorway (exits 6 or 7). The cathedral stands prominently to the south-east of the city centre, with the great gate of the

abbey immediately adjacent and the Fighting Cocks (said to be the oldest pub in England) near at hand: and about a mile further west (on the A414) are the extensive remains of Roman Verulamium, also well worth a visit.

great Benedictine abbey, officially recognised in the twelfth century as the most important in England.

The traveller who today retraces the steps of medieval pilgrims to the abbey church (which was raised to cathedral status only in 1877) will find it substantially as it was in the fifteenth century – with the important exception of the devastating Victorian "restorations" perpetrated by the odious Lord Grimthorpe. His, for example, are the west front and porches through which the church is entered, and where the millionaire architect is portrayed in the unlikely guise of St Matthew, flanked by a disgusted-looking lion of St Mark. Beyond is the immensely long nave, with no less than thirteen sets of great arches: the westernmost four on the north side and ten on the south being pointed Gothic, and representing either the extension of the church between 1195 and 1235 (which made the nave the lengthiest in Europe) or a slightly later rebuilding. These contrast sharply with the massive Norman pillars and round arches further east, the work of Abbot Paul of Caen who began the present building in 1077, and give the nave an unbalanced appearance characteristic of St Albans – whose monks rarely succeeded in completing the grandiose architectural projects they initiated. Yet to compensate both for this and for the severe plainness of the Norman work (which is constructed in Roman brick from the ruins of Verulamium and thus could not easily be carved) much fine thirteenth century wall painting survives here. The arches are striped and patterned in contrasting colours, and the north aisle pillars are painted on their west faces with Crucifixions and images of the Virgin Mary, intended as backdrops or "reredoses" for the altars which once stood against them.

To the eastward is the most impressive feature of the whole church, the soaring and tremendously powerful arches supporting the central crossing tower: which is the only major early Norman tower still surviving in Britain, perhaps due to the strength of the Roman bricks from which it is built throughout. Flanking it are the transepts, likewise substantially Norman but much altered by Lord Grimthorpe, who installed the ugly round "banker's window" in the north transept: and then comes the most sacred part of the building, the presbytery which housed the very

reason for its existence – the shrine of St Alban.

Rebuilt in the later thirteenth century, when the "protomartyr's" popularity with pilgrims was at its height, the presbytery also contains the rich tomb-chapels of the abbots and great men who (as at Canterbury and Ely) sought to be buried as close as possible to the shrine. Immediately south of it (and richest of all) is that of Duke Humphrey of Gloucester, Henry VI's powerful and turbulent uncle, which takes the form of an ornate two-tiered canopy carved all over with his arms and badges: the tomb intended to stand beneath it, however, was never built, doubtless because of the suddenness of the Duke's downfall and murder in 1447. East of this is the tomb-chapel of Abbot Whethampstead, carved with his wheat-head device: while opposite in the north aisle is the elaborate double-decker chantry of Abbot Ramryge (d.1521), its delicately traceried Perpendicular screen enlivened by visual puns on his name, crozier-bearing rams with "ryge" engraved on their collars. Near it stands the base of a shrine to the abbey's second saint, the priest whom St Alban protected and who was later known as "Amphibalus" – a name which probably arose from confusion with the Latin word for a cloak.

The focus of all this splendour, the shrine of St Alban himself, was destroyed at the Reformation: but its fourteenth century Purbeck marble pedestal, re-assembled from some two thousand broken fragments, now stands once again in the centre of the presbytery. Over eight feet high, and sumptuously sculptured, it depicts at its east end the scourging of the saint and at its west his beheading. On it rested the golden chest containing the martyr's bones, surrounded by the lavish gifts of royal and aristocratic pilgrims, including a silver-gilt image of Edward I and a jewelled necklace offered by Richard II. So fabulously rich was the shrine, indeed, that it had to be guarded night and day by relays of monks, posted in the two-storey timber "watching loft" which still overlooks it – a unique survival from the great days of pilgrimages, and a testimony to the reverence once inspired by England's senior saint.

See **Canterbury, Ely, The First Christian Missionaries, Monasteries and Religious Houses, Shrines and Pilgrimages.**

ST ANDREWS Fife
OS 59 NO 513168
The historic city of St Andrews is on the east coast of Scotland, some fifty-six miles north-east of Edinburgh via the A90, the Forth road bridge, the M90 and the A91. The cathedral is on the east side of the city, while the castle occupies a commanding position on the clifftop to its north-west.

102

St Andrews, long the ecclesiastical capital of Scotland, derives its name from the apostle whose relics were traditionally brought here from Greece by a monk named St Regulus or St Rule. Whether this event occurred in the fourth or the eighth century (or indeed whether it actually occurred at all) is uncertain: but by the latter date a settlement of the Celtic monks called Culdees ("servants of God") had been established here, and in 908 St Andrews became a bishopric, taking over

from Abernethy the spiritual leadership of the Scottish Church. The remains of a later Culdee church, St Mary's on the Rock, still survive on the clifftop to the east of the cathedral precinct wall. From the later eleventh century, however, the ancient Celtic style of monasticism came under increasing pressure from the Anglo-Norman and Romanising forms of ecclesiastical organisation introduced into Scotland in 1070 by St Margaret, the English wife of King

Malcolm Canmore: and it was most likely under her influence that the extraordinary little church of St Rule was built somewhat further inland, probably as a shrine for the apostles's relics. Its slender square tower tapers to an amazing height of 108 feet, and to this is attached a lofty narrow choir, which once had a steeply pointed roof: both are clearly in the tradition of the latest Anglo-Saxon churches of northern England.

St Rule's tower now dominates the whole site, but throughout the later middle ages it will itself have been dwarfed by the great cathedral immediately to the north-west. Also the church of an Augustinian priory (which at first used St Rule's, considerably adapted for the purpose) the new cathedral was begun in about 1160, and was built on a vast scale: at 355 feet long, indeed, it was much the largest in Scotland, and in Britain as a whole was only exceeded in length by Norwich. Comparatively little of this immense church, however, now survives; though its outline is marked out in the turf, and a good idea of its size can be gained from the distance between its two principal upstanding fragments, the west and east fronts. The former, dating from about 1280, retains one of its pinnacled turrets: while the earlier and much more complete east end (probably the first part of the cathedral to be built in 1160) preserves two such features, flanking a row of three Norman windows at the lowest level.

Originally it had nine of these in three tiers, but the two upper rows were replaced by the present much larger central window, inserted about half a century before St Andrews finally achieved promotion to an archbishopric in 1472.

To the south of the cathedral are considerable remains of the associated monastic buildings, set in a precinct which covered thirty acres, and is still surrounded by its towered and fortified wall, almost a mile long. This serves as a reminder that St Andrews was not only Scotland's premier cathedral, but also a place of great political importance. As such it was much embroiled in the troubles of the Reformation: within it, for instance, the Protestant reformer George Wishart was condemned to death by Cardinal Beaton, who watched his burning from the walls of the nearby castle. Two months later Beaton's own salted corpse hung from the same walls, after his assassination by Protestant rebels: and in 1559 the rebel leader John Knox preached his "Cleansing the Temple" sermons in the cathedral on four consecutive days, resulting in the destruction of its "Popish" images and furnishings. The final ruin of the great church, however, was encompassed not by Presbyterian zeal but by neglect and the elements, combined with its use as a handy source of building stone by the canny citizens of St Andrews.

See **Abernethy, The Reformation.**

Top, the nave of St Andrew's Cathedral is 355 feet in length. Above, the tower of St Rule's Church.

The Prayer Book Church

A Prayer Book Church is one that has been either built or adapted for worship according to the Book of Common Prayer, which is to say for Church of England services as they existed between 1560 and about 1850: and which has had the good fortune to escape "restoration" during the Victorian Gothic Revival. Such churches are comparatively few – there are perhaps two hundred of them – and they are nearly always to be found in out of the way places, but to visit them almost invariably brings surprise and delight. The surprise generally strikes as soon as the traveller enters the building, and springs from the marked contrast between the interior of a Prayer Book Church and that of a conventionally Victorianised place of worship: while the delight creeps up more slowly, arising from a close inspection of their sometimes haphazard-seeming but always charming furnishings, and above all from the timeless atmosphere that these churches so often possess. For in these unrestored places of worship the traveller can almost feel the presence of long-departed congregations, and understand their religious life with a clarity which no tidied-up church can convey, however ancient its fabric or fascinating its architecture.

Prayer Book Churches are of two basic types, namely medieval buildings adapted for Protestant services after the Reformation and later churches purpose-built for Anglican worship between the sixteenth and early nineteenth centuries. The first are more revealing, for they demonstrate how the concept of the Prayer Book Church arose. When Protestantism became firmly established in England at the beginning of Queen Elizabeth I's reign, the Church authorities were faced with the problem of how to convert thousands of medieval parish churches for the new form or worship. This was very different from the old Catholic ritual, which had centred on the celebration of Mass by a priest in the chancel, while the congregation stood or knelt in the nave, separated from the ceremony both by a decorated screen and by the convention that they should only set foot in the chancel on special occasions. The people were, indeed, simply spectators at a "holy mystery", and withal uncomprehending spectators, even if they could hear the words of the distant priest: for (apart from the sermon, if there was one) all services were invariably conducted in Latin.

The new order altered all this completely, laying down that; "It is a thing plainly repugnant to the Word of God, and the custom of the Primitive Church, to have Publick Prayer in the Church, or to minister the Sacraments in a tongue not understanded of the people". The people, moreover, were henceforth

expected not merely to understand the service, but actively to participate in it: a principle inherent in the title of the Book of Common Prayer, in other words prayer said communally by the minister and congregation. The standard Anglican service, indeed, now took the form of Common Prayer interspersed with readings from the Bible and concluded by a sermon, the last being regarded as the most important element: while Holy Communion services, the Protestant successors of the Catholic Mass, became increasingly infrequent.

These changes in practice necessitated a radical rearrangement of existing church interiors, which had been designed for the old forms of service. The first requirement was to find enough room for clergy and people to worship together, instead of separately as heretofore: and to this end services were henceforth held in the larger nave, instead of in the often cramped chancel. It was also necessary for everyone to be able to see and hear the minister, so that the pulpit from which he preached had to be both prominent and centrally placed. The pulpit, indeed, is the real focus of most surviving Prayer Book Churches, many of which possess exceedingly fine examples. Towering above the surrounding pews, their height is often increased by the provision of a lofty canopy, also called a "sounding board" because one of its purposes was to trap the parson's voice and thus help to project it towards the congregation. Nearly always made of wood, most such pulpits are finely panelled, and some are either elaborately carved (as at London's St Mary Abchurch) or richly inlaid (as at Gayhurst), while others (as at Shobdon) retain their sumptuous velvet hangings, all features designed to emphasise the importance of the Word of God being preached therefrom.

Some pulpits stand alone, in which case there may be a separate reading desk (or, as at Leighton Bromswold, a second pulpit) from which the parson would conduct the non-preaching elements of the service. During the seventeenth and eighteenth centuries, however, preaching pulpit and reading desk were often combined into a "two-decker" pulpit (as at Brougham), or more commonly into a three-tiered structure – such as survives at Parracombe, one of the finest of all adapted Prayer Book Churches. In this case the parson would read and conduct the prayers from the middle deck, mounting into the upper tier only for the sermon: while in the lowest deck sat the parish clerk, who gave out the notices and where necessary led the congregation in their "responses", the people's parts of the service.

Whatever their form, the pulpits of Prayer Book

Churches were frequently occupied by clergymen of formidable stamina, who thought nothing of delivering an hour long sermon and were quite capable of preaching for three hours on end. The congregation were therefore in urgent need of somewhere to sit, a facility comparatively rare in pre-Reformation churches outside East Anglia and the West Country, where finely carved benches had sometimes been introduced during the later middle ages. Where such medieval benches existed (as at Hailes) they were continued in service, and elsewhere new ones of similar "open" type were provided. But the favourite form of seating in the Prayer Book Church (and indeed one of its most distinctive and endearing features) is the high-sided and enclosed "box pew", literally a topless box with its own door and seating round three or even four sides. Such pews, crowding the interiors of churches like Whitby, were the private domains of the families that owned them, and varied in size, grandeur and position according to the family's wealth and social status. The pews of the squire and other leading men in the parish would generally be placed closest to the pulpit, and sometimes equipped (as at Shobdon) with a fireplace, wherein fire-irons could be rattled if the squire considered the sermon had gone on too long. As at Brougham and (most magnificently) at Rycote Chapel, squire's pews were sometimes both distinguished and made more private – perhaps for quiet repose – by being equipped with a canopy.

The lesser breeds who had no pews of their own, meanwhile, might be seated either on rough benches at the back of the church, or in galleries round its walls: though not all galleries were down-market, as witness the magnificent squire's gallery at Whitby. In many Prayer Book Churches, too, a special pew or gallery would be provided for the "church band" (or "playing quire") which, until organs became widespread in the later nineteenth century, provided the only accompaniment for hymns and psalm-singing: its heterogenous collection of instruments generally included a "serpent", a trumpet or cornet, and nearly always a bass viol – to accomodate whose bow a piece was cut out of the Parracombe musicians' pew. Another special pew, used only by a family whose baby was being christened was sometimes positioned by the font: which was usually placed near the entrance to the church.

While all this was going on in the nave, what was happening in the chancel, the side of the all-important Mass altar in pre-Reformation days? The altar itself, in the sense of a fixed stone structure against the chancel east wall, was held in deep suspicion by the early Church of England, who ordered its replacement by a simple and strictly movable wooden table

for use in Holy Communion services. Just where this table should be positioned, however, was the cause of much controversy. Queen Elizabeth decreed that it should be placed against the east wall and Archbishop Laud, in Charles I's time, caused riots by ordering it to be railed off, supposedly to prevent dogs defiling it. Both the arrangements were regarded by radical Protestants as smacking far too much of "Popish" altars, and Hailes (uniquely) still preserves their preferred alternative, a communion table set lengthways in the middle of the chancel, with pews for communicants round three sides of it. Generally, however, Prayer Book Churches have conventionally positioned communion tables, as opposed to "restored" Gothic Revival altars: and often their free standing nature is emphasised by placing them well away from the east wall, at Branscombe with rails round all four sides.

There, too, the chancel is shut off from the rest of the church by a screen with doors, which would originally have been kept locked. For in the heyday of the Prayer Book Church the chancel was used only for Holy Communion services, and these were comparatively rare, often being held only at Easter, Whitsun, Christmas and other major festivals, and in places more infrequently yet. This, therefore, is one of the major differences between Prayer Book and restored churches, where the chancel has once again become the focus for worship as the site of weekly or even daily Communions. In the older churches, by contrast, it often has a bare and somewhat disused air, and sometimes appears to have very little to do with the rest of the building: an impression which is particularly strong at Parracombe, where the chancel is concealed behind a great boarded screen, or at Whitby, where it is partly closed off by the Cholmley Gallery.

Prayer Book Churches which were built as such, therefore were rarely equipped with a pronounced chancel, often simply placing their communion tables in a slight projection at the east end. Otherwise they followed the layout made necessary by the Book of Common Prayer, whether its architectural setting was restrained Georgian (as at Gayhurst), extravagantly neo-Classical (as at Mereworth), or toy "Gothick", like Shobdon. Purpose-built or adapted, however, churches of the Prayer Book type attracted the scorn and in most cases the destructive "restorations" of the Victorian Gothic Revivalists. We are lucky that a precious remnant has escaped their attentions, to remind the traveller so graphically of an important and notable period in English church history.

See **The Medieval Parish Church,
The Reformation, The Gothic Revival.**

ST GREGORY'S MINSTER
Kirkdale, North Yorkshire
OS 100 SE 677858

*The minster is about twenty-two miles
north of York and about four miles
north-east of Helmsley, with its fine
castle and Rievaulx Abbey nearby: it is
clearly signposted from the A170
Helmsley–Pickering road. It is worth
visiting for its setting alone, and a
short walk from the church takes the
visitor onto the North York Moors.*

*The west end of the nave and its tall,
narrow doorway.*

The word "minster" has come to mean a
large church (or even a cathedral like York
Minster) rather than a tiny building like
St Gregory's Minster in Kirkdale – the picturesque "church valley" cutting into the
North Yorkshire Moors. In the Anglo-Saxon
times when St Gregory's was built, however,
a minster was simply a pioneering missionary
centre, such as was apparently first established here in about 664. Despite its remote
setting, this first minster probably fell victim
to the Vikings who ravaged Yorkshire in the
ninth century: and what happened thereafter
is recorded on the famous and unique
sundial set above the church door. "Orm
Gamal's son" (reads the inscription, in an
Anglo-Saxon not so far removed from this
translation) "bought St Gregorius's Minster
when it was all broken and fallen and he let
it be made anew then from the ground up
for Christ and St Gregory, in the days of
Edward the King and Tosti the Earl".

Orm's church, then, was built during

Edward the Confessor's reign, and during the
decade between 1055 and 1065 when Tostig
Godwinson – allegedly the murderer of
Gamal, Orm's father – ruled Northumbria.
Belonging therefore to the period immediately before the Norman Conquest, the core
of Orm's minster still stands as the nave of
the present church, and so does its tall, narrow west door – visible now only from within,
for the little nineteenth century turret masks
its exterior. The existing north aisle is also an
addition, built in about 1200; and so is the
chancel, largely reconstructed in 1881.
Within this most delightfully sited of
churches, however, is a relic from the earliest
minster – a seventh century tomb slab with
a cross, believed to commemorate Ethelwald,
son of St Oswald and King of Northumbria:
a second slab nearby, with a fine interlace pattern, is held to commemorate St Cedd the
bishop, but more probably belongs to Orm's
time.

See **The Anglo-Saxon Church.**

Rearing dramatically above the waters of Mounts Bay, and cut off by the sea at high tide, the great tower-crowned rock of St Michael's Mount must surely rank amongst the most romantic sights in Britain. The beginnings of its long history as a place of worship are shrouded in obscurity and legends of giants, tin-trading Phoenicians, and wandering Celtic saints: while an ancient tradition relates that Michael the Archangel – that haunter and patron of high places – appeared here to Cornish fishermen in 495. Certainly there was some kind of Celtic Christian sanctuary on the rock, as evidenced by the curious ninth century "Mount Cross" on the slope immediately west of the present buildings: but it is at least possible that its name and its connection with the archangel date only from 1044, when Edward the Confessor gave the place to the island abbey of Mont-Saint-Michel off the coast of Normandy. Thereafter the French monks built a monastery here, to which a castle was added in the twelfth century – for the Mount's inaccessibility made it an ideal refuge in times of trouble, and it was four times besieged, most notably during the Wars of the Roses and the Civil War.

Throughout the middle ages, however, its chief fame was as a place of pilgrimage, where pious travellers came to invoke the archangel's protection and, if sufficiently convinced of it, to test their faith by sitting in St Michael's Chair. "A bad seat and a craggy place . . . somewhat dangerous for access and therefore holy for adventure", this natural feature juts from the west side of the Mount, and pilgrims who braved it would sit poised above a sheer drop of several hundred feet to the sea. No content with this, moreover, some visitors also apparently insisted on hazarding themselves in a second Chair – in reality a stone beacon-holder on the battlements of the monastic church tower, with an equally terrifying drop below. Tradition held that the first member of a newly-married couple to do so would ever afterwards rule the household.

This beacon-chair – emphatically not recommended to modern travellers – is one of the comparatively few unaltered survivors of the medieval monastery: which from 1660 onwards was adapted, restored and much extended as the mansion of the St Aubyn family. The monastic church, for instance, became their chapel; and the monks' refectory the Chevy Chase Room, with its fine seventeenth century plasterwork hunting scenes: while the Old Lady Chapel was tranformed into a Gothick drawing room and boudoir. The castellated south-east wing (perhaps the most memorable of all the Mount's buildings) was raised only during the 1870s. For the lover of stately homes as well as of spectacular scenery and of ancient places of worship, therefore, St Michael's Mount amply repays a visit.

See **Shrines and Pilgrimages.**

The tiny oratory (or "prayer-house") of St Piran, remote and little-known among the shifting dunes of Penhale Sands, may well have been the oldest Christian place of worship in south-western Britain. It is said to have been built in the fifth or sixth century, either by or in honour of the saint who first brought Christianity to Cornwall, and who was buried with his mother and his companion St Ives beneath the altar. Where St Piran came from is uncertain, but both his oratory's position on the Atlantic coast and its construction (of rubble mortared together with clay in the early Irish fashion) suggest that he was one of the many Celtic evangelists who braved the hazardous sea-crossing from St Patrick's Ireland.

As early as the tenth century, however, the chapel was already being engulfed by the ever-encroaching sands, and the heads of the three saints were reverently removed to a new church built some half a mile to the east, at the site still marked by the Celtic cross known in 960 as "Christ's Mace". Thence these relics were from time to time carried in procession round the other Cornish parishes associated with the saint, such as Perranarworthal and Perranuthnoe: but at the Reformation, when relics fell out of favour, they were returned to the ancient oratory. Later still, in the early nineteenth century, the "new" church was

ST MICHAEL'S MOUNT
Cornwall
OS 203 SW 515299
Dramatically visible from many points along the south-west coast of Cornwall, the Mount lies immediately south of Marazion, which is three miles east of Penzance via the A394. It is accessible by a causeay at low tide, or at high tide by a ferry service which is continuous during the summer months. The mansion, in the care of the National Trust, is open all the year round: in April and May on Mondays, Wednesdays, and Fridays (10.30 a.m.–5.45 p.m.); from June until October, Monday–Friday 10.30 a.m.–5.45 p.m.; and from November to March for guided tours only, at 11 a.m., 12 noon, 2 p.m. and 4 p.m.

ST PIRAN'S ORATORY
Cornwall
OS 200 SW 768564
The site of the oratory is about a mile and a half north of Perranporth, via the B3285 east and then a minor road turning north through Gear Sands holiday camp: the excavated site of the later church, and the "Christ's Mace" cross, are about a third of a mile east of the oratory, at SW 772565. Perranzabuloe, with its nineteenth century church, is two miles south of Perranporth, off the A3075.

Left, Christ's Mace.

itself overwhelmed by the dunes, and yet a third place of worship was built still further inland, though it retained the old name of Perranzabuloe – "Perran-in-Sabulo", or St Piran's in the Sands. The original chapel had by then been lost and forgotten, but in 1835 it was rediscovered by archeologists, with the three skeletons and their separated skulls still lying under its altar. These have since been stolen, but the oratory's ruins remain beneath their protective building, a memorial to the seagoing saints who carried the Faith to the west long before Augustine came from Rome to Canterbury.
See **The First Christian Missionaries, Llandanwg, Whithorn.**

The cross of St Piran, amongst the dunes.

SALLE Norfolk
OS 133 TG 110249

Salle (sometimes spelt Sall and always pronounced "saul") is twelve miles north-west of Norwich, via the B1149, the B1145 (through Cawston, with its own splendid church) and a signposted minor road. The church of St Peter and St Paul can scarcely be missed, for its pinnacled tower is visible for several miles around.

If the traveller can visit only one East Anglian church, the choice should undoubtedly be Salle – which is indeed among the finest late medieval parish churches in all England. Towering over a small scattered village (which seems never to have been much larger than it is now) it was built during a single concerted campaign in the first half of the fifteenth century: and its size and grandeur are a tribute to the piety and generosity of a handful of local wool-merchant families – Boleyns, Rooses, Briggs and Founteyns – whose memorial brasses lie within. Grandest of all is its soaring 126 foot bell tower, with censer-swinging angels over the door, and square, beautifully traceried "sound-holes" half way up. But the rest of the exterior – a high, wide nave with matching two-storeyed porches to the north and south, balanced by transepts further east, with a lengthy chancel beyond – responds nobly to its challenge; and so does the vast, light-filled interior, a breathtaking sight.

First into view on entering is the splendid font, sculpted with the Seven Sacraments of the Church, raised on steps, and topped by an astounding pinnacled cover – which is so tall that it can be raised only by means of the painted crane-arm jutting from the ringers' gallery under the tower. Then the slender columns of the lofty nave arches carry the eye upwards to the angel roof high above, a daring and ingenious piece of engineering which spans the wide nave without the aid either of cross-ties or of hammer-beams – such as are employed at Cawston, Salle's neighbour and rival. Moving now up the central aisle (under whose carpet is the brass of Geoffrey Boleyn, ancestor of Henry VIII's unfortunate Queen Anne) the traveller comes to the "wine-glass" pulpit, a coloured medieval piece converted into a canopied three decker in Jacobean times. Nearby is the chancel screen, its painted saints much faded and now only a fraction of its original height – the marks of the saws which cut it down after the

Reformation are still clearly visible: originally it would have been surmounted by a great crucifix, whose canopy still survives above the chancel arch.

Within the chancel itself, lit by a noble east window, a series of central roof-bosses tell the story of Christ's life, from the Annunciation on the westernmost boss to the Ascension above the altar: and here too are twenty-six fine carved oak stalls, with a series of "misericords" under their folding seats – discreet supports for those who had to stand through long services. There is, moreover, much more to see in the transepts (with their cross-braced panelled roofs) and the nave side aisles: on the north transept floor is the brass (the best in the church) to Thomas Roos (d.1441) with his wife and twelve clustering children; in the south transept fragments of the original stained glass which once filled most of Salle's windows; and in the south aisle the brass of John Brigg (another of the church's builders) vividly portrayed as a shrouded corpse above the warning inscription "so schall ye be anothir day". Neither should the traveller miss opening the door at the west end of the north aisle and climbing to the "Old Maid's Chamber" above the porch, with its painted and swing-barred door, originally a chapel but afterwards the parish school.

Salle, then, is full of delights: yet it is no way commercialised or touristy, and those who visit it (especially in the winter or early spring) may have the feeling that they are its first discoverers. It is also much more than the sum of all its parts, possessing a powerful atmosphere of peace and serenity which cannot be defined, only experienced.

See **Cawston, The Great Wool Churches.**

Top, the font with its pinnacled cover at the west end of the nave, and above, a shrine in the south transept.

SHOBDON Hereford and Worcester
OS 149 SO 401628

Shobdon is near the Herefordshire border with Welsh Powys, seven miles east of Presteigne and eighteen miles north-west of Hereford, via the A4110 towards Knighton and then the B4362 turning west at Mortimer's Cross towards Presteigne. The church and the nearby Norman "arches" (a short walk from the church) are signposted from the B4362 east of Shobdon village, or may be reached from the village centre via a long estate drive. Nearby (five miles to the west) is the National Trust's Croft Castle.

The Normans founded a notable church at Shobdon, whose sad fragments attest that it was built in the very best style of the Herefordshire or Kilpack school of masons. During the early 1750s, however, the Honourable Richard Bateman of Shobdon Court (in whose grounds the church stood) swept away the old building and re-erected its ornately carved arches on a nearby hill as an eye-catching folly – a "conservation" measure much praised at the time, but one which has since resulted in their irreparable decay. He then built a new church which could perhaps be described as Gothic Revival – "modern Gothic" was the contemporary term – but one which entirely eschewed either the "High Seriousness" earnestly pursued later by Victorian Gothicists or any attempt to directly imitate medieval architecture. It is, indeed, essentially a church in the Georgian classical tradition, with decoration half Gothick and half fashionable Chinoiserie applied to its sur-face like icing on a cake.

Yet if it is difficult to take Shobdon's interior seriously, it is impossible not to be charmed by it. It is painted throughout in a delightfully frivolous colour-scheme of duck-egg white picked out in blue: and while the Gothick detail may be disgracefully inaccur-ate, it is certainly thoroughgoing. Everything is Gothick – the totally unstructural triple arches of chancel and transepts; the fine three-decker pulpit with original hangings; the pew ends and footstools; and even the chairs in the south transept, which served as the Bateman family pew and is equipped with a stove. Their servants sat stoveless in the opposite transept, and there too is some of the Georgian glass from the original east window, whose rather nasty Edwardian replacement is – except for the splendid Nor-man font – almost the only intruder into this otherwise elegant and unspoilt Gothick toy.
*See **The Gothic Revival.***

SILBURY HILL Wiltshire
OS 173 SU 100685

This instantly recognisable conical mound stands by the A4, some five miles west of Marlborough and fifteen miles south-west of junction 15 of the M4 motorway, via the A345 and Marlborough. A viewing area is provided by the side of the road, whence a footpath leads north to Avebury: while another path a few hundred yards eastwards along the A4 leads south to West Kennet Long Barrow, a dramatically restored Neolithic tomb.

Mysterious Silbury Hill.

The largest man-made mound in Europe, the awe-inspiring cone of Silbury Hill has per-plexed historians and archeologists ever since it was known to be pre-Roman by the fact that the straight Roman road to Bath (now the A4) deviates to avoid it. Covering some five and a half acres, the 130 foot high mound has a base diameter of about 550 feet, and it has been calculated that more than eighteen million man-hours must have been required to build it with prehistoric tools, perhaps over a period of decades or even centuries. Why it was raised and what it con-tains nevertheless remains a mystery, despite excavations ranging from a central summit-to-base shaft sunk in 1776 (which may have destroyed valuable evidence) to a thoroughgoing scientific investigation in 1968–70. The latter established that it was begun during the late summer of a year somewhere around 2700 B.C., when the ants perfectly preserved in the turf of its lowest level were growing wings: and that it was expertly constructed in seven steps, all except the topmost of which were carefully smoothed over to form a flat-topped cone. Yet it apparently houses no burial chamber, and it is badly positioned for an astronomical viewing platform: while only with the eye of faith can the traveller see it as a breast of the Great Goddess or a sighting point for flying saucers, two of the wilder "explanations" advanced for its construction.

It seems almost certain, however, that Silbury Hill was closely associated with the stupendous and slightly later Avebury stone circle (a mile to the north), and with the more ancient communal tomb called West Kennet Long Barrow, less than a mile to the south-west: and that, like them, this extraordinary feat of prehistoric engineering was in some now-mysterious way a sacred place of worship.
*See **Avebury, Prehistoric Religion.***

The British Church

In the first century A.D., much of Britain was conquered by Rome. The Roman administrative system was imposed upon the countryside, Roman fashions in architecture, dress, and manners were adopted, Celtic gods were worshipped in classical-style temples, and Latin was widely spoken, while the British tongue continued in use amongst the people. British culture flourished during the early centuries of Christianity. The Celts had always exhibited a remarkable cultural homogeneity despite the essentially tribal nature of their organisation. There was a powerful unity underlying the obvious diversities, and it was this unity, especially in the spheres of religion, art, law and language, which was to make the Celtic peoples adopt so eagerly the Christian faith which was to mould their archaic traditions into a new and powerful culture. The pagan Celtic priests, the Druids, were all-powerful, men of high birth and austere learning. They transmitted their sacred secrets to their acolytes in highly-organised schools, thus the early Christian missionaries encountered learned bodies in the Celtic lands, priests, poets and philosophers. In Ireland, unscathed by Roman conquest, the Druids came into close contact with the churchmen, and the fusion of the two traditions, achieved without a single martyrdom, resulted in the unique character of the insular Celtic Church.

The earliest Church in Britain was doubtless influenced by missionaries from Gaul, and the Near East, and possibly by soldiers from the Roman Army. By the second century, Christianity had already gained a foothold in the country. Three martyrdoms took place in Britain before the year 260. Three British bishops were summoned to the Council of Arles in 314, and to Rimini in 359, testifying to the existence of an organised Church in Britain at this early period.

The Celtic Church is usually thought of as monastic, but this was not always so. Christianity probably took root at first in the western and northern regions of the country, districts which had always strongly retained their Celtic character, and which now turned their pagan predilections into Christian fervour. By the fourth century, a diocesan structure was set up in Britain, whereby a district came under the pastoral care of a bishop. Ninian of Scotland and Patrick of Ireland were both called bishops by their biographers, while the priest Gildas refers to the Church of his time as though it were diocesan. This state of affairs would seem to have continued in Britain until the sixth century when the popularity of monasticism began to grow in the Celtic Church.

It is inevitable that, in the early centuries of British ecclesiastical history, our knowledge of the buildings and places set apart for Christian worship should be largely inferential. In pre-Roman times, the pagan Celts congregated in *temenoi*, sacred enclosures, in groves, or on open plains, where the priestly shrines would be set up, with their "holy of holies", and where the act of sacrifice would confer on all present the protection of the gods. Continuity of the sanctity of sites is well-known, new religions re-using existing shrines. Such places, hallowed by ancient tradition, would be purified, and re-consecrated by the priests of the new faith. This confronts the historian and the archaeologist with a number of problems for, if the earlier structure has not been entirely obliterated by later building, it is more or less impossible to excavate through existing structures without damaging them. Thus, only when repair work becomes necessary, or when a later church is abandoned or destroyed, can extensive work on the foundations be carried out. And, if the earlier structure was, as is so often, of wood, little trace of it can remain. We do have a certain amount of knowledge, however, regarding places of worship in early Christian Britain.

Here, as elsewhere, the first churches usually consisted of a room or rooms in private houses or villas, lent or given to Christians, and set apart for worship. Here they would gather to celebrate the Eucharist. In time, such places would tend to be made over for Christian purposes and their secular origins would be forgotten. As the barbarian raids on the continent became more disruptive in Britain and Europe, contact with the Church in Europe became increasingly difficult, and the British Church developed along its own, independent lines. As contact with the continental Church weakened, the only sources readily available for the British Church at this period are insular.

Wales had, in all probability, been Christian since the Roman period. The saints of the Celtic Church were as numerous as were the pagan deities, some of whose names and legends were adopted by Christianity. The earliest Welsh saint is Saint Dyfrig (Latin *Dubricius*), whose churches are sited on the River Wye. His most renowned pupil was Saint Illtud, who became the first abbot of the monastery of Llantwit Major, a man whose intellectual fame is supported by the number of inscribed crosses still preserved *in situ*, and by the written testimony of his contemporaries. The earliest *Vita* (Life) of a Welsh saint is that of Sain Samson of Dol, who was educated at Llantwit and became the most illustrious saint of the intellectually-superior Breton Church.

The first churches to be built in Celtic Britain are, in many ways, similar to pagan Celtic temples. That at Silchester, Hampshire, was small by Roman standards, but the early buildings conformed by having a nave flanked by side aisles, a *narthex* (vestibule or portico) and a semi-circular apse (an extension eastwards from the chancel). These early British churches are, in fact, less sophisticated than the Celtic Iron Age temples at, for example, Heathrow and South Cadbury. Stone buildings in the early Christian period in Britain were, on the whole, rare. Saint Ninian (Nynia), who converted the Southern Picts to Christianity, and was himself trained in Rome, had a base in Galloway known as *Candida Casa*, "The White House". There be built a church of stone which was unusual amongst the Britons. An important Christian community had been established at Whithorn in Roman times, and it had survived the Northumbrian conquest with no apparent break of the old bishopric in the early eighth century. An organised Church, then, existed in Wales, the north of England, Cumbria, and southern Scotland, during the fifth and sixth centuries, long before the mission of Saint Augustine to the heathen Saxons. Although actual church remains are few and far between, a fine series of inscribed memorial stones beginning in the late fifth century, indicates places of sanctity and worship.

So, for England and Wales, and southern Scotland, in the sub-Roman period, we find a Church, led by bishops, who held adjacent and continuous areas under control. As monasticism grew in popularity, the emphasis changed somewhat. Monastic, rather than diocesan organisation, suited the Celtic temperament better, for dioceses came into being in the Roman Empire, where Christianity was based on the towns. Celtic society was not, on the whole, urban, and a tribal organisation was well-suited to monasticism. Monasticism is, in fact, the great glory of the Celtic Church. The lives of the saints testify to all the virtues of the pastoral aspect of the Church, simplicity, self-sacrifice, missionary zeal, fervour. The concept was an import from the eastern Mediterranean, and there is little to indicate that it had gained much in popularity in Britain before the sixth century. The complex at Tintagel, Cornwall, for example, once thought to have been an early monastic site would now seem to have been an early secular settlement which later became monastic.

The first monasteries seem likely to have been established in Wales shortly before 500, and by the sixth century the monastic movement had spread to Ireland where it was to reach its apotheosis, and thus to affect much of later British Christianity. Northumbria was Christianised by monks, trained in the monastery founded in the sixth century on the little island of Iona, by the royal priest, Columba from northern Ireland. The earliest monasteries may have been set within rectilinear enclosures, exemplified at Iona. This ground-plan may have, in part, derived from Eastern monasteries, which had, themselves borrowed the base-plan of Roman forts. But it could also have been directly influenced by the Roman forts in Britain, some of which were, in fact, re-used as early monasteries. Celtic foundations evolved within the walls of Holyhead (*Caer Gybi*), Anglesey, and at Burgh Castle in Norfolk, where the monastery developed from an expedition from Ireland, led by Saint Fursa. But the Celtic monasteries soon reverted to a circular ground plan. They consisted of circular cells, ocasionally rectilinear, chapels, and other buildings for teaching purposes, or for such secular occupations as manuscript illumination, metalwork, and pursuits affecting the running and economy of the entire settlement. Large monasteries would have smaller offshoots. These monasteries of the Celtic Church served to keep learning alive during the gloomy, chancy, post-Roman phase of British history.

The great saint, Augustine, arrived in Britain in 597, the year of Saint Columba's death, but although his mission was ultimately to bring to an end the rival Celtic Church, it still had many glorious and independent years ahead of it. The differences between the Roman and the Celtic Church were, on the whole, trivial. The two questions that are most frequently mentioned are the fixing of the date for the celebration, and the nature of the Celtic tonsure, which may have been derived from that of the Druids. There were clearly other areas of conflict, possibly political, but there was no bitterness or real enmity between the contestants. There was certainly no clash of doctrine or of ideals, and no formal difference in the functions of the hierarchy, or in the basic order of the church services.

Bede movingly recorded the simplicity, sincerity and ascetic qualities of the life of Saint Aidan, who, with his monks, had founded the renowned monastery on Lindisfarne and established Celtic Christianity in Northumbria.

See **Monasteries and Religious Houses, The Anglo-Saxon Church, Iona, Lindisfarne.**

Anglo-Saxon church towers are not uncommon, but that of St Mary's at Sompting is probably unique in having retained the original form of its roof, and certainly unique for its famous and imposing "Rhenish helm" roof cap, the only one of its kind now surviving in Britain. So called because it resembles the helmet-like spires of Romanesque churches in the Rhineland, it is basically a pyramid resting on sharply pointed gables: and like the fine tower beneath (with its pairs of Saxon windows, triangular-topped on the east and west faces and round headed on the others) dates from around 1000. Within, the tower arch has capitals crudely but dramatically carved with foliage at the same period, and elsewhere in the church is more Saxon sculpture, notably a strange, primitive figure

of a sainted abbot in the south transept. The main body of the church, however, was rebuilt in the twelfth century by the crusading order of Knights Templars, with a long transept to the north and, to the south, a square chapel for their own private use: lower than the rest of the building, and originally quite separate from it, this was linked to the church as the south transept, only in Victorian times. When the Templars were suppressed in 1306 – allegedly for devil-worship, but more probably because kings coveted their immense wealth – St Mary's passed to their rival order of Knight's Hospitallers, who added another extension (now ruined) to the north of the tower, thus increasing still further the odd respect of this remarkable place of worship. See **The Anglo-Saxon Church.**

SOMPTING West Sussex
OS 198 TQ 162057
Sompting village is eight miles west of Brighton and two miles north-east of Worthing town centre, on the A27: St Mary's stands prominently to the north of this road, on the southern slopes of the Downs.

Though they are among the largest and most important in southern England, the great prehistoric stone circles of Stanton Drew are comparatively rarely visited by travellers: yet they have long fascinated the inhabitants of the place whose very name means "the homestead by the stones", and who once believed them to be a wedding party transformed into boulders as a punishment for dancing on the Sabbath. Even the village pub is called "the Druids' Arms", but the circles stood here long before the time of that semi-mythical Iron Age priesthood, being apparently raised by New Stone Age builders in about 2500 B.C. – and thus at roughly the

same period as the still vaster stone rings were being constructed at Avebury, thirty miles further east. That there was a close relationship between the two monuments seems indeed almost certain: for both contain the same elements – three circles, two "avenues", an outlying stone and a massive three-stone "Cove" – albeit arranged in a somewhat different manner.

That there was careful planning behind Stanton Drew's layout is equally clear, though its purpose is now hidden from us. For a line drawn through the centres of the south-western and the great central circle – the largest in England save only Avebury's

STANTON DREW Avon
OS 172 ST 601634
The extremely pretty village of Stanton Drew is seven miles south of Bristol, via the A37 and then the B3130 west. Both circles and Cove are well signposted in the village centre: the circles being reached (for a small fee) through a farm east of the church, and closed Sundays; while the Cove stands in the Druids' Arms garden, and is always accessible. Chewton Mendip is six miles further south, either via the A37 and A39 or by way of the B3130 and B3114, a picturesque route through Chew Magna and Chew Stoke.

outer circle, with twenty-seven of its original thirty stones visible, most of them fallen – points directly to an outlying marker stone a quarter of a mile away: while a line through the centres of the north-eastern and great circles once sighted directly onto the three huge stones of the Cove, now in the garden of the Druids' Arms. Significantly, however, this sight-line has long been blocked (almost certainly as a matter of deliberate policy) by the medieval parish church; whose positioning suggests that the Cove was once a particularly important feature of the prehistoric complex, perhaps a real or a symbolic burial chamber used in ceremonies of death and rebirth. Water was also apparently vital for Stanton Drew's worshippers, since converging stone "avenues" lead from the north-eastern and central circles to the River Chew in the valley below: while the wedding party legend may just possibly preserve ancient memories of dancing and fertility rites within the circles. But apart from these tantalising clues, the stones of Stanton Drew keep their secrets.
See **Arbor Low, Avebury, Prehistoric Religion.**

STOKE CHARITY Hampshire
OS 185 SU 488393
Stoke Charity is seven miles north of the historic cathedral city of Winchester, on a signposted minor road which turns west off the A33 (through Micheldever) or east off the A34 (through Sutton Scotney): the church is about a quarter of a mile east of the hamlet, in a meadow by the river Dever.

Standing alone in a situation as delightful as its name, amid lanes blue-purple in summer with comfrey flowers, the little church of Stoke Charity is one of the most charming and interesting in southern England. Part Saxon, part Norman and part later medieval, with a miniature spirelet on its tower, its light-filled interior is literally packed with medieval treasures of all kinds. Tombs and monuments abound, perhaps the most notable being the armoured brasses of Thomas Wayte (d.1482) in the nave, with its figure of Christ in Pity; and that of Thomas Hampton (who died in the following year and wears an almost identical suit of armour) between the chancel and the north chapel. Above Hampton's head is the Trinity – an old man for God the Father, the crucified Christ, and a dove for the Holy Ghost – and beneath his feet are his children, the married daughters in elaborate headdresses and the unmarried with flowing hair. A much rarer relic – and one which survived the Reformation only by being concealed in a wall recess, where it was rediscovered in 1849 – is the carving of St Gregory's legendary Mass in the north chapel, depicting Christ appearing as the saint raises the host, thus proving his "real presence" at the Mass to a doubting congregation: and unusual too are the iron staples on the font, allowing it to be locked against those who purloined holy water for curative or more sinister purposes.

These things alone would make the church worth visiting, and taken with its other treasures – sixteenth century paintings on the Waller tomb, medieval floor tiles and stained glass – they make Stoke Charity worth travelling many miles to see.

STOW-IN-LINDSEY
Lincolnshire
OS 121 SK 889828
Stow is nine miles north-west of Lincoln, via the A57 to Saxilby and then the B1241 north. Marton church (three miles west, on the A156) has a fine Saxo-Norman tower, and Gainsborough (seven miles north-west) is worth a visit for its late medieval and Elizabethan Old Hall: while Doddington Hall (eight miles south, via a turning off the A57) is a particularly charming and interesting Elizabethan historic house.

Vastly dominating its small village, the mighty Saxo-Norman church of St Mary at Stow-in-Lindsey was by tradition the cathedral of Saxon Lincolnshire: and though this is not strictly the case, Stow was indeed an important place in pre-Conquest times, being the "head minster" or mother church of a large block of ecclisiastical lands in this region. The early history of the present cross-shaped building is controversial, but its oldest surviving parts (the transepts or arms of the cross) appear to have been raised in about 975, and reconstructed after a fire during the mid eleventh century: soon afterwards, in about 1070, the nave was built by Remigius, the first Norman bishop of Lincoln, while the sumptuous Norman chancel belongs to about 1150 and the stubby tower to the later middle ages.

With its sheer, high-windowed rubble walls, the exterior looks like a true fortress of God, and the interior is astonishing: tall and narrow in the Anglo-Saxon tradition, its centrepiece is the magnificent Saxon crossing, whose four great thirty-foot arches are the largest of their period in Britain. Resting on heavy plinths at floor level, and flanked by pairs of columns whose bases rather awkwardly hang half-suspended in mid-air, the arches once supported a Saxon tower, possibly made of wood: but despite their massive appearance they were not deemed strong enough to bear the new stone tower added to the church in the fourteenth century, and a new set of reinforcing pillars and arches – this time pointed rather than round – were then built within them. This curious arrangement of two arched boxes, one within the other, is best viewed from the south transept; as is the sudden variation in thickness of the outer arch's decorative pillars, marking the division between the first Saxon arches and those rebuilt after the eleventh century fire. In the north transept, jammed between a pillar and the west wall, is a cinder which dropped from the tower roof during the fire, and there too are a fine Saxon doorway and the remains of a wall painting of St Thomas Becket.

The richly-carved decoration of the ornate Norman chancel – which was heavily and perhaps over-imaginatively restored by the Victorians – presents a startling contrast to the monolithic plainness elsewhere in the church: set into its floor are two thirteenth century coffin-lid memorials to ladies, the right-hand with an unusually early inscription in English to "Emma, Fuke's wife".
See **The Anglo-Saxon Church.**

The delightfully-named and peacefully-sited prehistoric ring at Sunhoney is perhaps the least altered of "recumbent-stone circles" – a type of monument frequent in north-eastern Scotland but unknown elsewhere in Britain. Constructed perhaps around 1900 B.C., it is composed of eleven red granite standing stones, carefully graded in height so that they rise from both directions towards the two tallest pillars flanking the "recumbent", a massive flat-topped stone which was always intended to lie horizontally. Special care, indeed, was taken that the top of the recumbent should be exactly level: as can well be seen at Sunhoney, where the great stone has fallen outwards to reveal that its once earthfast base has been laboriously shaped to fit its socket. Here, too, the upward face of the stone is pitted with the mysterious hollows called cup-marks: emphasising that the whole circle was focused on its recumbent.

How these distinctive circles were used – there is another fine example at Loanhead of Daviot, fifteen miles to the north – has long been a subject of controversy, but Aubrey Burl has suggested a convincing interpretation. He believes that the great recumbent (which lies towards the south-west of all such circles) was aligned on the summer setting of the moon – which at midsummer would be seen to pass between the two flankers and apparently disappear into the recumbent, as though the stone had captured the moon. The upward sweep of the circle-stones towards the flankers may well also be intended to symbolise the moon's rising and setting: while the cup-marks on the recumbent possibly represent the moon itself; though that is more doubtful, as is the significance of the burnt bones found within the circle. Ultimately, indeed, we can only guess at the exact nature of the rituals performed in any prehistoric place of worship: but at Sunhoney the traveller seems close to the spirit of Bronze Age man.
See **Prehistoric Religion.**

SUNHONEY near Echt,
Grampian
OS 38 NJ 716058
The circle is thirteen miles west of Aberdeen via the B9119, and lies just north of the road, to the west of Echt: it is on private land, and permission to view should be sought at Sunhoney Farm; boots are strongly recommended in wet weather. Five miles to the south-east (at NJ 785043) is a prehistoric circle of a different type at Cullerlie, which is signposted off a minor road running from the B9119 at Garlogie to Peterculter: and fifteen miles north is the fine recumbent-stone circle at Loanhead at Daviot (NJ 747288) signposted from the B9001 five miles north-east of Inverurie.

A fine large church of basically fourteenth century date, with a grand central tower – both unusual things hereabouts – St Peter's at Tawstock stands cheek-by-jowl with the remnants of a once-great mansion, now a school but long the seat of the Earls of Bath and their connections. It is this relationship, indeed, which gives the church its special character: for though its interior is literally packed with interesting and beautiful objects – the font, the rood screen and Tudor bench ends, the delightful coloured plaster ceilings in the transepts, and the roofed state pew and high gallery in the north transept – it is overwhelmingly dominated by the monuments of Tawstock Court's successive inhabitants. No less than fifteen major and many more lesser tombs crowd St Peter's east end and transepts, giving it the nickname of "the West-minster Abbey of North Devon".

The earliest and simplest of this remarkable collection is a fourteenth century wooden effigy of a lady in the chancel, near the grandest of them all, the vast alabaster tomb of the third Earl (d.1623) and Countess of Bath, with doll-like figures of their children kneeling at their head and feet. Opposite is the life-sized white marble statue of Lady Rachel (d.1681), the charitable fifth Countess: and in the chancel aisle stand both the oddest and perhaps the finest of Tawstock's monuments – the black marble sarcophagus of the fifth Earl (d.1654), borne by dog-like griffins; and the elegant effigy of Lady Frances Fitzwarren (d.1586), under a splendid Elizabethan canopied "six-poster".

TAWSTOCK Devon
OS 180 SS 559299
The attractive village of Tawstock stands amid wooded hills two miles south of Barnstaple, on a back road which runs parallel with the A377 but west of the River Taw, turning south off the A39 immediately west of Barnstaple station and rejoining the A377 south of Bishop's Tawton. Having reached the village, follow signs to the church and St Michael's School: if the church is locked, enquire for the nearby vicarage, where the key can be obtained. Chittlehampton is some six miles to the south-east, via the A377 and the B3227.

Throughout the prehistoric period, the area around Lochgilphead lay on an important trade and migration route between the Firth of Clyde and the Western Isles: and the many wandering peoples who passed or briefly settled here have left behind an almost unrivalled collection of evidence of their varied religious beliefs and practices. The Kilmartin valley north of Lochgilphead, indeed, contains more than twenty prehistoric monuments, including a henge and many standing stones and burial cairns. Among the most striking of them is the little stone circle in Temple Wood, hard by the Nether Largie standing stones and the chambered tomb of Nether Largie South. Far from any other known circle, this ring may have been raised by a migrating people coming from the south or the north-east; and consists of sixteen small local stones – one of them, to the north, carved with a double spiral. Within the ring is a floor of smaller stones, beneath which were buried three cremated bodies in stone boxes or "cists". Later, possibly when the original builders had moved on and been forgotten, more cremated remains were left here under cairns: and perhaps later still attempts were made to convert the stone circle into an unbroken ring with drystone walling. Like so many other prehistoric places of worship, then, this lonely ring on a Bronze Age highway clearly remained sacred for a considerable period.
See **Prehistoric Religion.**

TEMPLE WOOD
near Kilmartin, Strathclyde
OS 55 NR 826979
The circle is six and a half miles north of Lochgilphead and about a mile south of Kilmartin by a minor road turning west off the A816. Nearby are the Nether Largie standing stones (NR 831985), and further information about the many prehistoric monuments in the area can be obtained at Lochgilphead Tourist Information office.

The fortress-like preceptory at Torpichen.

TORPICHEN Lothian
OS 65 NS 968725

The preceptory church is sixteen miles west of Edinburgh city centre, via the A8, the A89 and the B792 through Bathgate. Five miles to the north is Linlithgow, with its fine church and medieval palace of the Scottish kings.

Looking more like a fortress than a church, the "preceptory" at Torpichen appropriately belonged to the crusading order of the Knights of St John of Jerusalem, better known as the Knights Hospitallers. Founded during the mid-twelfth century, it was probably their only priory in Scotland, and here members of the order – in the intervals of military service abroad – administered the surrounding estates which helped to support their work of guarding and caring for pilgrims in the Holy Land, and later of defending the island of Rhodes against the Turks. The church's odd appearance – a massive, almost windowless tower, sandwiched between two lofty blocks with typically Scots "crow-step"

gables – is due to the fact that it is by no means complete: and is in fact merely the central portion of the originally cruciform building, the chancel having disappeared and the nave being partly absorbed into the adjacent parish kirk. The twelfth century tower's flanking transepts, moreover, were much heightened in the later middle ages, probably as private burial chapels for the preceptory's knightly priors. One of these, Sir George Dundas, is commemorated within by a macabre panel depicting a skeleton in a shroud: and the impressive interior now also houses an exhibition illustrating the history of his order.

See **Monasteries and Religious Houses.**

WALSINGHAM Norfolk
OS 132 TF 935369

Walsingham – properly Little Walsingham, to differentiate it from its (smaller) neighbour Great Walsingham – is twenty miles north-west of Norwich, and five miles north of Fakenham via the B1105. All its places of worship are well signposted, the Anglican shrine being at the north end of the town and the priory ruins (closed in winter) set back off the main street behind a medieval gatehouse. The Russian Orthodox Church is west of the town centre, in Station Street, and the medieval parish church (rebuilt after a fire) to the south, near

the (privately owned) remains of a

There is nowhere in Britain quite like Walsingham. The unwary traveller's first impression is of a very pretty little Norfolk town, clustered round the Tudor brick conduit in its square or "Common Place": but a closer inspection reveals that every other shop seems to sell plaster images and other religious knick-knacks, while several of the houses are either pilgrim hostels or monasteries. For here is a fully operational shrine, a kind of English Lourdes – or indeed "England's Nazareth", as its votaries call it. This title, and Walsingham's fame, stems from a series of dreams experienced in the early twelfth century by a wealthy local widow named Richelde de Faverches: therein the

Virgin Mary appeared to her, carrying her in spirit to the "Holy House" in Nazareth where the Annunciation of Christ's birth had taken place. Richelde was given the house's measurements, and instructed to build an exact replica at Walsingham, which (with the aid of some angels) she set up near the site of two holy wells, building a chapel around it. Its fame grew, and in about 1169 an Augustinian priory was founded to care for it, while to its attractions were added a miracle-working statue of the Virgin and no less a relic than a phial of the Virgin's Milk, brought by Crusaders from the Holy Land – whence, some declared, the Virgin herself had fled from the Moslems to take up residence in her Norfolk "Holy House".

Throughout the later middle ages Walsingham's renown went on increasing, and the roads to it were thronged with pilgrims directed thither (so they believed) by the stars of the Milky Way – or the "Walsingham Way" as it became known. Henry III came many times, greatly adding to the shrine's prestige, and even Henry VIII, during his Catholic youth, walked the last mile to the Holy House barefoot and lit a candle there in 1511. Then, twenty-seven years later, the Reformation directed by that same king swept away the priory, smashed the Virgin's house, and carried off her famous statue to be publicly burned in London as "a superstitious idol, the Devil's instrument": leaving Walsingham to revert to a rural backwater, the only reminders of its past glory the scanty priory ruins and the occasional, furtive, Catholic pilgrim.

During the present century, however, Walsingham has experienced a remarkable revival, which began in 1897 when the Roman Catholics restored a medieval pilgrim chapel at nearby Houghton St Giles – supposedly the "Slipper Chapel" where devotees piously removed their shoes before entering "England's Holy Land". This now forms part of a "pilgrimage complex" with the recently-built Church of the Reconciliation – a large, simple, almost barn-like building which opens onto a concourse ringed with fifteen great crosses. Many thousands of Catholics come here to worship, either individually or – particularly on "Catholic Mothers' Day" – by the coachload: and from here processions are made to the site of the original Holy House, near the great arch which is virtually all that remains of Walsingham Priory church.

Perhaps a quarter of a million pilgrims, moreover, annually visit a replica of the House itself – and thus a replica of a replica – in Walsingham's most astounding place of worship, the Anglican shrine at the northern end of the town. Built during the 1930s by a vicar of extreme Anglo-Catholic views, this red-brick Italianate church contains no less than fifteen chapels, each with its highly-coloured saints' images and gold-candlesticked altar: while around and within the "Holy House" hundreds of candles flicker on wall-plaques recording thanks for favours wrought by Our Lady of Walsingham, or by the water from the adjacent "holy" well, which any visitor may drink. It is hard to believe, indeed, that this is a building at least nominally belonging to the Church of England, and not (say) to Catholic Spain: and the difficulty is still greater on Saturday evenings in the summer pilgrimage season, when a statue of the Virgin is borne round the shrine's garden by chanting processions.

Nor are Catholics and "High Church" Anglicans the only Christians who revere Walsingham: for part of the disused railway station is now the Russian Orthodox Church of St Seraphim of Sarov, complete with a little onion-domed tower and an ikon-screen separating the sanctuary from the rest of the tiny church. No student of holy places, then, can afford to miss "England's Nazareth", if only to compare its varying traditions of worship – and perhaps to marvel at the ironic contrast between the simple Catholic shrine and its ornate "Anglican" counterpart. For others, it may stir up strong emotions, either attracting or repulsing: travellers must decide for themselves.

See **Shrines and Pilgrimages.**

friary. The Roman Catholic Slipper Chapel and pilgrimage centre (TF 922354) is just over a mile south of the town, at Houghton St Giles: which also has an interesting parish church. Nearby, too, are Little Snoring (three miles south) and Binham Priory (four miles north-east).

Its hundred foot tower visible for miles across Sedgemoor, St Mary's at Westonzoyland serves an island of rich soil raised above the surrounding marshes, and was once the property of the great abbey of Glastonbury ten miles to the east. Outstanding even among the many splendid churches of the Somerset Levels, the greater part of it – the battlemented nave, aisles, transepts and porch – was built in blue-grey "lias" during the time of Richard Bere, abbot of Glastonbury from 1493 until 1524, whose initials appear both within and without: and of his time or shortly afterwards is also the mighty four-stage tower, with its three tiers of panelled windows rising to a pinnacled and battlemented crown. Still more glorious, however, is Westonzoyland's famous nave roof, one of the finest in the West Country and a masterpiece of wood-carving and of engineering: ornately decorated throughout, it is laterally secured by immense tie-beams, from whose perching angels central king-posts – flanked by bands of tracery – spring

upwards to support the roof ridge. Notable too, if less spectacular, is the rood screen separating the nave from the earlier and humbler chancel: for though its gallery (or rood loft) and Crucifixion figures (the rood itself) were added only in the 1930s, they furnish a good impression of how such screens appeared before the Reformation destroyed or defaced them.

St Mary's, then, is clearly worth visiting for itself: but many travellers are also drawn there by its sad associations with the Battle of Sedgemoor, fought immediately north of the village during the early hours of July the sixth 1685. Utterly defeated after a disastrously mismanaged night attack on James II's royal army, some five hundred of Monmouth's West Country rebels were herded into the church as prisoners, many of them having been stripped almost naked by the victors. "There was seventy-nine of them wounded", reported the Westonzoyland churchwardens, "and five of them died of their wounds in our church": while later in the day "were hanged

WESTONZOYLAND Somerset OS 182 ST 352348
Westonzoyland is four miles east of Bridgewater (which is easily accessible from exits 23 and 24 of the M5 motorway) via the A372. Glastonbury, famous alike for its abbey ruins and its alleged mystical associations, is some ten miles to the east, via the A372 to Othery and then the A361 through Street; and there are many other fine late medieval churches in this area, notably Langport and Huish Episcopi (to the south-east, via the A372) and Isle Abbotts (south of the A378).

with us twenty-two, of which four were hanged in gemmasses" (chains). Once itself a grotesque prison for men who had fought for a cause in which they passionately believed, this beautiful and tranquil church is again a place of worship and prayer for those who, with equal passion, seek forever an end to all fighting.

See **Cullompton, The Reformation.**

See **Cullompton, The Reformation.**

Below left, the fine angel roof of St Mary's, Westonzoyland, and below, the rood screen, extensively reconstructed in the 1930's.

WHITBY North Yorkshire
OS 94 NZ 902114

The picturesque port and seaside resort of Whitby stands on the north-east coast of Yorkshire, some twenty miles north-west of Scarborough and about fifty miles north-east of York via the A64 and A169: the A169 passes through Pickering (with its church wall paintings and castle) and then across wild moorland. The church stands high on East Cliff, and can be reached either on foot via the famous stairs from the town or by car following signs to the adjacent abbey: the abbey, also worth a visit, was a Christian power house in Saxon times, but the existing impressive ruins date mainly from the thirteenth century. The church is sometimes locked in winter, but is always open between 10 a.m. and noon on weekdays.

Three-decker pulpit and the barley-sugar twist pillars of the Cholmley family gallery.

Sharing its gale-swept clifftop site with the gaunt ruins of Whitby Abbey, St Mary's is without doubt one of the most unusual and delightful parish churches in all Britain. Most fittingly reached (for the comparatively agile) via the 199 winding steps from the fishing port in the cove below, it appears from the outside as a squat, spreading, battlemented building in a bewildering variety of architectural styles, combining Norman round arches with Gothic pointed lancets and sensible Georgian domestic windows, and sprouting white wooden staircases in unexpected places. Still more unexpected, however, is the stunning interior, jam-packed with shoulder-high Georgian box pews at ground level and fringed at every available point with raised and panelled galleries. Quite the most endearing of these is the late seventeenth century squire's gallery of the Cholmley family, with its fat-cheeked cherubs and barley-sugar twist pillars, set squarely across the chancel arch and effectively blocking off the dark Norman chancel from the light-filled main body of the church.

For St Mary's is most emphatically a Protestant and Prayer Book Church, whose focus is not the altar – indeed there is no altar proper, its function being supplied by the Elizabethan communion table in the chancel – but rather the fabulous centrally positioned three-decker pulpit. Here, during services, the

Church of England: and we must be profoundly grateful that Whitby's Victorian "quality" – who would otherwise surely have Gothicised the church – moved instead to the far side of town and built their own Gothic Revival church there.
See **The Prayer Book Church, The Gothic Revival.**

A view across the nave to the south transept.

parish clerk still occupies the lowest deck, while the minister leads the prayers from the middle deck and ascends to the uppermost "preaching box" for his sermon: clamped to its back are a pair of huge leather ear-trumpets, once used by the deaf wife of a Georgian minister. This pulpit has been compared to a rock rising above the wooden waves of the box pews, and there is much else in St Mary's – for instance the anchored brass chandelier and the Scoresby Chair in the chancel, commemorating a whaler turned clergyman – to recall Whitby's history as a fishing and whaling port, closely associated with the famous explorer Captain Cook. Perhaps most nautical of all, however, are the church's roofs, which were indeed built by Whitby shipbuilders and are equipped with great skylights like those of a ship's cabin, admitting so much light that artificial illumination is rarely needed: when it is, candles are used, for the church has no electric light.

St Mary's unspoiled and un-"restored" interior, in short, has no equal as a living memorial to the Georgian heyday of the

St Mary's, set high above the port of Whitby.

The Gothic Revival

The effect of the Victorian Gothic Revival on the present appearance of British places of worship was overwhelming. Something like half the existing churches in England, especially those in towns, were built according to its rules: while thousands of older churches were adapted or "restored" in accordance with its teachings, and what we now accept as the traditional church interior was the direct outcome of its beliefs. Indeed, the real or imitated Gothic style of the middle ages is now so inextricably connected with religion that a pointed window (even in a library or a suburban porch) irresistibly suggests a place of worship.

It needs first of all to be emphasised, therefore, that Gothic architecture was not originally used only for religious purposes: it was simply the ordinary building style of the later middle ages, employed alike for castles, mansions and merchants' houses as well as for parish churches, cathedrals and abbeys. As such it did not have a particular name, the term "Gothic" – meaning "barbarous" or more loosely "old fashioned" – being coined only after the medieval period had given way to the Renaissance, and medieval architecture had been largely superseded by imitations of the classical styles of Greece and Rome. Here and there, especially in remote country churches like Ninekirks at Brougham, simplified versions of the old style nevertheless persisted well into the seventeenth century, but these were continuations rather than imitations, "Gothic Survival" rather than "Gothic Revival". Far from being imitated, indeed, medieval architecture came to be rejected as antiquated and unfashionable: and if not thought actually improper (because of its connection with pre-Reformation Catholicism) for a Protestant church, it was at least held to be unsuitable for a building used for worship according to the Book of Common Prayer.

The Prayer Book Churches of the eighteenth century, therefore, were generally built in some version of the prevailing Georgian classical style. They were sometimes stupendously grandiose, like Christ Church, Spitalfields in London; and occasionally faintly comic – like Mereworth, a theatrical copy of a Roman basilica: but more often they were restrained, dignified, and finely porportioned buildings, redolent of Reason and Good Taste. By the middle of the century, admittedly, a few churches (most notably Shobdon) were being constructed in what was called the "modern Gothick" mode, but which in fact only involved adding vaguely medievalesque decoration to an ordinary classical building. Nor did such churches seriously intend either to imitate or to revive the Gothic style: they

were, rather the product of the contemporary fad – fostered by the sensational novels of the day – for regarding all things medieval (particularly monks and ruined abbeys) as deliciously Romantic and mysterious. The fashion was to continue into the early nineteenth century (when it was given new impetus by the voluminous "historical" fictions of Sir Walter Scott) and was to influence the design of the hundreds of new churches built in the decades after the Napoleonic Wars.

This flood of new places of worship, sometimes called "Waterloo or Commissioners' Churches", was the result of the realisation that though the population had grown immensely during the recent Industrial Revolution, the provision of churches had by no means kept pace with it. In the mushrooming cities and the new industrial towns of the north, particularly, it was said that only about a tenth of the people could be accommodated in existing churches, leaving the rest to debauchery, Methodism or – infinitely worse – to seditious freethinking which would probably lead to the bloody overthrow of the state. The only remedy was to rapidly build more Anglican churches, and in 1818 Parliament voted a million pounds for this purpose, setting up a body of Commissioners to supervise the work. Each of the three hundred or so new places of worship eventually built was approved by them, and naturally enough they favoured buildings which (if not particularly beautiful) were both capacious and cheap. Style did not so much concern them, though the prevailing trend was towards "Grecian" classical churches, which needed large and expensive stone porticos. For more modest buildings, therefore, the Commissioners recommended Gothic, which could be built in cheaper brick, and a number of at least nominally Gothic churches were built during the first decades of the nineteenth century. But the Gothic element in them was still only skin deep: in effect, they remained Prayer Book Churches in medieval disguise.

The change, and the real beginning of the real Gothic Revival, came with the revelation that churches should not be built in the Gothic style because it was Romantic, because it was cheap, or even because it was more British than the classical mode – though the last was an important consideration in many people's minds. They should – indeed must – rather be built in the Gothic style because Gothic was the only Christian style of architecture, and thus the only one which could even be considered for a Christian place of worship. Nor would lip-service to medieval forms suffice: churches must henceforth faithfully adhere to the true Gothic spirit, and reproduce accurately both the Gothic style and the Gothic plan of nave, aisles and transepts, preferably equipped with a full set of "medieval " fittings. They must, moreover, be designed by architects of irreproachable morals, and if possible built by labourers who refrained from swearing. For Gothic architecture was moral architecture, and all other styles were either pagan or merely frivolous.

This conviction proceeded partly from a more serious study of medieval architecture, and partly from a widespread sense of disgust at some of the duller and shoddier churches sponsored by the Commissioners, but most of all from the immensely influential works of Augustus Welby Northmore Pugin (1812–52). A practising architect, Pugin was one of the many Victorian converts to Roman Catholicism who looked back to an idealised (and almost entirely fictitious) medieval dream-world populated exclusively by saints and scholars, noble knights, and merry, honest rustics. Good men and good Catholics all, they had built good and beautiful churches as naturally as night follows day, and as surely as Victorian Protestants were bound to build bad and ugly ones. Less ludicrously, Pugin also preached that Gothic architecture was admirable because of its "Truth". By this he meant that it does not conceal its constructional features – for instance its buttresses, pillars and roof timbers – but rather displays and adorns them: and however richly decorated these features may be, they are uniformly and essentially useful rather than ornamental, unlike the plaster ceilings, sham domes and other "theatrical effects" beloved by classicists. In his "True Principles of Pointed or Christian Architecture", therefore, he insisted "that there should be no features about a building which are not necessary for convenience, construction, or propriety; and that all ornament should consist of enrichment of the essential construction of the building". Throughout his short life Pugin pursued his principles with ever-increasing fervour, and is said eventually to have been unable even to eat a pudding unless it was made in the Gothic style: perhaps not surprisingly, he died quite mad in 1852, but by then his ideas had taken firm hold.

They were most enthusiastically received, oddly enough, not by Roman Catholics but by sections of the Anglican church: where similar notions had begun to develop more or less independently, and where they were most effectively fostered by the influential Cambridge Camden Society. These followers of the "Tractarian" or "High Church" party agreed with Pugin that Gothic architecture was the only Christian style, but not that it could only be produced by Roman Catholics, "Roman" being the operative word. For their rediscovery of Gothicism had

been combined with the revelation that, though no longer "Roman", the Church of England was in fact "Catholic" (in the sense of "universal") Church, with a rich heritage of ritual and belief which had merely lain in abeyance since the Reformation. While advocating the revival of medieval architecture, therefore, they also favoured the re-introduction of many pre-Reformation practices and forms of service, taking advantage of ambiguities in the Book of Common Prayer in order to do so: and before long the Gothic Revival and the revival of "Anglo-Catholic" Ritualism became so inextricably interconnected that it is difficult to decide which begat which.

Many of the familiar features of present day Church of England worship, indeed, are the product of this Ritualist revival. By far the most frequently held Anglican service, for example, is now Holy Communion, which is held daily or at least weekly in many churches. Before the mid Victorian period, however, Communion services were comparatively rare, being generally celebrated only at major Festivals: the standard Sunday services were, rather, those of morning and evening prayer, each accompanied by a sermon. On entering the church at service time, moreover, the modern traveller may well witness members of the congregation bowing or even genuflecting towards the altar before taking their seat – a practice which would quite rightly have been viewed as shockingly "Popish and idolatrous" before the onset of Victorian ritualism. The altar itself will doubtless be decked with candles and a crucifix, unthinkable additions in pre Anglo-Catholic times, when the simple communion table bore only a white linen cloth and perhaps a Bible on a cushion.

When the ministering clergyman appears, he will most probably be wearing elaborate vestments coloured according to the ecclesiastical season of the year – white or gold for the greatest festivals, red for the feast days of martyrs, blue or purple during Lent, and green for other times. He will thus be following pre Reformation Catholic practice as reintroduced under the influence of the Camden Society, instead of observing the older Church of England tradition of officiating in an unadorned white surplice and black scarf, worn over a black cassock. The service having begun, the congregation will generally kneel on hassocks to pray, rather than leaning forward in their seats as they would once have done: and for the Creed they will stand and turn eastwards, sometimes crossing themselves in the Catholic manner at the conclusion of this part of the service. All these things – anathema to those who founded the Anglican Church at the Reformation – proclaim the triumph of the Ritualist view that the Church of England is essentially a Catholic institution, separated from

Rome only by an unfortunate historical accident.

At first, not unnaturally, the Protestant sections of the English church regarded both Gothic and Ritualist revivals as little better than a Catholic plot to subvert the nation. But the revivalists enjoyed immense influence, and most new churches built after the mid 1840s were built not only in the Gothic style, but in the type of Gothic style they favoured. For, with a truly Victorian moral certainty, Anglican "ecclesiologists" had decided that early Gothic (or "Early English") architecture was "immature", while the magnificent late Gothic (or "Perpendicular") style of the great wool churches was merely "debased". The only "correct" form of medieval architecture, therefore, was the middle Gothic or "Decorated" style of the early fourteenth century, and this all good Victorian architects must strive to imitate as closely as possible. They must, moreover, build churches that were symbolically as well as architecturally correct. Such churches should of course have a large chancel for the celebration of Holy Communion (they did not yet call it "Mass"), with an altar raised on three steps to symbolise the Trinity, which might also be suggested by three lights in the east window; they ought to have transcepts, so that their plan symbolised the Cross, but they need not have a tower; they should have an octagonal font, to symbolise regeneration, and so on almost ad infinitum.

All this was harmless enough (if faintly ludicrous) in a newly-built church: and if imaginatively applied by an accomplished architect – as was done at All Saints Margaret Street in London, the Camden Society's "model Church" – could produce a most striking place of worship. The revivalists, however, did not confine themselves to constructing a very large number of new churches, they also set about the wholesale "restoration" (at times amounting to virtual rebuilding) of old ones. Prayer Book Churches they particularly disliked as pulpit-centred rather than focussed (as was "correct") on the altar: here the despised galleries and box pews were ripped out and burnt; the musicians' pew was replaced by an organ; and the chancel cleared, raised, and floored in shiny tiles instead of the old flagstones. Nor was the architecture even of medieval churches safe, especially if it was considered not sufficiently Gothic, or Gothic of the wrong sort, in which case it was liable to "improvement". Medieval features, moreover, were introduced where they can never have existed; as in the case of altar rails, which originated in the seventeenth century but were often "restored" in the Gothic style, as were many fine Jacobean pulpits. And everywhere walls were scraped of their plaster and left bare, in the entirely erroneous belief that this was how they had appeared in the middle ages. What resulted, in short, was not a medieval church as it had been, but a medieval church as the revivalists considered it ought to have been: and in the process they probably did more irreparable damage to ancient places of worship than the post-Reformation Puritans they so much disliked. A few voices, it is true, were raised against this wholesale destruction. Here, for example, is an account of the "restoration" of Woodstock church in Oxfordshire, during the 1860s.

"An ominous begging-box, with a lock, stood out in the street asking for funds for the "restoration". One would have thought it almost a burlesque, for it wanted no restoration at all, and would have lasted for ever so many centuries; but the box was put up by those "who said in their hearts, Let us make havoc of it altogether". Within a few weeks of the time this interesting monument was perfect, no one beam was left; and now, as I write, it is "a heap of stones". Through the debris I could just distinguish a fine old Norman doorway that had survived ever so many scenes notable in history, but it was nearly covered up with ruins; and supposing it does escape the general melee, and has the luck to be inserted in the new Church, with open benches and modern adornments, it will have lost every claim to interest and be scraped down by unloving hands to appear like a new doorway."

It was the Gothic Revival, then, that produced the typical English church interior as we know it today. For only a few hundred churches – too remote to warrant interference, too poor to afford it, or in a few cases resolutely defended by vicar or parishioners – escaped Victorian "restorations", one of the most disastrous of which was that carried out by Lord Grimthorpe at St Albans. Yet for all its faults, the revival produced some splendid churches of its own, especially when the early passion for rigid "correctness" had run its course. Among them are J. L. Pearson's breathtaking St Augustine's at Kilburn in London, built for the highest of High Church congregations in the 1870s; and Bodley's gorgeously decorated church at Hoar Cross, raised for a wealthy and eccentric patroness during the last quarter of the nineteenth century. By that time, moreover, the principles of Gothicism had been extended not merely to Anglican churches but also to Nonconformist chapels: and had permeated not only other buildings associated with religion or general worthiness (like schools and hospitals) but also many that had no such connection, including town halls and even public lavatories. Even if he wishes, then, the traveller cannot escape the Gothic Revival in some form, and can only wonder at the power of the phenomenon that transformed British places of worship so comprehensively.

Whitchurch Canonicorum – St Wite's Church, once the property of the canons of Salisbury and Wells – is architecturally one of the finest parish churches in Dorset, with a noble fifteenth century tower of yellow-grey stone and a spacious interior mainly built some two hundred years earlier, in the first or Early English style of Gothic. Especially notable is the beautiful carving on the clustered pillar capitals of its north nave aisle – opposite and to the west of the entrance – which display a wonderful variety of foliage, including the aptly-named "trumpet scallops" and odd bulbous growths like campion or bladder-wrack seaweed.

It is not for architecture, however, that most travellers come to Whitchurch, as pilgrims have journeyed here for many centuries. They come rather to the shrine of St Wite, the only one in an English parish church which certainly still contains the bones of its original occupant, who is also Whitchurch's patroness. The thirteenth century stone shrine stands in the north transept, a tomb chest raised above three almond-shaped apertures: in the chest itself can be seen a mortared-up crack, and when this opened in 1900 (after a shift in the transept's foundations) a leaden casket was found, inscribed in Latin "Here rest the relics of St Wite": within were the remains of a small woman aged about forty, which were reverently replaced.

Just who St Wite was has never been satisfactorily established, though many theories have been advanced. Some say, for example, that she was a saintly Breton princess also called Gwen Teirbron ("three-breasted") whose body was brought here in the tenth century by refugees: but this theory is based on several false premises – for though "Gwen" is indeed Breton-Welsh for "white", the saint's Anglo-Saxon name "Wite" more probably means "wise"; while the suggestion that "he" was actually a monk called Witta was demolished by the discovery of the female remains. Far more convincing is the long-standing local tradition that St Wite was a Saxon holy woman, a hermitess who lived by the (recently restored) well named after her on the slopes of Chardown Hill, just over a mile south of the church: and that she was martyred by raiding Vikings, perhaps durinig the 830s – hence, it is said, the carved ship and axe high up on the south face of the tower, just below the window.

A church, at any rate, seems to have been built in her honour by 890; and she had doubtless long been attracting pilgrims when the present transept was reconstructed in about 1300, and she was provided with a new shrine. Its oval apertures were designed to allow pilgrims to reach in and touch her tomb-chest, perhaps with a diseased limb or other part of their body they hoped the saint would heal, or with a rag to carry home for

WHITCHURCH CANONICORUM Dorset
OS 193 SY 397954
The attractive village of Whitchurch Canonicorum is set in rolling countryside some four miles north-east of Lyme Regis, via the A35 and a signposted minor road running north-east beyond Charmouth. The church is in the middle of the village, and St Wite's Well – restored as a simple stone trough surrounded by wooden fencing – is a mile to the south: it is accessible via an unsignposted road turning south off the A35 opposite the Ship Inn, and then a (signposted) footpath. Abbotsbury is twelve miles south-east, via the A35 to Bridport and the B3157: and Branscombe thirteen miles west, via the A35 and the A3052.

White tulips in the south aisle of the church.

123

a sick friend: such "limb-holes" were a usual feature of medieval shrines, including those of the much more famous St Edward the Confessor at Westminster Abbey and St Thomas Becket at Canterbury. St Wite's renown was, of course, considerably more localised than either of these – though at least one wayside chapel, near Chard, was dedicated to her – and indeed she seems to have been rather a homely saint, whose votaries brought her offerings of cakes and cheese as often as gold and silver.

It was probably her very obscurity, however, that saved both her shrine and her relics at the Reformation, when all others in England (save only those of the royal St Edward) were destroyed by government command. The exact circumstances of this truly miraculous escape are uncertain, though the investigation of 1900 indicated that the relics may have been temporarily removed, according to one story by a vicar who could get no sleep until he restored them to the shrine. Thereafter St Wite seems to have been honoured more covertly, and at her well rather than in her church: but now pilgrims once again come openly – though without publicity – and the openings in the shrine are always full of written requests for prayers and petitions for relief from suffering, as well as with coins which are gathered for charity. Whether the traveller adds to these offerings must remain a private matter: yet even the most obdurate of doubters can hardly fail to be touched by the atmosphere of this place, the goal of pilgrims for perhaps a thousand years.
See **Holy Wells and Sacred Springs, Shrines and Pilgrimages,**

WHITHORN Dumfries and Galloway
OS 83 NX 444403

Whithorn town and cathedral priory stand near the south-west coast of Galloway, some sixteen miles south of Newton Stewart via the A714 to Wigtown and then the A746 south. St Ninian's Kirk at Isle of Whithorn (NX 479362) is another three and a half miles south-east, via the A750: while St Ninian's Cave (NX 422359) is reached via a signposted minor road turning south off the A747 some three miles west of Isle of Whithorn, and finally by a delightful walk down wooded Physgill Glen to the beach. The cave will then be seen to the traveller's right, and is easily accessible.

Well off the beaten track, and consequently little frequented by travellers, Whithorn nevertheless has a special claim on seekers after significant places of worship. For this small Galloway burgh was the centre of the earliest recorded Christian mission to Scotland, begun here more than 150 years before Columba came to Iona and two centuries before Augustine journeyed to Canterbury. Its leader was St Ninian, "a most reverend and holy man of British race", who was born (either hereabouts or, some say, in north Wales) when the Roman Empire still held sway, and who travelled to Rome itself for his learning. On his way home he also probably studied under the famous and saintly bishop Martin at Tours in France: and when he landed in Galloway in about A.D. 396 he dedicated his first mission church to that saint, who is said to have sent masons to help him construct it in whitewashed stone. A source of wonder to the local Britons, who knew only buildings of wood or rough rubble, it became known as the "Candida Casa" or White House, later Saxonised as "hwit aern" or Whithorn. From here Ninian extended his influence as far south as Westmorland (where Ninekirks at Brougham is named after him) and set out to convert the wild pagan Picts of southern Scotland: and though his success there was limited and short-lived, both the saint and the church where he was buried in about 432 long continued to be venerated by Christians all over Britain.

Whithorn's sanctity and fame as a centre of learning, indeed, preserved it from the many viscissitudes which overtook Galloway in the centuries after Ninian's death. In the eighth century, when the English of Northumbria expanded their power into the region, it became an Anglian monastery and the seat of a bishop, and when the Norsemen settled here in about 920 they too buried their dead round the shrine: both Anglian and Viking-age memorial stones survive among the sixty or so preserved in the little museum by the churchyard gate. A priory of Premonstratensian canons and the cathedral of the Scottish bishops of Whithorn and Galloway from the twelfth century onwards, it moreover enjoyed considerable immunity even during the bitter Anglo-Scottish wars of the later middle ages, when it became a renowned place of international pilgrimage.

Only after the Reformation in fact, did the cathedral priory begin to decline into its present moving but somewhat confusing state of decay. Entering via the gateway (adorned with the Scottish royal arms) of the delightful little burgh square, and passing (or better visiting) the fascinating museum in a house within, the traveller sees first a roofless and much altered medieval church. This was originally the nave or west end of the cathedral, and thereafter served as Whithorn's Presbyterian parish church until 1822, when the present towered and whitewashed kirk (worth inspecting in its own right) was built just to the north. Of the centre of the medieval cathedral nothing remains, the site having been used since the seventeenth century as a burial ground, containing many notable tombstones to Galloway seafarers. Walking to the east, however, the visitor may descend into "the Vaults", the series of crypts below the cathedral's now-vanished easternmost chapels. Here, most probably, were displayed the relics of St Ninian, wrapped in the silken garments given by the Saxon scholar Alcuin: and hereabouts was certainly the oldest part of the cathedral priory, dating from the Celtic period. The low wall immediately beyond the vaults, indeed, marks the foundations of a very ancient chapel, excavated in late Victorian times: its stone walls were found to be covered with a thick layer of cream plaster, and there seems little doubt that here stood Ninian's original "Candida Casa".
See **Brougham: The First Christian Missionaries: Shrine and Pilgrimages.**

Largely ignored by the traffic that rushes past on the A35, Winterbourne Abbas's two places of worship are widely separated in date and purpose, but perhaps somewhat alike in spirit. Bearly half a mile to the west of the town, in the roadside corners of a wooded glade that retains its serene atmosphere despite the adjacent road, is the Nine Stones prehistoric circle, a tiny but complete setting of two large and seven small stones dating possibly from around 1700 B.C.: the two tall stones stand at the exact north of the ring, which is no more than twenty-seven feet in diameter, and can never have been more than the Bronze Age equivalent of a humble parish church like St Mary's in the village. That attractively unspoilt building (essentially thirteenth century except for its neat little Perpendicular tower) is also comparatively small, with a curiously offset chancel containing a fine carved "piscina" for washing communion vessels and an eighteenth century gallery in the nave – where sat the "church band", the last of its kind in Dorset.
See **Prehistoric Religion.**

WINTERBOURNE ABBAS
Dorset
OS 194 SY 611904
The village stands among chalk hills, five miles west of Dorchester on the A35: the Nine Stones are half a mile further west, by the road. Abbotsbury is four miles to the south, via a signposted minor road; and Cerne Abbas about ten miles north, via Dorchester and the A352; while just south of Dorchester (off the A354) is the great prehistoric hillfort of Maiden Castle.

The startling appearance of Wymondham's church – which is basically a high clerestoried nave sandwiched between two mighty towers, one at each end – stems from its curious history as a parish church attached to the still vaster church of a monastery, yet not strictly belonging to the monks. This unsatisfactory and indeed unworkable arrangement, laid down by an optimistic founder in 1107, led to centuries of bitter disputes, which neither popes nor kings could resolve: and eventually to the construction of two rival belfries, the octagonal tower of c.1400 at the east end belonging to the monks and that at the west – built higher and broader than the other as a deliberate act of defiance – to the parishioners. It was the parishioners (with the help of Henry VIII) who triumphed in the end, for almost nothing now survives of the choir and transepts which constituted the abbey's portions of the church: while the people's nave and north aisle survive in all their very considerable glory.

Essentially fifteenth century (and thus Perpendicular Gothic in style) from without, the church displays within a fine sweep of Norman arches in two tiers – a lower arcade and an upper gallery – with a Perpendicular clerestory above again and over all a beautiful hammer-beam angel roof. This last was erected by the parishioners at much the same time as they extended their north aisle – likewise splendidly angel-roofed – again in defiance of the monks, who owned the south aisle opposite and cut windows in their dormitory above it to enable them to peer into the parish nave.

There was little the parishioners could do, however, to counteract the massive wall the monks raised across the east end of the nave, totally blocking the view into the abbey's choir: and it was not until the restoration of 1903 that the present great golden reredos was erected against this eastern wall, thus providing a more fitting focus for this confusing yet magnificent church.
See **Monasteries and Religious Houses.**

WYMONDHAM Norfolk
OS 144 TG 106015
The attractive town of Wymondham (pronounced "windham") is some ten miles south-west of Norwich, on the A11: and the abbey church, with its unmistakable two-towered silhouette, stands on the south-western outskirts of the town; it is open 10 a.m. – 12 a.m. and 2 p.m. – 4 p.m. in summer and 11 a.m. – 3 p.m. in winter. Nearby, in Church Street, is the fourteenth century chapel of St Thomas Becket (now a public library) and the pretty timbered Green Dragon Inn, once perhaps a hostel for abbey guests.

The medieval parish church of All Saints, North Street (one of nineteen such churches within the walls of York) possesses some of the most interesting stained glass in northern England – and moreover some of the most accessible, for it is all set at an easily visible level. Nine windows are filled with glass of the fourteenth and (mainly) the fifteenth century, perhaps the best and most delightful being the "Acts of Mercy Window", the second from the east in the north aisle. There a bearded early fifteenth century gentleman is seen obeying Christ's commandment to succour the needy: in the six panels he first distributes loaves to the hungry, then drink to the thirsty – one of whom is a cripple, with hobnailed knee pads and hand crutches. Next he greets travellers, including a blind man led on a belt; gives clothing to the (almost) naked; and visits the sick, casting a handful of coins on the bed: and finally he puts his hand to his purse to relieve a group of woebegone prisoners in the stocks, with the parish constable standing behind them. The next window to the east is equally remarkable, depicting in fifteen "strip-cartoon" panels the horrific events to be expected at the End of the World. While across the church (in the third window from the east in the south aisle) the Nine Orders of Angels are seen leading the various sorts and conditions of men into heaven: the grandest sort of angel, of course, conducts the kings, emperors and popes, and the lesser kind the lesser folk – one of whom, in the bottom right hand panel, wears a pair of medieval spectacles.

Angels likewise appear carved on the church's roof, plain in the aisles and vividly re-painted above the chancel: the colours there are based on original tints found during restoration, but their brightness has provoked some controversy. The twelve chancel angels (plus Gabriel facing the Virgin across the altar) are splendidly various, some being robed and others in feathery suits: many of them play instruments, and the third from the east on the south side holds a little naked soul in a sheet, representing the vicar who paid for the carving.
See **Pickering.**

YORK North Yorkshire
OS 105 SE 602517
The famous city of York is 193 miles north of London, via the A1 and A64: or can be reached by rail from London's Kings Cross station in just over two hours. All Saints church, easily identifiable by its slim stone spire, stands opposite the modern Viking Hotel in North Street, which runs along the west bank of the river Ouse. It is about five minutes walk from the magnificent Minster, from whose west door it can be reached by walking straight ahead down Duncombe Place and Museum Street, crossing Lendal Bridge, and then turning sharp left and right into North Street. York's many other attractions include its medieval walls; the Yorkshire Museum with the nearby ruins of St Mary's Abbey; the Jorvik Viking Museum; and the National Railway Museum.

GLOSSARY OF TERMS

ABBEY An independent monastery ruled by its own abbot or abbess, as opposed to a dependent *priory*.

AISLES Where a *chancel*, *nave* or transept is divided up by rows of pillars, the aisles are the corridor-like sections flanking the central space.

ALMSHOUSE Accommodation for the sick or aged poor, established as an act of charity.

ALTAR A block of stone, built-up slab, or fixed table, used as the focus for worship in pagan temples and in most Christian churches. *See communion table.*

AMBULATORY Semi-circular *aisle* leading round an *apse*, or round the east end of a church: used as a processional way.

ANGLICAN A member of the Church of England or one of its related Churches overseas: or something pertaining to that Church.

APSE The semi-circular end of a church, or of a chapel in a church.

ARCADE A row of arches, generally supported by pillars.

AUGUSTINIANS The oldest and largest order of *canons regular*, who followed the rule named after St Augustine of Hippo: they had more English houses than any other religious order.

BAROQUE An elaborate and exaggerated style of neo-*Classical* architecture or decoration, much in vogue during the seventeenth and eighteenth centuries.

BARROW A burial mound, generally prehistoric and invariably pre-Christian.

BAY Internal division of a building, separated by pillars etc., rather than solid walls.

BENEDICTINES The largest and earliest order of *monks*, founded by St Benedict of Nursia (d. 550): also called "black monks", they owned many of the richest British monasteries.

CANONS REGULAR Groups of priests following a monastic rule and living together in an abbey or priory: in practice almost indistinguishable from *monks*.

CANONS SECULAR Priests serving a *cathedral* or other great church, but owning individual property and neither bound by a monastic rule nor necessarily living communally.

CAPITALS Block-like heads of columns or pillars, often shaped or sculptured.

CARTHUSIANS A strictly contemplative order of *monks*, who lived separately as *hermits* within a monastery, meeting only for certain services or on major festivals. So called from their mother house of La Grande Chartreuse in the Alps.

CATHEDRAL A great church which is the seat of a bishop or archbishop.

CATHOLIC, ROMAN Member of the Church under the authority of the Pope, and claiming succession from the Christian Church established by the later Roman emperors.

CELTS The people who inhabited all Britain until the Anglo-Saxon invasions, and who still inhabit Wales, Ireland, parts of Scotland, and Cornwall.

CHANCEL The part of the east end of a church where the main altar is placed, or sometimes the whole eastern part of the church. *See choir; presbytery.*

CHANTRY CHAPEL A *chapel* attached to or within a church, used before the Reformation by priests saying Masses for the soul of the founder.

CHAPEL A place of worship without parish responsibilities, sometimes belonging to a private individual: a separate place of worship within a church, having its own altar: or a *Nonconformist* place of worship.

CHAPEL OF EASE A separate *chapel* subordinate to a parish church, built near an outlying settlement for the convenience of worshippers.

CHAPTER HOUSE The building in a monastery or cathedral where the monks or cathedral clergy met to discuss business, and in the case of monks to hear a chapter of the monastic rule.

CHOIR Strictly, the part of the church where services are said or sung: but sometimes used as a synonym for *chancel*.

CISTERCIANS Order of *monks* following the austere reform of the *Benedictine* rule which originated at Citeaux in France: stressing the importance of physical labour, these "white monks" grew rich on sheep-farming.

CLASSICAL Pertaining to ancient Greece or Rome: or a later imitation of their architectural styles.

CLERESTORY Uppermost storey of a church wall, generally containing windows and thus a "clear-storey".

CLOISTER The courtyard of a monastery, often surrounded by a covered walk where the monks took exercise.

COMMUNION TABLE A movable table used for celebrations of *Holy Communion* in *Protestant* churches, as opposed to a fixed *altar*.

CONGREGATIONALIST A *Nonconformist* sect which believes in the independence of each individual congregation, and its right to settle its own affairs.

CORBELS Blocks of stone projecting from a wall, supporting the eaves of a roof or some other feature.

CROSSING Space near the centre of a church, where the *chancel*, *nave* and *transepts* meet. In larger churches, the area under the central tower.

CRYPT Underground chamber beneath a church, generally at its east end.

CULDEES Early medieval Irish or Scottish *monks* following the *Celtic* as opposed to the Roman Catholic tradition: their name means "servants of God".

DECORATED Style of Gothic architecture which flourished in England from *c*.1280 until *c*.1340.

EARLY ENGLISH Style of architecture (also called early *Gothic*) which flourished in England during the thirteenth century, from the end of the Norman period until *c*.1280.

EFFIGY Sculptured statue placed on a tomb or monument. This usually represented the deceased as in life, but was sometimes accompanied by an image of a decaying corpse or "cadaver".

FACADE The "show front" of a building, often adorned with statuary or other elaborate sculptured decoration.

FONT Receptacle, often made of stone and elaborately sculptured, containing the water used in baptism.

GOTHIC The style of medieval architecture, distinguished in particular by pointed arches, which flourished in Britain from the thirteenth century onwards: though generally superseded by versions of the *classical* style in the sixteenth century, it never quite died out, especially in rural churches. The name (a synonym for barbarous) was originally coined as an insult by devotees of classicism.

GOTHIC REVIVAL The enthusiastic but not always accurate imitation of the *gothic* style, especially for churches, which became overwhelmingly popular during the mid and late nineteenth century.

HAMMER BEAM ROOF *See roofs*

HENGE Prehistoric circular earthwork enclosed by a bank and ditch, probably used for religious rituals: sometimes (but by no means always) a stone circle was raised within them.

HERMIT Person dwelling alone, and devoting themselves to prayer, meditation and penance.

GH CHURCH Name given to those within the Church of gland who favour elaborate ritual and (latterly) onciliation with the Roman Catholic Church.

LY COMMUNION The term used in *Protestant* rches for the service commemorating Christ's Last pper with His disciples. See *Mass*

OSPITAL Word used in medieval times to signify an nshouse providing accommodation for the sick or aged or, or a hospice for pilgrims: rather than simply a place ere the sick are cured.

IGHTS HOSPITALLERS Crusading order of knights ved to guard and care for pilgrims to the Holy Land: like *Knights Templars*, their work was financed by estates nted to them all over Europe.

IGHTS TEMPLARS Crusading order of knights sworn to fend the Christian holy places of Jerusalem against the racens, and guard pilgrim routes to Palestine: they took ir name from the Temple church, their headquarters in rusalem.

DY CHAPEL *Chapel* dedicated to the Virgin Mary, often the east end of a church or cathedral.

NCET Slender window topped by a pointed arch: one of e principal hallmarks of the *Early English* style.

AY BROTHERS Inferior grade of *monks* (especially in the stercian order), generally uneducated and occupied mainly manual work.

ECTERN Stand for the Bible, or another holy book read oud during church services: often ornamental, they equently take the form of an eagle on whose back the book sts.

ASS Name used by Roman Catholics for the service re-nacting Christ's Last Supper, which is the focus of their orship, and during which Christ is believed to be actually esent in the bread and wine used. See *Holy Communion*.

EGALITHIC Word (from the Greek "great stones") used describe the communal tombs and other monuments onstructed from massive stone slabs during the prehistoric eriod.

METHODIST Member of the *Protestant* church founded by e Reverend John Wesley (1703–91), originally as a ressure group within the Church of England: in 1795, owever, it broke away and became a separate enomination, which subsequently fragmented into groups uch as the Primitive and Wesleyan Methodists.

IISERICORDS Term (from the Latin for "mercy") for the helf-like brackets under hinged chair seats: when the seat as turned up, they provided a modicum of support for riests and others required to stand during long services. Misericords are often elaborately carved, sometimes with antastic monsters or realistic scenes from *everyday* medieval fe.

MONKS Men (not necessarily priests) living an enclosed life f poverty, chastity and obedience in a monastic *abbey* or priory.

NAVE Western section of a church, generally used to provide space for the congregation.

NEOLITHIC Word for the "New Stone Age" of the prehistoric period, generally held to have lasted from about 4000 B.C. until about 1700 B.C.

NONCONFORMISTS A blanket term for all those *Protestant* denominations which do not conform to the beliefs and style of worship of the Church of England.

NORMAN Style of architecture current in England from 1066 until the late twelfth century: often called Romanesque n Scotland, where it continued rather later.

NUNS Women having a life of poverty, chastity and obedience in a monastic *abbey* or priory, generally known as a nunnery whatever its status.

ORATORY Strictly, a building used for prayer by a priest, monk or hermit, and differing from a *chapel* in that it does not provide space for a congregation.

PERPENDICULAR Latest style of *Gothic* architecture, flourishing in England from c.1335 until c. 1540, and in Scotland continuing rather later.

PIER Solid support for a major arch, sometimes square in section but often a pillar.

PISCINA Basin for washing the vessels used in a Holy Communion service, often having a sculptured surround and set into the chancel wall near the altar.

PRECINCT Enclosed or semi-enclosed space containing monastic buildings, or surrounding a cathedral.

PREMONSTRATENSIANS Order of *canons regular*, more austere than the *Augustinians* and named after their mother house at Prémontré in France: also called "white canons" from the colour of their robes.

PRESBYTERIANS Members of a *Protestant* denomination, whose congregations are governed by a system of "presbyteries" composed of ministers and elders. In Scotland, presbyterianism was always the dominant form of protestantism, and after 1690 the presbyterian Church of Scotland (also known as "the Kirk") became the established national Church: in England and Wales, however, presbyterians constitute a *nonconformist* sect.

PRESBYTERY In greater medieval churches, the section lying east of the *choir* and containing the high *altar*. So called because it was reserved for priests.

PRIORY A dependent monastery ruled by a prior or prioress, but technically subordinate to a greater *abbey*. Cathedral priories were so called because their nominal abbot was the bishop or archbishop.

PROTESTANTS Name originally given at the Reformation to all those Christians who protested forcibly against the abuses of the medieval Church; and who established separate reformed Churches, basing their doctrine on Biblical guidance rather than on Roman Catholic tradition.

PULPIT Raised and partly enclosed platform where a minister or priest stands to preach. During the seventeenth and eighteenth centuries, when they were the principal foci of Protestant churches, pulpits were often equipped with canopies (or "sounding-boards") which aided the projection of the preacher's voice: and were sometimes triple-tiered (or "three-deckers"), the uppermost tier being used for preaching, the middle tier for readings, and the lowest for the parish clerk.

PURITANS Strictly, the militant *Protestants* of the sixteenth and seventeenth centuries, who wished to purify the Church of England from all trace of Roman Catholic ritual and doctrine, and to reform public life in accordance with Biblical principles.

QUAKERS The popular name for members of the Society of Friends, the denomination founded during the 1650's by George Fox. Emphasising the importance of individual experience of God ("the inner light"), they avoid fixed doctrines or set forms of service.

REFECTORY Room where monks or nuns ate communally.

REREDOS Painted or sculptured screen forming a backdrop to an *altar*.

ROOD Word (from the Anglo-Saxon) for a large crucifix, often flanked by figures of the Virgin and St John, erected in the archway between the *nave* and *chancel* of a church. It sometimes rested on a balcony or "rood loft"), which was used for preaching and often richly decorated: and this in turn was supported on a "rood screen", which effectively shut off the nave from the chancel, and was also carved and painted.

ROOF BOSS A projection, often elaborately carved, placed at the intersection of the ribs of a roof *vault*.

ROOF, HAMMER BEAM Roof whose main structural members are supported on short "hammer beams" projecting at right angles from the wall top: very popular during the later middle ages.

ROOF, TIE BEAM Roof whose main structural members are supported on a "tie beam" stretching from wall to wall, and thus preventing the roof timbers spreading outwards.

SCREEN Decorative feature, often richly carved, pierced and painted, dividing one part of a church (generally the choir or a chapel) from another. Sometimes used to support the *rood*.

SEDILIA Seating by the *altar*, often of carved stone and built into a wall, for priests officiating at services.

SHINGLES Small wooden roofing tiles.

STALLS Rows of permanent seating for priests or monks, generally of elaborately carved wood and placed in the *choir*

TRACERY Intersecting stone ribs, often taking very comple and highly decorative forms, used to support the glass in the upper part of a window, or applied decoratively to wall surfaces.

TRANSEPT The transverse projections, or "arms", of a cross-shaped church, Some very large churches have two se of transepts, forming a "cross of Lorraine" plan.

TYMPANUM In Norman doorways, the semi-circular space between the horizontal lintel of the door and the arch above

UNDERCROFT Vaulted basement, often semi-subterranean.

VAULT An arched stone roof.

FURTHER READING

Adair, John, *The Pilgrims' Way*, Thames and Hudson, 1978.

Betjeman, Sir John, *Parish Churches of England and Wales*, Collins, 1980.

Burl, Aubrey, *Rings of Stone*, Weidenfeld, 1979.

Butler, L., and Given-Wilson, C., *Medieval Monasteries of Great Britain*, Michael Joseph, 1979.

Chatfield, Mark, *Churches the Victorians Forgot*, Moreland Publishing, 1979.

Clarke, B. F. L., *Church Builders of the Nineteenth Century*, David and Charles, 1969.

Fawcett, R., *Scottish Medieval Churches*, H.M.S.O. (Edinburgh), 1985.

Frere S. S., *Britannia*, Routledge, 1973.

Platt, Colin, *The Parish Churches of Medieval England*, Secker and Warburg, 1981.

Ross, Anne, *Pagan Celtic Britain*, Routledge, 1967.

Soden R. W., *Welsh Parish Churches*, Gomer Press, 1984.

Stenton, F. M., *Anglo-Saxon England*, Oxford University Press, 1975.

The publishers acknowledge with thanks,
the cooperation of all those
in whose care the featured churches are held.
This book is dedicated to them.